NovaLogic Inc.
26010 Mureau Rd. Ste. 200
Calabasas, CA 91302

D1294115

CREATING COMPUTER SIMULATION SYSTEMS

AN INTRODUCTION TO THE HIGH LEVEL ARCHITECTURE

Frederick Kuhl
Richard Weatherly
Judith Dahmann

Prentice Hall PTR
Upper Saddle River, NJ 07458
www.phptr.com

Library of Congress Cataloging-in-Publication Data

Kuhl, Frederick, Dr.
    Creating computer simulation systems: an introduction to the high level architecture /
by Frederick Kuhl, Richard Weatherly, Judith Dahmann.
        p.   cm.
    ISBN 0-13-022511-8 (alk. paper)
    1. Computer simulation.   2. Computer architecture.   I. Weatherly, Richard.   II. Dahmann,
Judith.   III. Title.
QA76.9.C65K84   1999
003'.3--dc21   99-38888
                                                                                            CIP

Editorial/production supervision: *Kathleen M. Caren*
Acquisitions editor: *Mark Taub*
Cover design director: *Jerry Votta*
Manufacturing manager: *Alexis R. Heydt*
Marketing manager: *Kate Hargett*
Editorial assistant: *Michael Fredette*

©2000 The MITRE Corporation, published by Prentice Hall PTR
Prentice-Hall, Inc.
Upper Saddle River, NJ 07458

The proceeds from the sale of this book support U.S. DoD modeling and simulation research.
The views, opinions and/or findings contained in this publication are those of the authors and should
not be construed as an official Government position, policy, or decision, unless designated by other
documentation.
NOTICE
This technical data was produced for the U.S. Government under Contract No. DAAB07-99-C-C201,
and is subject to the Rights in Technical Data and Computer Software Clause 252.227-7013 (OCT 88)
and Alternate II (APR 93).
CORBA and OMG IDL are trademarks of the Object Management Group, Inc.
Pitch Portable RTI and pRTI are tradmarks of Pitch AB.
Java and Solaris are trademarks of Sun Microsystems, Inc.
JGL is a trademark of ObjectSpace, Inc.
Windows is a registered trademark of Microsoft, Inc.

ISBN   0-13-022511-8

Prentice-Hall International (UK) Limited, *London*
Prentice-Hall of Australia Pty. Limited, *Sydney*
Prentice-Hall Canada Inc., *Toronto*
Prentice-Hall Hispanoamericana, S.A., *Mexico*
Prentice-Hall of India Private Limited, *New Delhi*
Prentice-Hall of Japan, Inc., *Tokyo*
Prentice-Hall (Singapore) Pte. Ltd., *Singapore*
Editora Prentice-Hall do Brasil, Ltda., *Rio de Janeiro*

To my father, who got father and son started with computers.
–F.K.

To Taylor Rose.
–R.W.

To my children, who keep me up to date with just about everything.
–J.D.

TABLE OF CONTENTS

In many ways, computers are not yet fit for civilized use. In the future computers will properly fade into the background in at least two ways—into *appliances* that play some part in our lives, and into *simulations* that present us with intriguing environments in which to interact. Such environments range from the fanciful worlds of science fiction, interactive games, and animation; to engineering simulations of complex systems that exist only in a mind; and to environments in which individuals can learn and groups can be trained as teams.

Many technologies will play a part in realizing these simulations of the future. Virtual reality, video, animation, software development techniques, large display screens, wearable computers, cameras, (human) language translators, and high performance computers will all play a part. But it is the simulation technology that will bring all the other technologies together in a way so that the human is immersed in a mind-grabbing environment.

For this to come to pass, it must be the case that many independently constructed simulations can be composed together quickly and cheaply to create a larger simulation that is perceived by its users to be more than the sum of the components. The key enabler of such composition is an *architecture*, a simulation architecture with supporting interfaces and protocols.

Of course, not just any architecture will do. It must engender software engineering discipline and provide a basis for the exchange of information between the simulation components. At the same time, it must not micro-manage and unduly constrain the simulation components and their developers. It must be of and by the community that uses it.

This book describes such an architecture, the *High Level Architecture* for simulation. The architecture arose to meet a community need. It happened to be developed under the sponsorship of the U.S. Department of Defense. The military community had developed training simulations with some sophisticated aspects that are not even yet matched by commercial simulations. In particular, it was and is routine for thousands of military participants to interact with one another in a single, shared training exercise. Such a simulation sets a scene in which to train and exercise even high-level decision-makers in solving problems and in taking complex actions. Civilian simulation counterparts handle only handfuls of participants. However, I expect commercial simulation to shortly mature to the same, or a higher level—particularly in the entertainment industry.

In the early 1990s there were so many military simulations that no one had an accurate count of them. Certainly, they numbered in the thousands, but no one knew for sure how many existed. Each organization that saw a need for simulation "rolled their own," with little reuse of what already existed. There was a clear need for simulations (built by different organizations) to be *interoperable*, and for simulation components to be *reusable* for multiple purposes.

I gave the Defense Modeling and Simulation Office (DMSO) the job of "assuring interoperability and reusability of defense models and simulations." One necessary component in achieving that objective was the creation of a simulation architecture standard. DMSO catalyzed the creation of the HLA, but it was the community that first created it and that continues to evolve it today. Those who were interested and had a stake joined in. Of particular importance were the critical and constructive contributions of the industrial and academic communities who had developed the Distributed Interactive Simulation protocol known as DIS. Most appreciated that it was time for a quantum step forward and they wielded their criticism and their constructive support quite effectively.

By the time an architecture working group had hammered out a first draft version of the architecture, the construction of experimental federations of simulations commenced. These so-called "protofederations" necessitated early implementations of the architecture, its application programming interfaces, and its runtime support. These federations spanned engineering applications, training, analysis, and platform development simulations.

The federations tested the architecture specification. They also performed another function. Military Service experts (in government and industry) were involved; those stakeholder organizations gained in-depth, hands-on knowledge. As a result, the Services had a cadre of their own knowledgeable people who could render judgement about whether it was in a Service's interest to support the High Level Architecture. When the time came for a DoD-wide policy requiring compliance with the architecture, the Services unanimously agreed to a compliance policy, even after I accelerated by one year the compliance dates that they had proposed.

At the same time a high degree of industry and IEEE involvement ensured that those stakeholders were knowledgeable as well. The active IEEE standards balloting on the HLA, the active adoption by the Services, the adoption of the HLA by the NATO countries, and the academic analysis of HLA all contribute to its position today.

It is historic accident that the HLA emerged with DoD support. It is the same sort of historic accident that caused DoD to foster the TCP/IP protocols that later enabled the Internet. In both cases DoD had a need, and some individuals had a vision. Had civilian simulations outpaced military simulations in the early 1990s or had the telephone companies envisioned an

Internet, the requisite standards could have grown up in the commercial world, as they have with Windows, CORBA, VRML, and Linux.

Today, there is a growing *civilian* need for a simulation standard of some sort. The HLA architecture is the front runner. Civilian critical mass or critical need has not been reached. Neither vendors nor purchasers of training and entertainment simulation products are demanding the kind of interoperability and reusability that DoD now requires. But it must come.

Neal Stephenson's science fiction novel, *Snow Crash*, depicts a simulated civil environment whose components are built by individuals at will. In that context many individuals interact. There is a precursor, the Multi-User Domain (MUDs) games; they are mainly played by informal communities, and have yet to become a substantial market. What is lacking is the economic impetus to demand interoperability and reusability. I expect it to rise with the emergence of a rich variety of entertainment products.

When civilian simulations become complex enough—and they will—the same need for an underpinning architecture to support composition and reuse of components will arise. At some time in the future, industry products will be required to meet a standard in order to compete. In the DoD, one uses policy to force acceptance of a standard. And today that policy exists. The challenge for the HLA is whether it is flexible enough to serve civilian, as well as military, purposes, and whether transition of ownership out of the DoD into appropriate, civilian community hands takes place as it did with the Internet protocols, TCP/IP. The international standards activities are crucial.

Only a few standards have successfully pursued a path of being driven by need, and being developed and owned by a community that could organize itself to advance the standard despite all the myriad conflicts of interest and of opinion that arise. Simulation technology advancement *depends* upon the existence of a standard like the HLA. May it grow, prosper, and serve.

HONORABLE ANITA JONES
UNIVERSITY PROFESSOR
UNIVERSITY OF VIRGINIA
FORMERLY DIRECTOR, DEFENSE RESEARCH AND ENGINEERING,
U.S. DEPARTMENT OF DEFENSE

GUIDANCE TO THE READER

Suppose you have several computer simulations that you wish to combine to create a single simulation system. For example, you have simulations of various manufacturing machines and simulations of conveyors. You desire to create a simulation of a complete factory floor while minimizing the changes needed to the existing simulations. Or perhaps you have a simulation of air traffic controllers in a region and another simulation of civil aircraft. You wish to create a complete simulation of air traffic in your region, and you expect you'll need to add a simulation of military air traffic later. The High Level Architecture for modeling and simulation, or HLA, is the glue you need to combine existing simulations and accommodate new ones.

The HLA is a software architecture for creating computer models or simulations out of component models or simulations. The HLA has been adopted by the United States Department of Defense (DoD) for use by all its modeling and simulation activities. The HLA is also increasingly finding civilian application. This book is a comprehensive introduction to the HLA.

"High Level Architecture" might seem an ambitious name. When the name was adopted by the DoD, the context was a variety of military simulation programs with little in common and little that could be reused. The HLA was the "high level" architecture from the perspective of the simulation programs of the time. While the HLA contains much that is generic to distributed computer systems, its intended application is to modeling and simulation.

AUDIENCE

This book will be useful to you if you are one of the following:

- The systems engineer or integrator of a simulation system comprising several components

- The developer of a simulation or model to be used as a component in a larger simulation system
- A decision-maker, someone who has to decide to commit money and resources to a project employing the HLA
- A student of simulation in the context of computer science
- A student of technology transfer

If you are an integrator or developer, we expect you are an experienced programmer. You'll get the most out of the book if you can run and modify the software presented in the text, but most of the discussion of the HLA is designed to be independent of the code samples. Furthermore, we have provided tools that will allow you to experiment with the HLA without writing software.

SCOPE AND CONTENTS

The book consists of text and a CD-ROM. The text contains tutorial material and exercises with the HLA. The tutorial material can be read without the exercises. The two are differentiated visually, to make it easy to skip the exercises. The CD-ROM contains reference documents, software, and installation instructions.

What This Book Covers

The text of the book beyond the Preface is divided into the following chapters:

1. Introduction: defines the HLA
2. The Story Behind the HLA: the reasons for the definition of the HLA and its development, how it came to be, how the HLA has been promoted as an architecture, and why it has succeeded
3. An Overview of the HLA: the HLA considered as a software architecture, its large pieces, its chief functions, and some things it is not
4. The Sushi Restaurant Federation: the beginning of a tutorial on using the HLA to integrate a set of simulations in substantial technical detail
5. Synchronizing the Federation: a continuation of the tutorial
6. A Sample Implementation: a guide to a complete implementation of the simulation system developed in The Sushi Restaurant Federation and Synchronizing the Federation
7. Extending the Federation for a New Purpose: a tutorial that builds on The Sushi Restaurant Federation and Synchronizing the Federation
8. Advanced Topics: further technical detail to be approached after you've read the tutorial parts

This book aims to be a tutorial, rather than an exhaustive reference. The index will make this book useful as a reference as well, but our main aim is to guide you in applying the HLA in the most common circumstances.

Contents of the CD-ROM

The CD-ROM contains the HLA specification (all three parts), software, installation instructions, and programming notes. You can find installation instructions and other documentation by starting with the file `index.html` in the top directory of the CD-ROM. Software includes the following:

- An implementation of the HLA Runtime Infrastructure (RTI) suitable for use with the sample code. This implementation, called the Pitch Portable RTI (pRTI™) Exploration Edition, is from Pitch AB of Linköping, Sweden [Pitch 1999a]. The pRTI Exploration Edition implements the entire HLA Interface Specification but is limited in capacity. An unlimited version is available [Pitch 1999b].
- A "Test Federate," software that can be used to invoke the various HLA services manually. You can use the Test Federate to explore the HLA without writing any software yourself [MITRE 1999].
- A complete implementation of the simulation system developed in the tutorial, included as Java source code and as executable files [MITRE 1999].

HOW TO READ THIS BOOK

Regardless of your interest, you should go through the rest of this preface and Chapter 1, "Introduction," thereby furnishing yourself with terms and definitions you will need for the other parts of the book.

- If your interest is chiefly managerial, we recommend that you continue with Chapter 2, "The Story Behind the HLA," and perhaps Chapter 3, "Overview."
- If your interest is chiefly technical, we suggest Chapter 2, "The Story Behind the HLA," for general background and strongly recommend Chapter 3, "Overview." That will give you a high-level technical understanding of the HLA.
- If you're an integrator or developer, you'll want to continue into the tutorial parts: Chapter 4, "The Sushi Restaurant Federation," Chapter 5, "Synchronizing the Federation," and Chapter 7, "Extending the Federation for a New Purpose." The tutorials are designed to be read from beginning to end; they are not very amenable to sampling in the middle. You'll definitely want to have read the tutorial parts before tackling Chapter 8, "Advanced Topics."
- If your interest extends to the details of programming with the HLA, you should read Chapter 6, "A Sample Implementation," in the order it appears among the tutorial parts.

TYPOGRAPHIC CONVENTIONS

Java code, pseudocode, and web URLs are spelled with a `monospaced font`. Names of HLA services are spelled in small caps, as REGISTER OBJECT INSTANCE. HLA services that are initiated by the RTI are adorned with a dagger, as DISCOVER OBJECT INSTANCE †.

ACKNOWLEDGMENTS

Something as large and successful as the HLA is clearly the result of technical skill, leadership, and dedication by many individuals. The authors gratefully acknowledge the opportunity to work with these talented members of the growing HLA community. The authors are particularly grateful to have worked as members of the early RTI development teams. The members of the first five RTI development teams are:

- RTI 0.X – Gary Bisaga, Jim Calvin, Carol Chiang, Bernadette Clemente, Paul DiCaprio, Sean Griffin, Curtis Holmes, Cris Hutto, Tim Hyon, Fred Kuhl, Steve McGarry, Jack Ogren, Steve Rak, Scott Shupe, Dan Van Hook, Richard Weatherly, Annette Wilson, and Harry Wolfson.

- RTI-S – Paul Barham, Steve Boswell, Jim Calvin, Carol Chiang, Steve Kolek, Steve McGarry, Paul Metzger, Steve Rak, Dan Van Hook, Harry Wolfson, and Sue Yao.

- RTI F.0 – Rich Briggs, Rob Head, Cris Hutto, Tim Hyon, Fred Kuhl, Kurt Louis, Dave Meyer, Gordon Miller, Jack Ogren, Jeff Olszewski, Jeff Pace, Russ Richardson, Scott Shupe, Richard Weatherly, and Annette Wilson.

- RTI 1.0 – Mark Boriack, Rich Briggs, Mike Daren, Bob Gibson, Sean Griffin, Je-Nien Hancock, Rob Head, Chris Heaps, Cris Hutto, Tim Hyon, Jamal Karerat, Fred Kuhl, Kurt Louis, Mike Mazurik, Greg McDonald, Jack Ogren, Jeff Olszewski, Russ Richardson, Scott Shupe, Thuc Vu, Richard Weatherly, and Chul Yoon.

- RTI 1.3 – Steve Bachinsky, Steve Boswell, Rich Briggs, Jim Calvin, Carol Chiang, Bob Gibson, Jack Harrington, Rob Head, Chris Heaps, Tim Hyon, Steve Kolek, Fred Kuhl, Kurt Louis, Steve McGarry, Sylvie Platre, Steve Rak, Russ Richardson, Joe Seward, Scott Shupe, Allen Skees, Ed Skees, Michael Starkie, Don Theune, Dan Van Hook, Richard Weatherly, Annette Wilson, and Harry Wolfson.

The authors gained increased understanding of the HLA Interface Specification and Object Model Template through membership in the informal "Onion Group" of HLA technical advisors. The "Onion Group" included Jim Calvin, Dan Van Hook, James Ivers, Andreas Kemkes, Reed Little, Bob Lutz, Katherine Morse, Dave Seidel, and Susan Symington.

The authors also thank Tim Hyon, James Ivers, and Annette Wilson for their patient response to a stream of questions while we wrote this book. We thank Ernest Page for background material on modeling and simulation, spontaneous tutorials on simulation, and references to the literature; and Eric Blair, Andreas Kemkes, Jayne Lyons, and Juergen Schulze for reading the drafts and making constructive suggestions. John Schleith drew the picture of the restaurant. We thank Madge Harrison, our editor at MITRE, for a thorough review under very tight time constraints.

CHAPTER 1

Introduction

1.1 WHY A HIGH LEVEL ARCHITECTURE FOR MODELING AND SIMULATION

The HLA is the glue that allows you to combine computer simulations into a larger simulation. For instance, you might have simulations of several different manufacturing machines and material-handling machines. The HLA helps you create a factory floor simulation from the pieces. You might want to combine simulations of air traffic control in several different regions of the country with simulators of individual aircraft. The HLA helps you combine these simulations into a single, comprehensive simulation. The HLA also helps you extend your simulation later, by adding, for example, another manufacturing machine or an additional airport.

The HLA defines some terms that will be used throughout this book:

- The combined simulation system created from the constituent simulations is a *federation*.
- Each simulation that is combined to form a federation is a *federate*.
- A *federation execution* is a session of a federation executing together.

A federation contains the following elements:

- Supporting software called the *Runtime Infrastructure* (RTI)
- A common object model for the data exchanged between federates in a federation, called the *Federation Object Model* (FOM)
- Some number of federates

A federate is a member of a federation, one point of attachment to the RTI. A federate could represent one platform, such as a cockpit simulator. Or a federate could represent an aggregate simulation, such as an entire national simulation of air traffic flow.

1.2   AN HLA FEDERATION HAS SOFTWARE AND DATA COMPONENTS

Federates and the RTI are software. Typically the federation developer furnishes the federates and gets an RTI implementation from some other source. (An RTI implementation is furnished on the CD-ROM in this book.) The FOM is data created by the federation developer.

The FOM is a description of the kinds of and relationships among data that the federates will exchange in a federation execution. It expresses agreement about data between the federates. The FOM is a significant tool for communicating design decisions between federate and federation developers. Part of it is furnished to the RTI during federation execution, effectively parameterizing the RTI for the federation.

The relationship of the software components is depicted in Figure 1–1. Federates are shown in the figure as either simulations, surrogates for live players, or tools for distributed simulation. A federate is defined as having a single point of attachment to the RTI. A federate might consist of several processes, perhaps running on several computers. A federate might model a single entity, like a vehicle, or a federate might model many entities, like all the vehicles in a city. From the perspective of the HLA, a federate is defined by its single point of attachment to the RTI.

As shown in Figure 1–1, a federate might model some number of entities, or it might have a different purpose. It might be a collector and/or viewer of data, passively receiving data and generating none. A federate might act as a surrogate for human participants in a simulation. In this role, the federate might reflect the state of the larger simulation to the participant via some user interface, and might convey control inputs or decisions from the participant to the rest of the federation.

The RTI used by a federation may be implemented as many processes or as one. It may require many computers to execute, but conceptually it is one RTI. An RTI may support several federations executions at once.

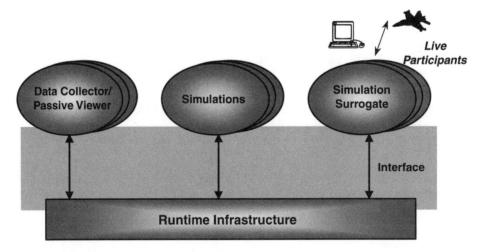

FIGURE 1-1   Software Components in the HLA.

1.3   THE HLA AS A STANDARD

The HLA is foremost a software architecture, rather than a particular implementation of its infrastructure or tools designed to work with it. The HLA embraces a variety of implementations. Consequently, it is defined not by software but by a set of documents. This book is written to reflect version 1.3 of the HLA specification as adopted by the U.S. Department of Defense (DoD). The full text of the specification is included on the CD-ROM. The HLA standard has three parts:

- HLA Rules
- Object Model Template (OMT)
- Interface Specification

1.3.1   HLA RULES

The HLA Rules are principles and conventions that must be followed to achieve proper interaction of federates during a federation execution. They are design principles for the Interface Specification and OMT. They also describe the responsibilities of federates and federation designers.

1.3.2   OBJECT MODEL TEMPLATE (OMT)

Every federation has an FOM. The OMT prescribes the allowed structure of every FOM. The OMT is the meta-model for all FOMs.

1.3.3   INTERFACE SPECIFICATION

The interface specification is the specification of the interface between federates and the RTI. The RTI is software that allows a federation to execute together. The interface between the RTI and federates is standardized. Implementation of the RTI could take a variety of forms.

1.3.4   HOW THE SPECIFICATION IS EVOLVING

At the time of writing, there are two parallel efforts under way to pursue the adoption of the HLA by standards bodies. One effort is through the Object Management Group (OMG), a consortium of software vendors and users pursuing standards for distributed object computing. Version 1.3 of the interface specification has been adopted by the OMG as a standard called the "Facility for Distributed Simulation Systems" [OMG 1998]. The other standards adoption effort is through the Institute of Electrical and Electronics Engineers (IEEE). The draft IEEE standards are P1516 (HLA Rules), P1516.1 (Interface Specification), and P1516.2 (OMT) [IEEE 1999].

1.4   YOU CAN RUN YOUR OWN FEDERATION

The accompanying CD-ROM contains all the software you need to run your own HLA federation:

- A version of the RTI suitable for the samples in the book and for limited experiments with federations of your own design

- A FOM for the restaurant federation to be described later
- Three kinds of federates

The three kinds of federates on the CD-ROM are:

- The basic federates developed in "The Sushi Restaurant Federation" and "Synchronizing the Federation." We suggest you read your way through that part of the book before running them.
- The manager federate described in "Synchronizing the Federation." This federate would be useful for your own projects as well as our sample implementation.
- A test federate, which allows you to invoke manually any HLA service. You can start any number of test federates at once to create a federation without any programming.

You can also create your own federates by modifying the sample implementations. You can also experiment by mixing your federates with instances of the test federate.

The Story Behind the HLA

2.1 INTRODUCTION

The goal of this section is to explain the genesis of the High Level Architecture (HLA) and the approach its proponents have taken to ensure its success. We start by describing the broad problem that the HLA is intended to solve. We then describe the development of the HLA as an application of technology transition principles.

2.2 HOW THE HLA GOT STARTED

The HLA is technology born of necessity: technology developed in response to management needs, technology driven by shrinking resources, and technology envisioning a higher level of simulation capability. The setting for our story is the U.S. Department of Defense (DoD). However the situation that led to HLA development had less to do with defense work than it did with the circumstances facing many large organizations in the early 1990s. Fewer resources were available to cope with mounting needs and increasing uncertainty. Decisions needed to be made before there was sufficient information to satisfy decision makers. This picture could characterize the automobile industry, the health care establishment, or the banking enterprise. In this particular case it was the DoD.

By the late 1980s, the cold war was clearly over and the political realm less interested than ever in increased defense expenditures. Nonetheless, the public continued to expect national security support against new and unpredictable threats over a wider range of geography than ever before. Many assets in the defense inventory were nearing the end of their productive life, and many were no longer appropriate for the new threats. At the same time, there was little patience on the part of the public or the U.S. Congress with the costs of military systems, the lengthy product development process, or the increased difficulties of modernizing the forces in a cost-effective way.

A solution to these problems was seen in information technology. The view of many was that by leveraging advanced computing hardware, software, and network communications, more could be done with less. Simulation in particular was seen as providing technical opportunities. It offered the DoD the opportunity to conduct many operations in simulation first before facing the realities of war. This included:

- Training of fighting forces
- Experimentation with new force structures, warfare tactics, and doctrine
- A chance to create new weapons systems in simulation first, the "try before buy" procurement approach

The DoD had used simulation as a war planning tool for decades, so the idea of applying simulation was not a new one. Sand tables, where small-scale force representations were maneuvered through alternative scenarios, have been used for option assessment ever since warfare was viewed as a manageable enterprise. Some of the earliest computer simulation developments were found in defense applications. Over the previous decade, computer-based "board" games had become a staple in the military training community, allowing commanders to exercise their trade without the costs of men and materiel. In the 1980s, real-time simulator networking, using SIMNET protocols, had opened up a new way of training, using linked man-in-the-loop simulators. In the development of weapons systems, models and simulations had created situations that are almost impossible, or undesirable, to achieve in reality. Weapons system simulators costing as much as many civilian systems have become a routine part of military systems development. Physical stimulators, creating complex electronic environments, have been developed to test systems in environments comparable to those they will encounter in complex conflict situations. All these represent large investments in what have been termed "synthetic environments."

However, in the cost-conscious 1990s, it was clear that if these simulated environments were going to be used in the future, they, too, needed to be developed in a more cost-effective way. No longer was it affordable to develop a new simulation to address each new problem. Investments in simulators to support development alone were no longer tolerated; these costly items needed to be put to work supporting training and mission rehearsal. It was no longer acceptable for multiple organizations to create simulations of similar systems. To be useful, the authorities on those systems had to invest their time to ensure that the simulations provided an acceptable representation of the systems. Often the largest expense of developing simulations was the hidden costs: understanding the system characteristics and validating the simulation, that is, ensuring that the simulation reflected the system characteristics. These costs needed to be managed.

Simulations were being recognized as defense assets that needed to be managed like other assets of the organization. This led to the DoD-wide objective of finding ways to support reuse of defense simulations, both individually and in combinations. The driving idea was that if you could reuse simulations in combined applications, you would get added flexibility in the application of simulations and more benefit for the investment made. This was the management and economic push for the development of the HLA.

However, no specific agency was responsible for taking the actions and paying the costs to support the shared basis that would support reuse. The Director of Defense Research and Engineering (DDR&E) assigned the Defense Modeling and Simulation Office (DMSO) the objective of assuring the interoperability and reuse of military simulations. This assignment substantively changed DMSO's mission. Until the early 1990s, it accomplished its task by funding or co-funding projects with the Services, improving their technology and simulation products in a piecemeal fashion. The new mission demanded the creation of a simulation architecture as a construct on which to base the interoperability of components built by different organizations and the reuse of simulation components by organizations other than the developers.

2.3 THE MODEL OF TECHNOLOGY TRANSITION

It was recognized very early that the HLA would never achieve its purposes unless it gained broad acceptance in the DoD and beyond the DoD. Mandates are good, but in most cases transition to general use is not accomplished through mandates alone. Work at the Software Engineering Institute (SEI) [Levine and Fowler 1993, 1995] has characterized successful technology transitions as occurring in three broad phases, which are depicted in Figure 2–1. The phases are (with slight modifications of the names):

- Technology development
- Product development
- Customer transition

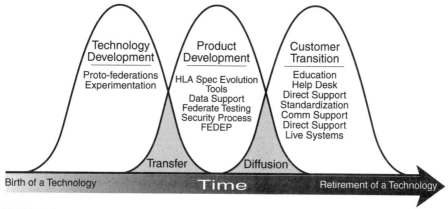

FIGURE 2-1 HLA Technology Transition and Technology.

The strategy to develop and promote the HLA approximates this model of technology transition. Accordingly, we will discuss the HLA story in terms of the phases presented above. However, the SEI work suggests that the more concurrency there is across the phases in the technology development process, the greater the likelihood of technology transition and adoption. These phases have been pursued, and indeed continue, in a highly concurrent way. Many of the activities we describe here have occurred in parallel.

2.4 TECHNOLOGY DEVELOPMENT

As is typical in many large organizations, the DoD identified the broad objective of promoting reuse and interoperability and then turned to the technical community for the technical means to achieve this end. In this case, the vision for modeling and simulation in the DoD was formulated by high-level decision makers:

> Defense modeling and simulation will provide readily available, operationally valid environments for use by DoD components:
>
> - to train jointly, develop doctrine and tactics, formulate operational plans, and assess war fighting situations,
>
> - as well as to support technology assessment, system upgrade, prototype and full scale development, and force structuring.
>
> Furthermore, common use of these environments will promote a closer interaction between the operations and acquisition communities in carrying out their respective responsibilities. To allow maximum utility and flexibility, these modeling and simulation environments will be constructed from affordable, reusable components interoperating through an open systems architecture [DMSO 1995].

This vision was then followed by a strategic plan, the DoD Modeling and Simulation (M&S) Master Plan [DMSO 1995], which identified critical areas where investments were needed if the vision was to become a reality. The first objective was to create a common technical framework for M&S development. The cornerstone of this framework was HLA. The HLA fulfills one of the objectives of the M&S Master Plan: "Establish a common high-level simulation architecture to facilitate the interoperability of all types of models and simulations among themselves and with C4I systems, as well as to facilitate the reuse of M&S components…" The HLA was given a broad mandate: "Simulations developed for particular Department of Defense Components or Functional Areas must conform to the High Level Architecture…" But that mandate was limited: "Further definition and detailed implementation of specific simulation system architectures remain the responsibility of the developing [armed forces] Component" [DMSO 1995]. What the HLA was, and even whether it was a technically feasible, was not a consideration at this stage. The need for this technical capability was recognized first, and its development proceeded thereafter.

2.4.1 DIVERSE TEAM PRODUCED INITIAL HLA CONCEPT

Development of the HLA proceeded in several stages that involved a diversity of teams from industry, government, and laboratories. First was the development of an underlying approach or concept. This development began with a call to industry. In the summer of 1995, three technical contractor teams were commissioned to conduct six-month investigations of technical options and approaches. Another team, called the program evaluation team, worked closely with the technical contractor teams to explore the options for meeting the objective. This team was composed of government, laboratory, and university technologists who used or applied simulation across the full range of areas to be covered by the HLA. The idea was to bring together a cross-section of the simulation technical community to assess the options and focus on technical development. The result was an initial technical architecture in March 1996.

2.4.2 BASELINE HLA SPECIFICATION GUIDED BY USERS

This initial technical architecture defined the concept of a basic HLA. The next step was to move from concepts to sufficient technical detail that the architecture could be assessed against the objectives. It was crucial for acceptance that further development be guided by prospective users. This baseline development phase of the HLA was done by an organization called the Architecture Management Group (AMG). The AMG was made up of sixteen major defense programs that covered the range of uses for defense simulation. Programs were selected because they represented the major simulation requirements ranging from analysis to training to test and evaluation, and from detailed engineering representation to campaign-level warfighting to man-in-the-loop interactive vehicle simulators. As programs, they had specific system requirements, users, budgets, and schedules. They represented the community that would use the HLA. The members of the AMG brought their technical teams from government, industry, and academia to the table. Their job was to take the initial HLA concept, develop it to the point that it could be applied, prototype its use in their application area, and provide feedback to the architecture development as a result of the prototype application experience. They were asked to consider both the needs of their own program and the broader needs of the defense community. The assumption was that it would be possible to support both without large technical or management compromises.

AMG members, along with their supporting government and industry teams, meet every six to eight weeks to address the key HLA issues, to conduct cooperative prototyping efforts with other AMG members, and to participate in technical working groups to evolve cross-cutting technical aspects of the HLA.

Supporting the AMG was a small, focused technical support team (TST) with the task of maintaining the technical underpinnings of the architecture. Team members were drawn from across the simulation technical community based on their technical expertise and experience base. The TST members were tasked with developing the HLA specifications and the prototype infrastructure software, as well as conducting technical analyses of issues critical to the AMG.

2.4.3   PROTOFEDERATIONS PROVED THE CONCEPT

The primary purpose of the HLA baseline development period was to take the initial HLA definition and develop the specifications and tools needed to use the HLA to support actual prototype applications. The development approach was based on the idea that by building applications that employed the HLA, users would be in a position to evaluate its potential for their work. Consequently, this prototyping was directed toward answering a common set of questions and evolving the HLA to meet a broad set of needs. The questions covered the following requirements:

- Technical viability of a single interface specification to support the wide range of applications of the HLA
- Technical feasibility of building a runtime infrastructure (RTI) with the necessary range of tools needed by those applications
- Impact of the HLA on simulation internal development
- Utility of the object model concept and formats throughout the HLA lifecycle
- Ability to specify common testing methods
- Ability to operate HLA federations securely
- Applicability of the HLA to address the wide range of DoD simulation applications

There were four major prototype implementations of federations ("protofederations") that supported the HLA baseline development process. The simulations incorporated in these protofederations were made available, along with their supporting technical development teams, by AMG members. Each protofederation addressed a different corner of the simulation application domain, and as such, typified one way simulations would be used in an HLA context.

Several overall observations are warranted before the protofederations themselves are described. First, the purpose of these prototypes was to develop the HLA through hands-on experience, not to solve a particular problem. Secondly, all four prototypes used the same architecture, the same interface specification, the same object model template, and, in fact, the same implementation of the RTI.

To serve the HLA baseline development, it was decided to develop one prototype implementation of the RTI and use that implementation with all the protofederations. This was seen as both the most cost-effective approach and the best strategy for examining the desirability of having not only a common interface specification, but also a common implementation to serve the entire community. The primary objective of the RTI prototyping was to provide the protofederations with the functionality needed to use the HLA. The RTI prototype also allowed assessment of the functional and performance requirements for RTI services. This assessment guided RTI development and transition.

The four protofederations are described below.

- *Platform Prototype Federation.* The first protofederation was called the Platform Prototype Federation. This was a federation of real-time platform-level simulators and simulations that had used IEEE Distributed Interactive Simulation (DIS) 2.0 [IEEE 1995]. The key issues addressed by this protofederation were the ability of HLA to replace DIS and the adaptation of DIS-based systems.

- *Joint Training Protofederation.* The second federation, called the Joint Training Protofederation, was a federation of discrete event simulations. The key issue for this prototype was the coordination of multiple discrete event simulations.
- *Analysis Protofederation.* The third prototype federation was the Analysis Protofederation. This protofederation was composed of closed-form analytic applications. Hence, runtime efficiency and repeatability were important here, since these simulations required multiple executions for analysis purposes. The interest in this protofederation was in the time management and data management services.
- *Engineering Prototype Federation.* Finally, the Engineering Prototype Federation examined whether the HLA could federate simulations to support system acquisition. Acquisition support requires validated, engineering-level simulations. This protofederation was particularly interested in the performance required to support hardware-in-the-loop applications.

2.4.4   BASELINE DEFINITION: FOUNDATION FOR FURTHER DEVELOPMENT

These prototypes exercised the HLA with applications that typified its ultimate uses, with the goal of furthering its definition. The results of the prototypes were fed into the specification and testing procedures through working groups. The experiences of the individual federate developments afforded insight into the effect of the HLA on simulations and offered an experience base for future users. The tangible result was the basis for a baseline HLA definition, HLA 1.0, which was completed in August 1996 and approved as the standard technical architecture for all DoD simulations on 10 September 1996 [DoD 1996].

Acceptance of the HLA baseline accomplished two important things that aided technology transition. First, it defined a stable standard that could serve as a foundation for further development. Technologies sometimes fail because they cannot be defined clearly enough to be adopted. The baseline was good enough to start; further standardization would come later. Second, the baseline, with its mandate for use across the DoD, created a base of users that justified investments from private industry.

2.5   PRODUCT DEVELOPMENT

Once the HLA technical approach had been adopted, efforts began in earnest to implement the architecture for the end-user community. Because the benefits of a common architecture depend on a critical mass of users, substantial investments were made in freely available supporting software, user training, and support.

The focus for HLA development was on its capabilities as a runtime architecture for simulation interoperability. However, it became quite clear from the first days of the protofederations that users who are faced with this new way of doing business need support in understanding both the process of applying the HLA to their problems and the automated tools required to lessen the time, tedium, and cost of building federations.

Ultimately the HLA would succeed only if it were supported by an entire software economy characterized by:

- Software producers
- Software consumers
- Publicity, training, and support
- Timely response to competition
- Perception of economic benefit

In effect, the government created a temporary microcosm of the desired software economy during the product development phase of the transition, harnessing the enthusiasm of "early adopters." The microcosm demonstrated the desired economy on a small scale and facilitated the full-scale transition. Product teams for the needed tools and infrastructure software acted as software producers. Early adopters inside and outside the defense community acted as software consumers. Publicity, training, and support were handled by government, industry, and federally funded research and development centers (FFRDCs). DMSO handled perceived competition to the HLA by incorporating good ideas and refuting bad ones. Finally, by creating the economic microcosm, DMSO demonstrated to private users and industry that the HLA could bring economic benefit. It demonstrated that an economy was forming around the HLA, and the government's supplier role was temporary.

Two activities of this phase might appear contradictory at first sight. The first was making available some form of the necessary software and tools as early as possible. The second was encouraging the development of software and tools by private industry. The quickest way for the government to make versions available early was to pay for their development. At the same time, the government had to convince private industry that government-furnished software would not constitute competition for private development. The government combined these goals by using a team of FFRDCs and industry to prepare initial versions, and by announcing limits to support for government-furnished software.

2.5.1   A USER VIEW OF THE FEDERATION DEVELOPMENT PROCESS

For many prospective users of the HLA, its adoption would mean changing their way of doing business. DMSO facilitated adoption of the HLA by defining a development process for federations. To start, the protofederation developers began to document their process for applying the HLA. Over time, this process view evolved into the HLA federation development and execution process (FEDEP) [Scrudder *et al.* 1998]. In this view, the process covers five basic steps: concept development, federation design, federation execution implementation, testing, and operations. The basic elements of these steps are then articulated in more detail to define the basic activities which constitute the end-to-end process of developing and fielding an HLA federation. The FEDEP continues to evolve as HLA users gain experience building federations. The FEDEP is depicted in Figure 2–2.

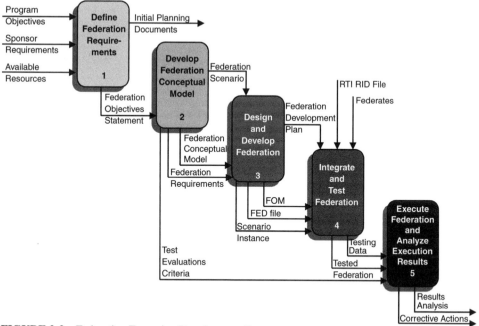

FIGURE 2-2 Federation Execution Development Process.

2.5.2 AUTOMATED TOOLS TO SUPPORT THE USE OF THE HLA

Another lesson learned from the baseline prototyping was that automation was needed to support the federation development process itself, if HLA was going to be usable. Thus adoption of the HLA would depend on the extent to which cost-effective supporting software was available for the creation, development, and operation of HLA federations. Work began on the development of key supporting software as soon as the baseline HLA specification was adopted.

Since the FEDEP gave a view into the key steps a user would follow in applying the HLA, it served as a framework for examining the places where automated support could be applied to save the user time and resources in building a federation. This resulted in the development of an "HLA tools architecture" [Scrudder *et al.*1998b], which pointed out the places in the process where tools could be developed and used, as well as the types of information interchanges that could be anticipated among tools of various types.

The tools architecture was determined early in the HLA development process. Consequently this framework of tools and data interfaces was available to guide tools development by the HLA developers, independent HLA users, and commercial tools developers.

2.5.2.1   Object Model Tools

Users of the HLA will be developing object models for their simulations, as well as for other federates and their federations. While straightforward in concept, HLA object models can be cumbersome to develop and share as they grow in size and complexity. To aid in this process, automated tools have been created to develop, fill, and share object models. In particular, there were three components in an Object Model Tool set developed early in the HLA transition process and made broadly available in the public domain:

- Object Model Development Tool. Automated support for developing HLA object models, generating RTI federation execution data, and exchanging object models with the web-based Object Model Library.
- Object Model Library. Web-accessible library of Federation Object Models (FOMs) and Simulation Object Models (SOMs).
- Object Model Data Dictionary. Web-accessible repository of common data components for object model development mapped to DoD data standards, having linking capability with Object Model Development Tools.

As with the RTI software, these tools were made publicly available via the web. Over 200 users accessed these in the first six months they were available. These tools are supported by a set of publicly available data interchange formats (DIFs), which allow the exchange of object models [Scrudder *et al.*1998b]. These DIFs have allowed the development of commercial tools to meet these and other HLA object model development functions tailored to the needs of particular HLA users. Several companies in the U.S. and elsewhere have plans to market comparable tools that use the DIFs for data exchange.

2.5.2.2   Planning Federation Execution

Automation is also being applied to the process of planning federation execution and to the testing and monitoring of federation runtime operations. A federation execution planner's workbook has been developed [Dahmann *et al.* 1997], which provides a structured approach to compiling the data needed to configure an HLA federation execution. An automated tool set is in development to support the development and exchange of completed workbooks, along with supporting DIFs for sharing this data with other related tools. Tools supporting the verification that federates are adhering to the FOM are being developed, as are runtime data collection and monitoring tools. These runtime tools monitor the progress of the federation using the HLA Interface Specification, and hence can be used for different federations.

2.5.2.3   Adaptation of Simulations to Use the HLA

As experience with the HLA has grown, so have the software tools to support the development and adaptation of simulations to use the HLA. There has been considerable experience with the adaptation of simulations that had been designed to operate DIS protocols [Braudaway and Harkrider 1997], and several tools have been developed to provide automated support for this transition [Belanger *et al.* 1997]. Other tools have been developed to aid the transition to the

HLA through the provision of reusable middleware [Paterson *et al.* 1998] and through the incorporation of HLA functions into new or existing simulation development environments and tools.

2.5.3   RTI SOFTWARE DEVELOPMENT

RTI software was viewed as the most critical software element to make available as soon as possible. The philosophy was that confidence would be built in the user community by getting working software to users as soon as possible, with basic capabilities first and incremental improvements over time. The initial emphasis was on correctness and robustness. Performance was recognized as important but functionality came first.

The RTI prototypes were developed by an integrated product team consisting of FFRDCs (The MITRE Corporation and MIT Lincoln Laboratory) and industry (SAIC and Virtual Technology Corporation). Use of the FFRDCs had these benefits:

- The work was undertaken quickly.
- The FFRDCs were able to interpret ambiguities in the specification in the government's interest.
- The FFRDCs posed no continuing competition to private industry.

RTI software was initially developed as part of the prototyping for the HLA baseline definition. This initial RTI software, known as the 0.X series, was developed with an OMG Interface Definition Language (IDL) application programmer's interface (API) using Common Object Request Broker Architecture (CORBA). With the acceptance of the HLA baseline, the 0.X series RTI software was retired and the 1.0 series development began. The 1.0 series was developed in C++ and supported APIs (Java, OMG IDL) through bindings or software caps. The first release, known as the familiarization release (F.0), came out in December 1996. It implemented all the HLA services except certain federation management functions and Data Distribution Management (DDM) services. The next RTI 1.0 release, in May 1997, supported all but the DDM service group. DDM services were first implemented experimentally in another RTI prototype, RTI-S. RTI-S was used with an advanced concept technology demonstration called the Synthetic Theater of War (STOW). The STOW exercise supported over 300 federates and 5,000 objects operating in perceived real time. The STOW prototype software and experimentation guided the evolution of the HLA specification in the DDM service area. Experience with RTI 1.0 and RTI-S was incorporated into RTI 1.3, the first full-service RTI implementation. RTI 1.3 implements HLA specification 1.3, released in March 1998. RTI 1.3 is in the public domain and can be accessed via the web. In the first eighteen months of availability, this software was downloaded by over 1,200 users worldwide, about 30 percent outside the United States.

As part of HLA experimentation, RTI 1.0 was implemented again in Java. The goal of the experiment was to demonstrate the robustness of the architecture to new implementation approaches, and the use of HLA for web-based applications. The Java RTI 1.0 version successfully interoperated with federates using RTI 1.0 implemented in C++. Further experiments are underway with RTI 1.3 to support federates operating in shared-memory and multiprocessor environments, again to ensure the flexibility of the HLA to support a range of implementation options.

Development of RTI implementations continues in and outside the United States. A current list of available implementations is maintained on the DMSO website.

2.6   CUSTOMER TRANSITION

A facility to support testing the compliance of federates to the HLA was established early in the HLA development process. Compliance with the HLA was established with the baseline definition along with test procedures [DMSO 1998a; DMSO 1998b; DMSO 1998c]. A federate compliance testing process and supporting system was developed and was fielded in the fall of 1997. This web-based test facility allows federates to be tested for compliance over the network in a straightforward four-step process. A comparable approach for testing RTI software for compliance with the HLA is in development.

Finally, a suite of user services accessible from the web was provided to users of the HLA. An on-line HLA resource center is available for access to HLA documentation and public-domain supporting software. Accessible via the web, this resource center is an open source for use by implementers of the HLA. The resource center includes information on HLA training and education. It also includes on-line user support both on the HLA in general and on use of the RTI and other supporting software.

Training in the HLA is available in several forms. DMSO sponsors monthly regional U.S. training events and select overseas events, as well as open hands-on RTI training offered twice a month near Washington, D.C. There are a growing number of privately offered courses as well. To foster use of the HLA in university curricula, DMSO is developing a graduate course curriculum module and a researcher support package [McLeod Institute 1999].

2.7   WHY DOES HLA PROGRESS WHEN OTHER (EQUALLY) GOOD IDEAS HAVE NOT?

In the period of less than four years, HLA has moved from a vision to a mature architecture with substantial and growing numbers of active users, and a suite of basic freeware automated tools, followed closely by commercial products to support the HLA user community. HLA is OMG adopted technology [OMG 1998] and a draft IEEE standard, and it has been adopted by the NATO technical community. Adoption at this rate can be attributed to a number of factors. HLA is a good idea, but there are numerous equally good ideas that have not been adopted as quickly or as widely. Understanding how this has happened is important to understanding the HLA and the technology transition process.

First, the HLA has a strong institutional proponent in DoD in general and DMSO in particular. DMSO is responsible for guiding the development and supporting the transition. It has actively pursued this mission by bringing to bear the key technical expertise and by furnishing resources to the key software and user support mechanisms.

The requirement for HLA to be used across the DoD has also been an important factor. For architectures to be successful, they need to be adopted and used by a critical mass of users. Without this, the incentives for commercial developers and the opportunities for real reuse do not exist. By providing the mandate for broad use, the base set of users is expanded, and acceptance can proceed on this basis.

All this was aided by the fact that HLA was not a technology in search of a problem. The problem existed, the potential customers were apparent. What was sought was a technical approach, and the supporting products to meet this recognized need.

By defining standards in terms of interfaces and rules, not products, the HLA has another advantage. The HLA avoided the pitfall of depending on current technology—or worse—locking out new technology developments. Rather, it has provided a framework for evolving implementations that take advantage of new technologies. As new approaches to computing and networking evolve, the HLA can take advantage of them.

Finally, another key to the progress has been that active user participation in HLA development was coupled with a strong, focused technical team which held the cogency of the architecture as their priority. The technical support team worked through the full lifecycle of the HLA development and transition. As inputs would come from users, the technical support team investigated possible ways to address these user requirements from the perspective of the architecture as a whole. No change was made without consideration of the impacts on the other aspects of the architecture. Formal and informal methods for analysis were used. This led to the integrated nature of the specification. As a result, the HLA was not a solution designed by committee or an exercise in technology for its own sake. Rather it was a focused technical development driven and harnessed by real users.

CHAPTER 3

An Overview of the HLA

3.1 INTRODUCTION

This chapter gives an overview of the High Level Architecture (HLA). Drawing on the definition of the HLA standard from the introduction, the overview discusses the HLA as a software architecture and summarizes the functions of the Runtime Infrastructure (RTI). If you don't plan to continue into Chapter 4, "The Sushi Restaurant Federation," this overview affords you a summary of the HLA and its goals. If you do plan to continue reading through Chapter 4 and beyond, the overview will show you the shape of the forest before you encounter the trees. If you understand the HLA as an architecture, you'll find it easier to use effectively.

3.2 THE HLA DEFINES A SOFTWARE ARCHITECTURE

3.2.1 GOAL OF THE HLA: BUILD SIMULATION SYSTEMS FROM COMPONENTS

The HLA defines a software architecture. To understand that architecture, it is helpful to know what the HLA is intended to do. Its chief intent is to allow simulation applications to be created by combining other simulations. In this way the HLA supports component-based simulation development, where the components are federates (not entities being simulated).

The design of the HLA is based on several premises or assumptions.

- No single, monolithic simulation can satisfy the needs of all users. Users differ in their interests and requirements for fidelity and detail.
- Simulation developers vary in their knowledge of domains to be simulated. No single set of developers is expert across all details even in one domain.
- No one can anticipate all the uses of simulation and all the ways simulations could be usefully combined. Even if a developer were able to satisfy a comprehensive set of require-

ments in a domain of application (by building the monolithic simulation), the developer could not anticipate the requirements for such a system. The world changes continually; nobody knows all the future uses for simulation, even in one domain.

- Future technology and tools must be incorporated. Were developers able to build the comprehensive simulation, and their crystal ball enabled them to anticipate requirements, computer technology would change underneath them. If their crystal ball could reveal the future of computer technology, they would still face the problem of incorporating it as their customers demanded to benefit from its advances.

These observations led the HLA designers to the following goals:

- It should be possible to decompose a large simulation problem into smaller parts. Smaller parts are easier to define, build correctly, and verify.
- It should be possible to combine the resulting smaller simulations into a larger simulation system.
- It should be possible to combine the smaller simulations with other, perhaps unanticipated, simulations to form a new simulation system.
- Those functions that are generic to component-based simulation systems should be separated from specific simulations. The resulting generic infrastructure should be reusable from one simulation system to the next.
- The interface between simulations and generic infrastructure should insulate the simulations from changes in the technology used to implement the infrastructure, and insulate the infrastructure from technology in the simulations.

The HLA is fundamentally an architecture to support component-based simulation, where the components are individual simulations. The architecture also supports building simulations that are distributed across multiple computers, but that is a happy side effect of its support for components. Nothing in the architecture assumes or requires a distributed implementation.

If the HLA is a Component Architecture, What Are the Components?

When we say that the HLA is a component architecture, the "component" in view is a federate. A federate is a simulation or tool that can be used in other federations beyond the federation for which it was originally designed. Federations are constructed from federates, so the federate is the unit of construction. The federate is also the unit of software reuse.

Federates typically are larger than common software components. Federates are complete running programs, rather than routines or objects in a library.

Describing the HLA as a component architecture may lead to another misunderstanding. "Model construction environments" often have associated graphical tools for discovering components' interfaces and for combining the components. The HLA is not a model construction environment. It supports the interaction of simulation components at federation execution time and to some extent at design time. But it is not an environment for constructing models.

It seems reasonable to believe that model construction environments can be designed to construct federates that adhere to the HLA. The HLA services provide mechanisms for accomplishing certain things and avoid dictating policy regarding their use. The design of an environment for federate construction will require adoption of policies in many cases, thereby specializing the HLA.

3.2.2   THE HLA DEFINES A SOFTWARE ARCHITECTURE

3.2.2.1   An Architecture Involves Elements, Interactions, and Patterns

Shaw and Garlan [Shaw and Garlan 1996] define a software architecture as follows:

> Abstractly, software architecture involves the description of elements from which systems are built, interactions among those elements, patterns that guide their composition, and constraints on those patterns.

The three parts of the HLA standard map to elements, interactions, and patterns as follows:

- *Elements*. The rules and the interface specification define the elements of an HLA federation to be the federates, an RTI, and a common object model.
- *Interactions*. The rules and the interface specification define the interactions between federates and the RTI, and between federates (always mediated by the RTI). For a given federation, the federation's object model defines the kinds of data carried by interactions between federates and RTI. The object model template (OMT) is a meta-model for all FOMs (federation object models), that is, it defines the structure of every valid FOM. That structure is assumed in the interface specification.
- *Patterns*. The allowed patterns of composition in the HLA are constrained by the rules and defined in the interface specification.

3.2.2.2   HLA, an Architecture, Not an Implementation

The HLA defines an architecture, not an implementation. In particular, the RTI is defined by its interface. Many different implementations of the RTI could meet the interface as specified. This is also true of federates. The interface specification defines not just the interface the RTI presents to federates, but also the interface federates present to the RTI. Every federate is yet another implementation of that interface.

The interface specification is abstract. The services (in both directions) are defined as procedure calls that take and return parameters, by pre- and post-conditions on the calls, and by exceptions. The definitions of the services make no reference to any programming language. Only after the services are defined does the interface specification define (in appendices) application programming interfaces (APIs) to various programming languages.

Why define things so abstractly? One goal of the HLA is to standardize an approach to the persistent problems in federating simulations, and to avoid defining the HLA in terms of transitory technology. One may say with confidence, and hope, that the evolution of programming languages will continue. We haven't yet found the ultimate networking technology. The HLA will keep pace with new technology by defining APIs for new languages, and by incorporating new networking technology into implementations of the RTI.

3.2.2.3   The HLA Exhibits Several Architectural Styles

Shaw and Garlan describe several architectural styles that appear frequently in software systems. As you look at a set of software systems of the same style, you see common idioms of organization, interactions, and constraints; these idioms are architectural styles. As we identify the architectural styles one finds in the HLA, you will understand better why it is organized as it is and how to exploit it.

As Shaw and Garlan point out, "most systems typically involve some combination of several styles." The HLA is no exception. Of the several styles they describe, the HLA exhibits features of three: layered systems; data abstraction systems; and event-based, implicit-invocation systems. The HLA combines these styles to exploit benefits specific to each.

The HLA Is a Layered Architecture   As Shaw and Garlan describe it,

> A layered system is organized hierarchically, each layer providing service to the layer above it and serving as a client to the layer below. In some layered systems inner layers are hidden from all except the adjacent outer layer, except for certain functions carefully selected for export.

From the perspective of a federate, the RTI appears as a layer below it that completely encapsulates the RTI's functions. For instance, in a distributed federation, the RTI contains the network functions needed to accomplish distribution. The distribution functions are hidden from the federate behind the RTI's interface.

This separation of RTI functions from the federate accomplishes two important things. First, it removes what is generic in simulation interoperability from the federate. The federate's code need not duplicate the services needed for interoperability. Secondly, the layer insulates the federate from changes in technology that may be reflected in the RTI. If the RTI must be modified to accommodate a new kind of network, the federate is unaffected.

The HLA Is a Data Abstraction Architecture   Shaw and Garlan describe a data abstraction architecture:

> In the style based on data abstraction and object-oriented organization, data representations and their associated primitive operations are encapsulated in an abstract data type or object. The components of this style are the objects—or, if you will, instances of abstract data type.

The layering principle in the HLA actually works in two directions: from the federate looking toward the RTI, and from the RTI looking toward the federate. This constitutes data abstraction. The RTI presents an interface to the federate behind which all its state is hidden, and each federate also presents an interface to the RTI behind which its state is hidden. From the RTI's perspective, there are multiple federates, each with the same interface but distinct identities. This is the essence of a data-abstraction or object-oriented organization.

The benefit of this style looking toward the RTI has been discussed. The benefit looking toward the federate is similar: the RTI is unaffected by changes in federates. The same RTI implementation can be used with various federates. And the federates may themselves contain complex systems (such as an entire vehicle simulator) or be connected to other systems (for instance, sensors).

Shaw and Garlan mention as a disadvantage of such systems the fact that objects must know about each other in order to invoke operations on each other explicitly. This is certainly as true in the HLA as it is in object-oriented programming in general; a federate must find its RTI implementation to join a federation, and the RTI must maintain a reference of some sort to each federate. However, this is no great limitation.

We should point out here that, according to the HLA Rules, one federate *never* interacts with another directly, but always through the federation's RTI. Federates need not retain any sort of reference to other federates, and indeed need not be aware of other federates' existence.

The HLA Is an Event-Based Architecture Event-based architecture is also called implicit invocation, reactive integration, or selective broadcast. As Shaw and Garlan say:

> The idea behind implicit invocation is that instead of invoking a procedure directly, a component can announce (or broadcast) one or more events. Other components in the system can register an interest in an event by associating a procedure with it. When the event is announced, the system itself invokes all the procedures that have been registered for the event. Thus an event announcement "implicitly" causes the invocation of procedures in other modules.

Implicit invocation pervades the design of the RTI's services. HLA Rule 3, which says no federates interact directly, but always through the RTI, has given rise to an architecture where federates are, generally speaking, unaware of each other's existence. Instead, the pattern is that one federate invoking a service on the RTI will cause the RTI to invoke services on other federates. It is the RTI's task to decide which federates it will call.

The easiest illustration of this is the sending of an interaction (the HLA's name for an occurrence communicated from one federate to others). One federate sends an interaction of a certain class. The RTI then calls all the federates that have subscribed to that class. The sending federate need not concern itself with which federates will receive (be called back with) the interaction. Thus the sending federate implicitly invokes all the receiving federates. Implicit invocation appears in all the groups of services. In a time-managed federation, one federate's request to advance its logical time may well cause other federates to be granted permission to advance theirs. The former need not know about the latter. Each group of services exhibits similar examples.

Shaw and Garlan mention as the chief benefits of this architectural style the support for reuse and the ease with which a system may be evolved. Those are precisely the purposes of this style in the HLA: a federate written to expect a certain federation object model (FOM) is able to combine with other federates with the same FOM. The number and identity of the other federates should be irrelevant. And with a well-written federate, that is the case.

What do we mean by well written? Shaw and Garlan give as the primary disadvantage of implicit invocation the fact that components relinquish control over the computation of the system. In particular, they can make no assumptions about the order in which things happen. A well written HLA federate avoids assumptions about ordering, except as ordering is mediated through RTI services, and it avoids assumptions about other federates in favor of dealing strictly with the FOM. Here is an example: a federate that operates on objects of a certain class, say, sushi boats, should subscribe to the class of sushi boats and deal with all the sushi boats it is informed of by the RTI. It should not assume anything about the number and kind of federates that are used to model the boats.

3.2.3   THE ARCHITECTURE SPLITS SIMULATION AND INFRASTRUCTURE FUNCTIONS

The software elements of an HLA federation are an implementation of the RTI and some number of federates. The RTI is the software that allows a federation to execute together. The HLA partitions functions in a federation between simulation-specific functions and the infrastructure. The intent is that all behavior specific to a given model or simulation is in the federate that implements it, and that the infrastructure contains functions generic to simulation interoperability. Thus the same implementation of the RTI can be used to support many different simulation applications. And federate developers are freed from worry about most infrastructure matters.

In Figure 3-1, you see the interface between the RTI on the bottom and the various kinds of federates above. Notice that the federates do not talk to each other directly. They are each connected to the RTI, and they communicate with each other using only services provided by the RTI. Notice also that the federates may be of various kinds: some are simulations in the usual sense; some may be merely passive viewers or loggers of the federation's progress; some may be surrogates for external systems or live participants; some may be controllers and managers of the federated simulation and not simulations at all. Each federate uses those RTI services appropriate to its purpose; the RTI does not otherwise distinguish federates. Finally, notice that each federate has a single point of contact with the RTI. The single point of contact is the definition of a federate from the RTI's perspective. The federate might consist of multiple processes, perhaps running on several computers; but it maintains one connection to the RTI, and it communicates with other federates only through the RTI.

In Figure 3-1, we show the names of the interfaces between each federate and the RTI. The RTI offers an interface called RTIambassador to each federate. The federate invokes operations on that interface to request services of the RTI, for instance, a request to update the value of an attribute of an object. These are called *federate-initiated* services. Each federate also presents an interface called FederateAmbassador to the RTI. The RTI invokes operations on that FederateAmbassador when it must call the federate, for instance, to pass to it a new value of an attribute. These are called *RTI-initiated* services. Thus some RTI services are defined as part of the RTIambassador interface, and some are defined as part of the FederateAmbassador interface.

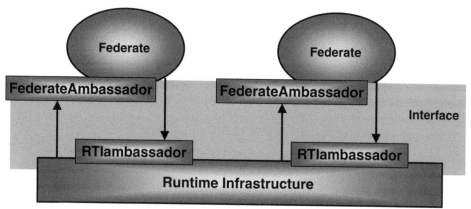

FIGURE 3-1   Interfaces Between RTI and Federates.

These interfaces take slightly different forms in the APIs defined in the interface specification in various programming languages. In C++, RTIambassador is a class with methods corresponding to the federate-initiated services. The FederateAmbassador is an abstract class with abstract methods corresponding to the RTI-initiated services. As part of an RTI implementation, a federate developer receives an implementation of RTIambassador that is linked into the federate process. The developer also receives the abstract class FederateAmbassador, and is responsible for implementing a concrete class derived from it. In the Java API, RTIambassador and FederateAmbassador are Java interfaces. An implementation using Common Object Request Broker Architecture (CORBA) defines these as interfaces in the Object Management Group (OMG) Interface Definition Language (IDL) [OMG 1996]. Ada 95 defines the interfaces as limited private types.

3.2.4   HLA'S INFORMATION MODEL: THE OBJECT MODEL TEMPLATE (OMT)

The OMT prescribes the structure of all FOMs. Each federation has a FOM that is the vocabulary of that specific federation. Each execution of a federation uses the federation's FOM. The FOM defines the names of things and occurrences that federates speak to each other about. The FOM does not describe things internal to a single federate, only things that are shared with other federates. The FOM is the vocabulary of data exchanged through the RTI for an execution of the federation.

The FOM is a parameter to the RTI, in the sense that the FOM is supplied as data to the RTI at the beginning of an execution. The RTI does not change when the FOM is changed or the RTI is applied to another federation. This is a significant feature of the HLA. The designers of each federation are free to adopt their own object model without changes to the RTI or to the HLA standard.

The main components of the OMT are the following:

• Object classes
• Interaction classes

3.2.4.1   Interactions: A Collection of Data Through the RTI

An *interaction* is a collection of data sent at one time through the RTI to other federates. An interaction may represent an occurrence or event in the simulation model of interest to more than one federate. An interaction may be defined to occur at a point in simulated time.

A federate *sends* an interaction; other federates *receive* the interaction. The interaction has no continued existence after it has been received. Each interaction carries with it a set of named data called *parameters*.

A FOM defines classes of interactions; when a federate sends an interaction, it is an interaction of a specific class. Interaction classes form a single-inheritance hierarchy. The hierarchy has a single root called InteractionRoot. Each interaction class defines the parameters that may be sent with it. Each class inherits the parameters defined for all its superclasses. InteractionRoot defines no parameters by default. The *fully qualified name* of a class is formed by concatenating the class names from the root to the class, separating the names with periods. The fully qualified name of each class must be unique in the FOM. All the foregoing are illustrated in Figure 3-2.[1]

---

1. This figure, and similar figures to follow, use the notation of the Unified Modeling Language [UML 1997].

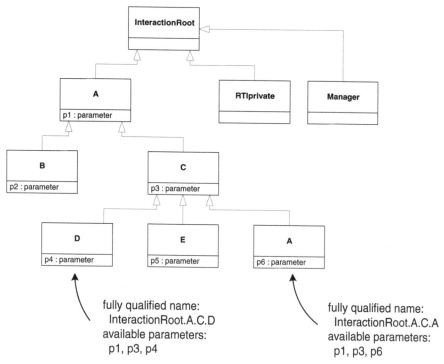

FIGURE 3-2   Interactive Class Hierarchy.

3.2.4.2   Objects: Simulated Entities That Endure

Objects in the RTI refer to simulated entities that:

- Are of interest to more than one federate and thus handled by the RTI
- Persist or endure for some interval of simulated time

The OMT defines classes of objects. Each class has a name. Each class defines a (possibly empty) set of named data called *attributes*. Federates create instances of these classes, each of which possesses a separate identity in the federation, and each of which has distinct instances of its attributes. Federates evolve the state of an object instance in simulation time by supplying new values for its attributes.

Federates converse with the RTI in terms of interactions and objects. Since federates converse with each other through the RTI, they converse in terms of interactions and objects. Each federate must make some translation from its internal notion of simulated entities to HLA objects as specified in the FOM. If the federate was written with the intention of HLA-compliance, the translation may be very straightforward; if the federate is being adapted to the HLA, the translation may be more involved. The FOM represents the common, agreed vocabulary between members of a federation.

Object classes form a hierarchy. Each object class has exactly one immediate ancestor or superclass. Object classes form a single-inheritance tree. The root class is called ObjectRoot. The *fully qualified name* of a class is formed by concatenating the class names from the root to the class, separating the names with periods. The fully qualified name of each class must be unique in the FOM.

Each class inherits all the attributes of its superclasses. The set of attributes declared for a class and those inherited from above is called the set of *available attributes*. The root class, ObjectRoot, has one required attribute, called privilegeToDeleteObject. Consequently, every class has at least one available attribute. See Figure 3-3.

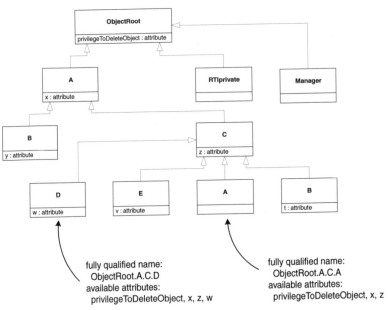

FIGURE 3-3   Object Class Hierarchy.

When attributes are the subject of an RTI operation, they are either the attributes of an object class, considered as a class, or they are the attributes of a specific object instance:

- The attributes of an object class, considered as a class, are called *class attributes*.

- The attributes of a specific object instance are called *instance attributes*.

Here are some examples. A federate wishing to subscribe to information regarding all instances of a certain object class subscribes to class attributes. A federate wishing to supply a new value for an attribute of a specific instance will update the appropriate instance attribute. The attributes that appear in the object class diagram in Figure 3-3 are class attributes.

Class and instance attributes are referred to by the same identifiers, names, or handles. RTI services that specify class attributes specify an object class and attribute identifiers, but never identify an object instance. Services that specify instance attributes always specify an object instance and attribute identifiers.

HLA Objects Are Not Entirely Object-Oriented

The term "object" as it is used in the HLA may be confusing, because it means something somewhat different from "object" in the usual object-oriented sense. The terms are the same in the following ways:

- HLA objects are instances of object classes, with distinct identity.
- Object classes form a hierarchy, with defined attributes inherited from superclasses.

The terms are different in these ways:

- HLA objects have *no* behaviors associated with them in the FOM.
- The "class attribute" notion does *not* correspond to "class variable," as in Smalltalk, or "static member," as in C++ and Java. In the HLA, a class attribute is an attribute of a class considered as a class and not with respect to an instance. There is no notion of a value for a class attribute.

With respect to RTI implementations:

- The term "object" does not imply that either the RTI or any of the federates must be implemented in an object-oriented language.
- The term "object" does not imply that HLA objects exist as object constructs in any API for an object-oriented language. In fact, HLA objects are not "language objects" in the APIs.

3.2.4.3   Interactions Versus Objects

Should you model with objects or interactions? In a sense, objects and interactions are interchangeable. Any federation model could be written entirely in terms of objects or entirely in terms of interactions. The change of state of an object attribute is an instantaneous occurrence (when the attribute's value is updated), so a designer could always achieve the effect of an interaction by creating attributes whose state changes are noticed and treated as interactions. Similarly, the evolution of the state of an object could be conveyed by a series of interactions that represent changes in the values of attributes. The following is general guidance:

- Any occurrence or event can be modeled as an interaction.
- If an entity is to be modeled that has persistent state, the entity should be represented as an object.

Taken together, objects and interactions represent a very general scheme that can be applied flexibly within a federation design.

3.2.4.4   Hierarchies of Classes Protect Federates From Change

You might think that the hierarchical structure of object and interaction classes is intended as an organizational aid for federation designers: like things may be grouped together, and attributes or parameters common to several classes can be factored out and placed in superclasses. The inheritance hierarchy is useful that way, but that isn't its chief purpose. The chief purpose of inheritance in the object model is to protect federates from change. To put it briefly, federates that were written to expect and use certain object and interaction classes can continue to use them even if the FOM is extended with subclasses not there originally.

Consider the inheritance diagram in Figure 3-4 representing an object class tree.

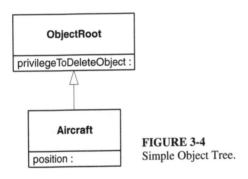

FIGURE 3-4
Simple Object Tree.

Suppose you had a federate written to publish or subscribe the Aircraft class. The federate might subscribe to the Aircraft class and discover instances of Aircraft registered by other federates. It might also register instances of the Aircraft class and update their position attribute. Now suppose that the federate is going to be used in a new federation, for which the FOM must be extended by adding subclasses, as depicted in Figure 3-5.

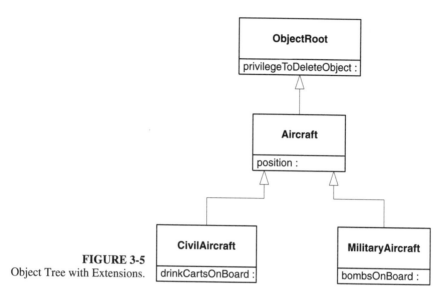

FIGURE 3-5
Object Tree with Extensions.

Can the original federate still operate? As far as the RTI is concerned, the answer is yes. The original federate subscribes to class Aircraft. As other newer federates register instances of CivilAircraft or MilitaryAircraft,[2] the federate will discover corresponding instances of class Aircraft. If a newer federate updates the position and drinkCartsOnBoard attributes of an instance of CivilAircraft, the original federate will be notified of the update of the position attribute of the instance, but not the update of drinkCartsOnBoard, which would be meaningless to it. The HLA is designed so that a FOM can be extended without invalidating federate software that was written assuming the earlier FOM.

3.2.5   HLA RULES

The HLA rules are one of the three parts that constitute the HLA standard. They express design goals and constraints on HLA-compliant federates and federations. The benefit for the developer of considering the rules here is that they summarize the way the HLA is intended to be used. The first five rules deal with federations, the latter five with federates.

3.2.5.1   Federation Rules

Rule 1. Federations shall have an HLA FOM, documented in accordance with the HLA OMT. The FOM is the common vocabulary of a federation. It describes the objects and interactions that one federate exposes to others in the federation. Agreeing on the FOM is an important step in the design of the federation. The OMT requires more information than the RTI needs to oper-

---

2. In earlier versions of this material, the attributes on the new classes were, respectively, transponderCode and radarCrossSection, which certainly sound more sophisticated. However, we found that someone in the audience inevitably would point out that many military aircraft have transponder codes, and civil aircraft all have radar cross-sections. So we chose silly names to avoid the distraction.

ate. The additional information in the template aims to ensure semantic consistency across the federation.

Rule 2. In a federation, all simulation-associated object instance representations shall be in the federates, not in the RTI.
This expresses a crucial design goal of the HLA: the RTI services are generic to simulation interoperability and can be used without modification across a variety of domains of application. The same RTI services will support cockpit simulators, manufacturing scheduling simulations, and urban traffic analysis tools.

This rule also gives rise to the following design constraint on the RTI: the RTI never functions as a database of present or previous attribute values. This constraint is sometimes oversimplified as "The RTI never keeps state." Any RTI implementation keeps a great deal of state associated with its services, but it always relies on federates to supply values for instance attributes and parameters when needed.

Rule 3. During a federation execution, all exchange of FOM data among federates shall occur via the RTI.
The goal of this rule is interoperable, reusable simulation components. The infrastructure cannot be bypassed by a compliant federate. Thus all federate exchanges are available for reuse.

Rule 4. During a federation execution, federates shall interact with the RTI in accordance with the HLA Interface Specification.
This Rule acknowledges the place of the interface specification in the HLA. Not only shall federates interact only through the RTI, their interactions shall observe the interface specification. This protects federates from peculiarities in RTI implementations and makes it more likely that one RTI implementation can be replaced successfully with another.

Rule 5. During a federation execution, an instance attribute shall be owned by at most one federate at any time.
There is an important idea latent in this rule. To own an instance attribute is to be responsible for updating it, and to be allowed to furnish new values. The interface specification makes it clear that, if a federate does not own an instance attribute, any attempt to update its value will be rejected by the RTI. The RTI will enforce this rule.

3.2.5.2   Federate Rules

Rule 6. Federates shall have an HLA Simulation Object Model (SOM), documented in accordance with the HLA OMT.
For a federate, part of HLA compliance is that all its simulation functionality be documented in HLA terms, at least all the data that the federate might expose in any federation. That documentation is its simulation object model (SOM). The OMT establishes the minimum set of information needed to characterize a federate during the design of a federation.

Rule 7. Federates shall be able to update and/or reflect any attributes and send and/or receive interactions, as specified in their SOMs.
This rule defines HLA-compliance with respect to data: attributes and interactions mentioned in the SOM must be fully supported in RTI terms. A federate will initiate the appropriate behavior with the RTI and will respond to RTI-initiated services with respect to each attribute or interac-

tion in its SOM. A federation designer can expect correct behavior from the federate with respect to any data it offers in its SOM.

Rule 8. Federates shall be able to transfer and/or accept ownership of attributes dynamically during a federation execution, as specified in their SOMs.
Data in the SOM must be supported not only as to production and consumption, but the federate must implement its part of the ownership transfer protocols defined in the interface specification. A federate's willingness (or unwillingness) to transfer ownership must be indicated in its SOM.

Rule 9. Federates shall be able to vary the conditions (for instance, thresholds) under which they provide updates of attributes, as specified in their SOMs.
The SOM indicates the conditions (passage of time, passage of a threshold, etc.) that cause the federate to update a given attribute. The federate should behave as advertised.

Rule 10. Federates shall be able to manage local time in a way that will allow them to coordinate data exchange with other members of a federation.
This rule requires a federate to use some set (possibly empty) of the time management functions of the RTI to manage its logical time coherently and to allow other federates to manage theirs. The federate may decide not to use any time management services. The RTI supports several different time management schemes and it allows a federation to include federates that vary in their approach.

3.2.6   THE MANAGEMENT OBJECT MODEL (MOM): THE RTI DESCRIBES THE FEDERATION

HLA federations are typically distributed systems. The federates often run on many computers. Thus federations are subject to the usual ills of distributed systems and must be managed. The RTI, being a sophisticated system for maintaining a shared view of some set of entities, can be used to maintain and manage a shared view of the federation as a distributed system. Management data can be described and distributed just like simulation data. The MOM is a standardized, mandatory part of every FOM that allows the RTI to describe and manage the state of a federation.[3]

The RTI itself creates the instances and updates attribute values associated with the MOM. For instance, as each federate joins the federation, the RTI creates an instance of class Manager.Federate and provides values for the instance's attributes. A federate wishing to know how many other federates have joined can subscribe to the class Manager.Federate using the same mechanisms as for any other FOM data. Thus system management can be accomplished through the use of federates designed for the purpose. Because the MOM is the same in all federations, management federates can be reused.

The MOM also defines a set of interactions that can be used to affect the state of other federates. The RTI is required to respond correctly to MOM interactions. These interactions are used to adjust federation operation, request information, and report on federate activity.

---

3. The MOM is defined in the interface specification. Its use is discussed to some extent in Chapter 5, "Synchronizing the Federation." It is more fully described in Chapter 8, "Advanced Topics."

A federation designer can extend the MOM, either by adding attributes to the HLA-defined MOM classes, or by adding subclasses to the MOM classes, or by adding interactions to the HLA-defined MOM interactions. The generation and reception of data in extensions to the HLA-defined MOM becomes the responsibility of one or more of the federates.

3.3   THE HLA OFFERS SERVICES IN SIX AREAS

The overview of the HLA concludes with a summary of the functions of the interface, that is, the services the RTI offers to federates and *vice versa*. HLA services fall into six groups that are defined by similarity of interest.

3.3.1   FEDERATION MANAGEMENT

Federation management services manage a federation in two ways:

- By defining a federation execution in terms of existence and membership
- By accomplishing federation-wide operations.

To define a federation, there are services to create a federation execution and to permit a federate to join the execution or resign from it. Every federate must join a federation execution, so no federate can completely ignore this group.

Federation-wide operations include the coordination of federation saves (checkpoints) and restores. There are also services to allow a federation to define and meet a federation-wide synchronization point.

3.3.2   DECLARATION MANAGEMENT

The HLA is characterized by an implicit-invocation style of data exchange. Federates don't send data to other federates by name; they make it available to the federation, and the RTI ensures its delivery to interested parties. The *declaration management* services are the way federates declare their intent to produce (publish) or consume (subscribe to) data. The RTI uses these declarations for routing data, transforming data, and interest management.

Regarding routing, the RTI uses subscriptions to decide what federates should be informed of the creation or update of entities.

Declarations are used to transform data received by a federate. Received data undergoes pruning and promotion (re-labeling) in accordance with the federate's subscriptions before being delivered. This is one of several mechanisms for protecting federates from extensions to the FOM and encouraging federate reuse.

Finally, the RTI uses declarations to indicate interest to publishing federates. The RTI can tell a federate whether any other federate is subscribed to data it intends to produce, so that it can cease producing when no other federate needs the information.

3.3.3 OBJECT MANAGEMENT

Object management services are those used for the actual exchange of data. A federate uses services from this group to send and receive interactions. These services are also used to register new instances of an object class and to update its attributes. Other federates will have services from this group invoked on them to receive interactions, discover new instances, and receive updates of instance attributes.

Other services of this group are used to control how data are transported, to solicit fresh updates of attribute values, and to inform a federate whether it should expect data.

3.3.4 OWNERSHIP MANAGEMENT

In HLA terms, simulating an entity means furnishing values for instance attributes. The *ownership management* services in the RTI implement the HLA's notion of responsibility for simulating an entity. They allow that responsibility to be shared or transferred among federates.

As stated above, HLA rules 5 and 8 require a federate to own an instance attribute before it can update its value. The RTI ensures that at most one federate at a time owns a given instance attribute. The owning federate is responsible for updating it. Responsibility for simulating an entity can be shared between federates in two ways.

First, the complete modeling of an entity may be shared among federates. If the entity is represented by an instance with several attributes, different federates may own various attributes of that instance, and thus be responsible for updating the attributes that they own. Ownership management services support the acquisition of ownership to allow this.

Second, the modeling of entities may pass from one federate to another in the course of a federation execution. Ownership of an instance attribute may be transferred from one federate to another. Transfers of ownership may be initiated by the present owner or the prospective owner.

Ownership management can be ignored if a federation does not need it. This service group is an example of the effort to make the service groups independent; the default behavior regarding ownership of the object management services is reasonable.

3.3.5 TIME MANAGEMENT

With federates executing in their own threads of control, the proper ordering of events between federates is a significant problem to be solved. In the HLA, ordering of events is expressed in "logical time." Logical time is an abstract notion; it is not necessarily tied to any representation or unit of time. The RTI's *time management* services do two things:

- They allow each federate to advance its logical time in coordination with other federates.
- They control the delivery of time-stamped events so the federate need never receive events from other federates in its "past," that is, events with logical times less than its logical time.

The RTI allows a federate to choose the degree to which it participates in time management. A federate may be time-constrained, in which case its advance of logical time is constrained by other federates. A federate may be time-regulating, in which case its advance of logical time regulates other federates. A federate may be time-constrained and time-regulating, or either alone, or neither. Federates will make different choices depending on their purpose and the requirements of the federation. The RTI allows federation executions whose federates make differing choices.

3.3.6   DATA DISTRIBUTION MANAGEMENT

Data distribution management (DDM) services control the producer-consumer relationships among federates. Whereas the declaration management services manage those relationships in terms of interaction and object classes, DDM manages in terms of object instances and abstract routing spaces. DDM provides powerful tools to refine producer-consumer relationships.

3.3.7   THE GROUPS OF SERVICES ARE AS INDEPENDENT AS POSSIBLE

It is a goal of the design of the HLA services that a federate developer who does not need the functions of a group of services can ignore it safely. The services in one group can be used without reference to another, and the default behavior is reasonable and useful. This goal is realized in the case of ownership, time, and data distribution management. The federation, declaration, and object management groups, however, are always required for the exchange of data.

3.4   SUMMARY

Here are some important points from our overview of the HLA:

- The HLA standard contains three parts: the Rules, the OMT, and the interface specification.

- The goal of HLA is to allow simulation systems to be built from components that are themselves simulations.

- HLA is a software architecture in the common sense. The HLA exhibits several architectural styles: layers, abstract data types, implicit invocation, and support for distribution.

- HLA is an architecture, not an implementation.

- HLA addresses the persistent problems of simulation interoperability and it avoids standardizing transitory technology.

- The object model and standardized interfaces to the RTI insulate federates from change.

- RTI furnishes its own management data through the MOM.

The HLA's Relation to CORBA

CORBA is an architecture for "middleware"—software that occupies a layer somewhere between the operating system and applications—that allows computing with objects distributed across computers [OMG 1996]. The CORBA standard is a product of the OMG, a consortium of software vendors and users. It is the most widely used standard of its sort. There are other middleware products that do somewhat similar things, such as Microsoft's Distributed Common Object Model.

CORBA defines an Object Request Broker (ORB), which is infrastructure that implements the CORBA functions. To some people being introduced to the HLA, the RTI sounds like an ORB. They are similar, in that ORBs mediate interactions between distributed objects, and the RTI mediates interactions between federates. But the similarity is superficial. The following will help to point out the architectural differences between an HLA federation and a CORBA-based system:

- CORBA is for building object-oriented systems in the architectural sense. As Shaw and Garland point out, in object-oriented systems (at the ORB level), all elements interact explicitly. In the HLA, federates interact implicitly.

- The RTI supports a component model at the federate level. CORBA does not. CORBA is a platform on which one could define a component model. OMG is currently working on a definition for a CORBA-based component model.

Even though CORBA and the HLA are both used to build distributed systems, they aren't very similar. Nevertheless, there is a relationship between CORBA and the HLA:

- The interfaces between federates and the RTI can be cast as CORBA interfaces. OMG IDL is one of the APIs: using that API, the RTIambassador and FederateAmbassador are instantiated as CORBA objects. In fact, version 1.3 of the interface specification and the IDL API have been adopted by the OMG as their "Facility for Distributed Simulation Systems" [OMG 1998].

- ORBs and CORBA services are candidate tools for implementing RTIs. Their use in an RTI is effectively hidden behind the RTI interface. Likewise, federates are free to use CORBA in their implementations. Implementations exist of both RTIs and federates using ORBs.

CHAPTER 4

The Sushi Restaurant Federation

4.1 BUILDING A FEDERATION: BEGINNING AN EXAMPLE

This chapter begins a tutorial introduction to building a federation. It describes the integration of simulations into a High Level Architecture (HLA) federation and uses that description as a vehicle for explaining the application of the HLA. It does not cover all the things the runtime infrastructure (RTI) can do; instead, its goal is to present useful ideas for applying the HLA to common tasks. The following groups of HLA services are discussed in this chapter:

- Federation Management
- Declaration Management
- Object Management
- Ownership Management

The time management service group and coordination of the federation lifecycle are discussed in Chapter 5, "Synchronizing the Federation." The data distribution management service group and further applications of the HLA are described in Chapter 8, "Advanced Topics."

When you have read this chapter, you will know enough to build a running federation that can do a variety of useful things. In Chapter 5, "Synchronizing the Federation," you will learn how to ensure the ordering of events in logical time and synchronized start-up of federates.

We assume you've read the Preface, Introduction, and Overview. We also assume that you are a programmer, though not perhaps conversant with Java.

4.1.1 EXAMPLE: A "SUSHI BOAT" RESTAURANT

Now we introduce our running example, a "sushi boat" restaurant modeled after establishments in San Francisco, Denver, and elsewhere. The restaurant serves, among other things, various kinds of sushi but uses a novel means of conveying the servings, depicted in Figure 4-1.

FIGURE 4-1   The Sushi Boat Restaurant.

In a "sushi boat" restaurant, the chefs work on an island in the middle of the restaurant. They are surrounded by counters and other space on which to prepare their delights. The chefs' work area is surrounded by a water-filled moat or canal about a foot wide. The diners sit at a bar that surrounds the canal, which is at the height of the bar. The canal experiences a gentle current; wooden boats or barges several feet long and about as wide as the canal float with the current. As the chefs prepare servings, they place them on rectangular plates of elegant Japanese design. When they have finished a batch of servings, which may fill several plates, the chefs place the plates on empty boats as the boats float by. Diners who spy an attractive serving floating toward their seat at the bar remove the plate as the boat comes by and sample its contents.

Sushi comes in many kinds and prices. The price of each serving is indicated by the design and color of its plate. The diner's bill is determined by the stack of empty plates carried to the cashier at the end of the meal. The chefs typically will try to keep a supply of all the kinds of sushi available on the boats. They spread out a batch of sushi across several boats, rather than placing all the plates of one batch into the first boats with space for them. The experience of the diner then—so unlike the experience of normal life—is of a succession of boats floating past with a variety of pleasant tastes.

Our example is typical of the intended use of the HLA in that we will construct a federation from models that were built by different organizations, probably for different purposes. To begin with, we will work with three federates, as depicted in Figure 4-2.

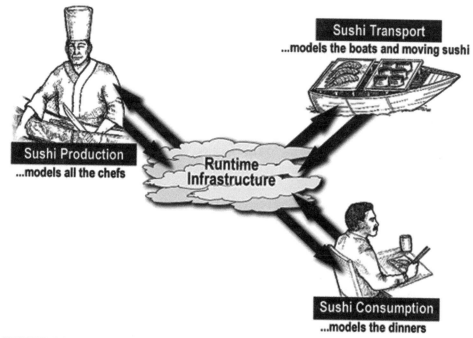

FIGURE 4-2   The Restaurant Federation.

- The Object-Oriented Culinary Institute of San Francisco has developed a simulation of sushi chefs.
- The Center for Concerned Sushi Patrons of Washington, D.C., has developed a model of sushi diners.
- The International Brotherhood of Sushi Transporters of Chicago has a model that conveys sushi servings from chefs to diners in a restaurant.

As is typical in HLA applications, these simulations already exist. Owing to a striking exercise of forethought, they are already HLA-compliant, and therefore will require little or no modification to act as federates. The program structures of these simulations may be quite different, they may turn out to manage simulation time very differently, and their internal representations of simulation entities may diverge. The HLA is used as an integration mechanism, defining a federated model for the combined simulation, defining the representation of common objects, isolating the differing program structures, and accommodating the various time-management schemes.

We'll assume that the models will be executed at the sites of their developers, that is, in San Francisco, Chicago, and D.C., respectively.[1] Thus the federation execution will be distributed geographically. The RTI implementation may be distributed across the sites of the federates and perhaps some facility for system management of the simulation. An important consequence of distribution is that the relative ordering of many occurrences in the federation execution depends on processing and communications latencies. Therefore the ordering cannot be guaranteed without recourse to the RTI mechanisms designed to achieve ordering or synchronization. But those mechanisms exist, and we will show as we go along how the RTI is used to guarantee the correct ordering of the crucial events.

4.2 FEDERATION MANAGEMENT: DEFINING THE FEDERATION

Before a federation execution exists, it must be defined to the RTI. The federation execution must be created and associated with a Federation Object Model (FOM), and the federates must join the federation execution. Accordingly, we'll discuss first the services defined in the RTI for these purposes.

An RTI may have several federation executions defined in it simultaneously. This circumstance might arise, for instance, in a laboratory, where several combined simulations might be conducted at the same time, or where production work is performed at the same time as development or testing. Within a given RTI, all federation executions existing simultaneously are distinguished by unique names assigned by the federation execution developers. Uniqueness is enforced by the RTI; an attempt to create a second execution with the same name as a current execution will cause an exception. A federate joins a specific execution by supplying the execution name when it joins. The RTI ensures that there is no interference between simultaneous federation executions.

4.2.1 MECHANISM, NOT POLICY

The RTI services support the notions of the federation execution and of being joined to the execution. But the RTI makes no assumptions about what software invokes these services. The

---

1. While the geographical distribution makes the problem more difficult in some ways, it has the virtue of keeping the federate development in the hands of the people who developed the models originally. We're also assuming a strong, competent, tactful integration agent. This agent, endowed with the wisdom of Solomon, and the patience of Job—or the authority of Napoleon—will ensure that the necessary design agreements are reached and respected.

intent of the RTI is to provide the necessary mechanisms but not to impose a policy for their use, thereby supporting many different policies. (This is a theme that recurs throughout the RTI's design.) As we discuss the example, we'll have to choose some strategy of using each set of services, in order to be concrete, but we'll try to indicate other possible choices of strategy.

4.2.2   LIFECYCLE OF RTI AND FEDERATES

Before the first invocation of an RTI service, the RTI software and the federates' software must begin executing. After the federation execution is finished, the RTI and federates eventually stop execution. These concerns and the allocation of processes to hosts, are often referred to as *lifecycle* matters. The HLA is deliberately silent about the lifecycle of the RTI and the federates, thereby allowing a range of approaches.

In our example, we assume that the federates will run in three locations, and we make no assumptions about the RTI. We do assume, however, that the RTI is running before any of the federates, and that the federates begin execution somehow. Perhaps this is done by human operators at consoles. Or perhaps the lifecycle is under the control of a tool that can activate processes on remote hosts.

4.2.3   FEDERATION EXECUTION DATA AND RTI INITIALIZATION DATA

The RTI will require certain information to support a federation execution. Some of that information is part of the HLA standard and does not vary from RTI to RTI. This information is called the federation execution data, or FED. Some information is specific to the RTI implementation employed and is not standardized. This is the RTI initialization data, or RID.

The syntax of the FED is part of the HLA interface specification. A FED conforming to the standard should be usable with any RTI. The FED contains the extract of the FOM that is needed for the RTI to function.

The content and syntax of the RID is determined by the supplier of the RTI implementation you're using. The RID is supplied typically when the RTI software is started; how and when is a lifecycle matter.[2]

4.2.4   CREATING THE FEDERATION EXECUTION

The first order of business is to create the federation execution. The service is straightforward; some software invokes the service CREATE FEDERATION EXECUTION,[3] supplying the execution name and a location of the FED. The important thing is to ensure that the federation execution is created before federates attempt to join it.

There are two ways to cause the creation and joins to occur in the right order. One way is to distinguish some federate and give it the responsibility of creating the federation execution.

---

2. The Pitch Portable RTI furnished with this book does not use a RID file. There are some user-definable configuration parameters that are described in the CD-ROM documentation on the Pitch Portable RTI.
3. We'll render all HLA service names in small caps. Service names adorned with a dagger (†) are initiated by the RTI. Sometimes we refer to the invocation of an RTI-initiated service as a callback.

However, that approach relies on the creation and the joins being ordered. In a distributed system it's difficult to guarantee the ordering of the creation and joins. The RTI supports an easier approach. The RTI ensures that a federation execution is created only once. If a second creation is attempted with the same name, the CREATE FEDERATION EXECUTION service reports an exception, and no harm is done. So one strategy is to require each federate to attempt to create the federation execution. If the federate receives the exception reporting that the federation execution already exists, it ignores it.

4.2.5   JOINING THE FEDERATION EXECUTION

After each federate has ensured that the federation execution exists, the federate joins it by invoking JOIN FEDERATION EXECUTION on the RTI. The federate must supply the name of the federation execution and a "type," which we'll explain in a moment. The federate gets back from the service a "federate designator" that uniquely identifies the federate in the federation execution. In the APIs for C++, Java, and Object Management Group (OMG) Interface Definition Language (IDL), this "designator" is a federate handle consisting of a small positive integer. The federate designator is used chiefly in system management mechanisms (the management object model or MOM) that will be described in Chapter 8, "Advanced Topics."

The federate type that is supplied for JOIN FEDERATION EXECUTION is part of the mechanism for restoring the state of an execution, which is described fully in Chapter 8. In the various APIs, the type is a string of some sort. Types need not be unique within a federation execution. We will use the type as a name for each federate. Each federate will use a descriptive string for a type, for instance, "Production."

4.2.6   JOINING LATE

Our discussion thus far could lead you to believe that the RTI demands that all federates join before anything interesting happens. This is not the case. The RTI fully supports federates joining at any point in the course of a federation execution. They may also resign (leave the federation execution) at any point. There are consequences of joining and resigning for time and object management, and indeed for all the RTI functions, but the behavior of the RTI is clearly defined in all cases. In fact, because the RTI has no intrinsic notion of phases of execution, all joins may be said to be "late."

So are there phases of execution? Yes. In many applications it is useful to have all the federates join before the simulation proceeds. This is particularly the case if the federation is characterized by strict time management. The RTI contains mechanisms to support a variety of phased-start policies. These are discussed at length in Chapter 5, "Synchronizing the Federation." The point is that these are policies for the use of the RTI, not required behavior.

4.2.7 CLEANING UP AT THE END

At the end of the simulation, the federation execution should clean up after itself. We must postpone discussion of some of the details here, but you should be aware that there is a clean-up procedure that reverses the procedure we've just described. Each federate resigns from the federation, and then some software destroys the federation execution.

A federate resigns from the federation by invoking RESIGN FEDERATION EXECUTION on the RTI. After the resign invocation has completed, the former federate cannot invoke any services on the RTI except to destroy the execution (or to create a federation execution or to join one). The former federate is no longer counted in the RTI's time management or other schemes.

A tidy federation designer may wish to end the federation execution after all its federates have resigned. This can be accomplished by some software, perhaps a former federate, invoking DESTROY FEDERATION EXECUTION, supplying the name of the execution to destroy. This service will raise an exception if some federates are still joined. The service raises a different exception if the federation execution named in the invocation does not exist, perhaps because it has already been destroyed.

Joining and Resigning with the Test Federate

This is a good time to try the services we've just described. The test federate is software supplied with this book that allows you to invoke all the federate-initiated HLA services "by hand" without doing any programming. The CD-ROM describes how to install and run the test federate and the supplied RTI. It also describes how to create a federation and join one or more test federates to it.

Sample Java Code

Here is some Java code that performs the functions we've just discussed. This code is adapted from the sample implementation of the restaurant federation that is included on the CD-ROM. That implementation is described in greater detail in Chapter 6, "A Sample Implementation."

Before a federate can invoke any RTI services, it must obtain a reference to an implementation of the Java interface, `hla.rti.RTIambassador`. How the federate does this may vary depending on the RTI implementation. In the case of the Pitch Portable RTI (pRTI), the federate invokes a static method on the implementation-supplied class RTI:

```
String hostname;
int portNumber;
RTIambassador rti = RTI.getRTIambassador(hostName, portNumber);
```

See the programming notes on the pRTI (on the CD-ROM) for more details about this call. Once the federate has acquired an `RTIambassador` reference, the federate can create a federate execution, if necessary. In the code below, the federate detects and ignores the pre-existence of the federation execution.

```
String federationExecutionName;
java.net.URL fedURL:
try {
   rti.createFederationExecution(federationExecutionName, fedURL);
}
catch (hla.rti.FederationExecutionAlreadyExists e) {
   System.out.println("Federation execution " + federationExecution-
Name
   + " already exists.");
}
```

The federate can now join the federation execution. We assume the federate has constructed an instance of some implementation of the Java interface hla.rti.Federate-Ambassador. In our sample implementation, each of the federates contains an implementation called FedAmbImpl.

```
hla.rti.FederateAmbassador fedAmb;
int federateHandle;
String federateType = "MyFederate";
try {
   federateHandle = rti.joinFederationExecution(
      federationExecutionName,
      federateType,
      fedAmb);
}
catch (hla.rti.RTIexeception e) {
   System.out.println("Exception on join:" + e);
}
```

4.3 THE FEDERATION OBJECT MODEL:
A COMMON DESCRIPTION OF THE WORLD

The purpose of this section is to describe the federation object model (FOM) we will use with the restaurant federation. We draw on our earlier description of the object model template and show how it is applied in the case of this federation. We conclude by discussing ordering and transportation, which apply to all federations.

4.3.1   CLASSES IN OUR RESTAURANT FEDERATION

To begin with, our sushi boat restaurant federation will have three classes in its FOM: Restaurant, Serving, and Boat. These are depicted in Figure 4-3. The graphical notation, as before, is that of the Unified Modeling Language.

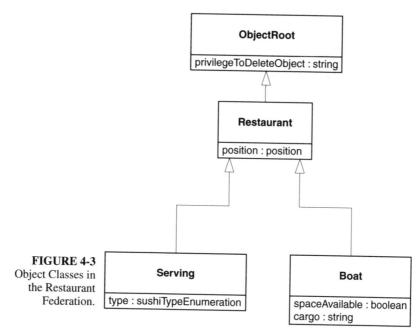

FIGURE 4-3
Object Classes in
the Restaurant
Federation.

Serving represents a serving of sushi, usually several pieces, that is conveyed on a plate from a chef to a diner. Serving is represented as an object because instances of Serving are created, manipulated, and consumed in the federation and—this is most important—they are of interest to more than one federate. Servings are created by the Production federate, manipulated by the Transport federate, and consumed by Consumption federate. Thus Servings persist and affect more than one federate. Therefore, they are represented in the FOM as an object class.

The Serving class has position and type attributes, with position inherited from Restaurant. The position attribute indicates the physical location of the Serving. The type indicates the type of the serving (California Roll, various kinds of fish, etc.). The type is assigned by the Production federate which creates the instance. Ultimately the type may affect the choice of a diner modeled by the Consumption federate.

Why Boat objects? As with Servings, all the federates act upon or interact with Boat instances. The Transport federate moves Boats, and the Production and Consumption federates must interact with the Boats' positions and loads. Boats are not private to one federate; therefore they are represented in the FOM.

Boat objects have position, spaceAvailable, and cargo attributes, with position inherited from Restaurant. The position attribute tells where the boat is on the canal, and thus whether it is in reach of a chef or diner. The spaceAvailable attribute indicates whether there is room on the Boat for more Servings. In our implementation of the restaurant federation, we make the simplifying assumption that each Boat can carry only one Serving; thus spaceAvailable is boolean. The cargo attribute (again with the simplifying assumption of one Serving per Boat) is a designator that identifies the Serving riding on the Boat.

Why the Restaurant class? It is defined to allow us to declare the position attribute once and cause it to be inherited by all the subclasses of Restaurant. One might declare position in each of the subclasses, but defining it once in a common superclass is a way to enforce the fact that the attribute has the same meaning and representation in all the subclasses. Now Serving and Boat must also have the common superclass ObjectRoot. You could move the position attribute up to ObjectRoot. It is legal to add attributes to ObjectRoot. With that arrangement the classes Serving and Boat would both inherit position without interposing Restaurant. However, it is probably unwise to do so from the standpoint of modeling, and it would make it harder to evolve the FOM. If it became necessary to add other subclasses to ObjectRoot later on, they also would inherit the position attribute, and that is unlikely to be desirable.

Why are there no Chef or Diner objects? Our conceptual model of the federation includes a notion of chefs creating servings of sushi and diners consuming them. The Production and Consumption federates may indeed model chefs and diners internally, but there is no aspect of chefs or diners that need be exposed to other federates. Therefore, there are no corresponding classes in the FOM.

4.3.2   INTERACTIONS IN THE RESTAURANT FEDERATION

Strictly speaking, the model of the restaurant doesn't need any interactions. However, we'll need a way to indicate that the simulation has gone far enough and can stop. We'll use an interaction of the class SimulationEnds to signal quitting time. The place of this interaction class in the hierarchy is indicated in Figure 4-4.

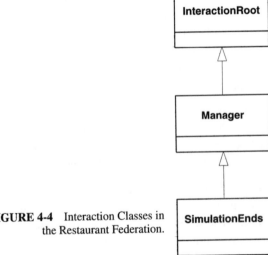

FIGURE 4-4   Interaction Classes in
the Restaurant Federation.

All interaction classes are subclasses of InteractionRoot. SimulationEnds is a subclass of Manager because it is an extension of the MOM. We'll describe that in Chapter 8, "Advanced Topics." An execution of the restaurant federation is defined (somewhat arbitrarily) as complete when some predetermined number of Servings have been consumed. The Consumption federate will be responsible for noticing that condition and sending SimulationEnds. The other federates must receive SimulationEnds and cease simulating when they receive it.

4.3.3   DATA: ATTRIBUTES AND PARAMETERS

To complete our description of the FOM we'll use for the restaurant federation, we discuss several topics not mentioned in our discussion of the HLA's object model.

4.3.3.1   Types, or Lack of Them

The formal presentations of FOMs in the various object model tools describe the types of attributes and parameters, that is, whether they are integers, floating-point numbers, strings, etc. You may have noticed that the FED does not. Attributes and parameters have no types associated with them in the FED. This is because the RTI also has no notion of the type of an attribute or parameter. The RTI deals with attributes and parameters as uninterpreted sequences of bytes: it delivers the supplied bytes in their supplied order. If a federate on a "big-endian" computer updates an attribute understood to be a four-byte binary integer, and that attribute is reflected on a "little-endian" machine, the reflecting federate will perceive an unintended value, unless it makes some adjustment. The RTI conveys the four bytes without regard to their interpretation by the federates' hosts.

This puts the burden of interpreting attributes and parameters on the federates, and more importantly, puts the burden of agreeing to the interpretation on the federation designers. In the case of a binary integer, a sensible approach is to decree that the attribute will always be supplied to the RTI in "network order." This is sensible because: (1) it's unambiguous; and (2) most programming languages have available library routines that will convert to and from this data format.

4.3.3.2   Ordering

One of the RTI's strengths is its ability to sequence the arrival of time-stamped events, such as attribute updates and interactions, in accordance with logical time. The RTI can ensure that events are delivered to each federate in correct time order regardless of the origin of the event and regardless of the vagaries of communication. When the delivery of events is so ordered, events are said to be delivered in *time-stamp order*. The RTI can also deliver events to a federate as they arrive, without regard to logical time. In this case, events are said to be delivered in *receive order*.

The federation designer can decide what ordering applies to the update of each attribute of an object class and the receipt of each interaction class. The designer specifies in the FED the ordering of each class attribute, and each interaction class. (Note that these are not symmetric;

individual class attributes are assigned an ordering, but it is an entire interaction class, not its parameters, that is assigned an ordering.)

4.3.3.3   Transportation

In addition to ordering, each attribute and each interaction class have another "quality of service," namely, transportation type. As with ordering, transportation is a property of attributes (not object class) and of interaction classes (not parameters). Transportation is defined in the FED and must appear for each class attribute and each interaction class.

For network-based RTI implementations, the choices for transportation are *reliable* and *best-effort*. The idea of reliable is that transmission of the event occurs over a reliable underlying network mechanism, such that the RTI guarantees that the event will be delivered or an exception will be indicated. Best-effort transportation makes no such guarantee; an attribute update or interaction sent best-effort may not arrive at any or all of its destination federates, and no exception is indicated upon failure. Best-effort transportation, however, typically uses the network more efficiently than reliable. In network-based RTI implementations, reliable transportation often is implemented with TCP streams and best-effort transportation with UDP datagrams or IP multicast.

4.3.4   READING THE FED FILE

Before we present the FED file for the restaurant federation, here are some observations that apply to all FED files.

All names mentioned in a FED file are construed by the RTI without regard to case. Thus the class names "serving," "Serving," and "seRvInG" are indistinguishable to the RTI. This is also true for attribute names and other FED names we've mentioned (including spaces and dimensions). The keywords in the FED file syntax—for instance, *FED*, *objects*, *class*—are recognized without regard to case.

The arrangement of the FED file into lines is arbitrary, as with most modern programming languages. However, a double semicolon turns everything to the right of it into a comment up to the end of its line. Indentation is entirely arbitrary, so you may adopt any scheme of indentation you wish.

Every valid FED file contains three required object classes:

- The root of the object class tree is called ObjectRoot.
- ObjectRoot has a required subclass called RTIprivate. RTIprivate is used by RTI implementers. It must be present but cannot be extended (subclasses) by a federation designer.
- ObjectRoot has another required subclass called Manager. It is the root of a further tree that defines the object portion of the MOM. All the subclasses of Manager that you see in the sample FED files are required to be there. We'll discuss this more later.

Every valid FED file also contains three required interaction classes: InteractionRoot and two subclasses, RTIprivate and Manager.

A FED file for the restaurant federation looks like Figure 4-5. Note that the subclasses of object class Manager and the subclasses of interaction class Manager have been omitted for brevity. Their full definition is depicted in Chapter 8, "Advanced Topics," and is included in the FED for the sample implementation.

```
(FED
(Federation restaurant_1)   ;; we choose this tag
  (FEDversion v1.3)             ;; required; specifies RTI spec version
  (spaces                       ;; we define no routing spaces
  )
  (objects
    (class ObjectRoot          ;; required
      (attribute privilegeToDeleteObject reliable timestamp)
      (class RTIprivate)
      (class Restaurant
        (attribute position reliable timestamp)
        (class Serving
          (Attribute type reliable timestamp)
        )
        (class Boat
          (attribute spaceAvailable reliable timestamp)
          (attribute cargo reliable timestamp)
        )
      )
      ;; Manager class and subclasses are required
      (class Manager....
    )                             ;; end ObjectRoot
  )                             ;; end objects
  (interactions
    (class InteractionRoot reliable timestamp
      (class RTIprivate reliable timestamp)
      (class Manager reliable receive
        (class SimulationEnds reliable receive)
    )                      ;; end InteractionRoot
  )                        ;; end interactions
)                          ;; end FED
```

FIGURE 4-5   FED File for Restaurant Federation.

4.4 OVERVIEW OF SHARING DATA

In an HLA federation, federates share data among themselves using services from the declaration management and object management groups. These services all go together, and trying to explain one group without the other is confusing. The functions we need for the basic restaurant federation are fairly simple, so we'll try to give you an overview in this section, and postpone a fuller discussion to following sections.

4.4.1 SHARING IS GOOD

As we have said before, the data in a federation take one of two forms: objects and interactions. Objects are simulated entities of interest to more than one federate that persist for some interval of simulated time. Interactions represent simulated occurrences. They occur at a point in simulated time but don't persist. Objects and interactions are instances of object and interaction classes that are defined in the FED. An object class defines named data called class attributes; an interaction class defines named data called parameters.

How is data sent with an interaction? When a federate *sends* an interaction, it supplies data for some or all of the parameters available to the interaction. When the RTI delivers the interaction to subscribing federates, those federates are said to *receive* the interaction. The RTI delivers the values of the parameters that were sent with the interaction.

In the case of objects, the sending of data is a little more complicated. It happens in several stages. First, a federate *registers* a new instance of some class of objects. The registration of the instance is a signal to the RTI that a new instance is entering the federation execution. Other federates that have subscribed to some or all of the attributes of that object class are informed by the RTI of the registration; they are said to *discover* the instance. After the instance is registered, the registering federate supplies values for some or all of the instance's attributes. It is said to *update* the attributes. Federates that have subscribed to some or all of the attributes are informed of the new values; they are said to *reflect* the new values. The updating federate will continue to update the values of the attributes from time to time (however the federation designers have agreed this should be done); the reflecting federates will continue to reflect the updates. At some point the updating federate may decide to remove the object instance from the federation execution. It signals the RTI to *delete* the instance; subscribing federates are informed of the deletion and they are told to *remove* the instance.

The RTI thus provides the mechanisms by which a federation can maintain a shared database of object instances. More precisely, each federate interested in certain classes of objects can maintain a database containing instances of those classes. The federate is told by the RTI when to discover new instances and when to remove old ones, and it reflects new values of attributes as they become available.

In our restaurant federation, the Transport federate will create and maintain a set of Boat objects. Because the Production and Consumption federates are both interested in Boats (the one to load Servings, the other to take Servings off), they will subscribe to the attributes of Boats. As the Transport federate creates Boats, the other federates will discover the Boat instances and set aside the space needed to store the attributes of the Boat instances internally. As the Transport federate updates its Boats' position and spaceAvailable attributes, the other federates will reflect those updates.

4.4.2   WHAT YOU NEED TO KNOW

In the foregoing, we've alluded to federates subscribing to class attributes and classes of interactions. The services for registering, discovering, updating, reflecting, deleting, and removing objects all belong to the Object Management group of services, as do the services for sending and receiving interactions. The behavior of all these services is controlled by the publication and subscription services from the Declaration Management group, which we will explain now.

Any component-based simulation system can be overwhelmed by data if all data produced by all components is transmitted to other components. This wastes both network bandwidth (in the case of a distributed simulation) and the recipients' processor cycles. Some mechanism for routing data only to interested parties is necessary to maintain efficiency as the size of a component-based simulation increases. The declaration management services of the RTI accomplish coarse filtering of data based on expressed interest.

Declaration management also establishes the notion of publication and subscription. The idea, which appears in many information systems today, is to decouple producers of data from consumers. The producer of a certain kind of data is relieved of having to know (and manage) the set of recipients. The producer merely declares its intent to publish a certain kind of data, and the publish-and-subscribe facility ensures that data is routed to interested recipients. Similarly, consumers are relieved of having to know about producers. The consumer announces a desire for a certain kind of data, and the publish-and-subscribe facility will route to the consumer data of that kind from any source. Declaration management is a keystone of the RTI's publish-and-subscribe function. As you will see, publish-and-subscribe is a powerful tool for reducing the complexity of simulations, for allowing them to grow with less pain, and for reuse of simulation components.

Figure 4-6 illustrates the publish-and-subscribe idea. In it, federates A and B publish one class of object, and A, B, and C all subscribe to the same class of object. Federate C is unaware of which federate registered the objects it discovers. Likewise, federates A and B are unaware of what federates discover the objects they register.

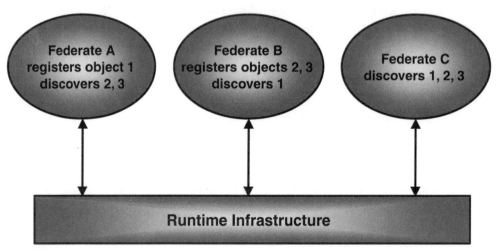

FIGURE 4-6   Publish-and-Subscribe.

There is a final purpose of declaration management that is just as important as the foregoing, but not as obvious. These services constitute a mechanism for protecting federate software from later changes to the FOM. If federate code is written to subscribe to attributes of a certain object class, and the FOM is extended later to contain subclasses of the subscribed class, the federate code will run without modification. The RTI will deliver the subscribed attributes as if they were attributes of the originally subscribed class. We will cover this in detail in Chapter 7, "Extending the Federation for a New Purpose." To summarize, declaration management is used for isolating the effects of change, as well as for routing.

Table 4–1 lists the attribute publications and subscriptions needed for our restaurant federation. The contents of this table, and the similar table for interactions, represent a significant matter that must be established as part of federation design. These decisions are part of translating the "conceptual model" of the federation—what the federation will simulate—into responsibilities for each federate.

Table 4-1   Object Class Publications and Subscriptions in Restaurant Federation

	Production	Transport	Consumption
Serving privilegeToDeleteObject position type	Default publish publish publish	Default publish publish	Default publish publish subscribe
Boat privilegeToDeleteObject position spaceAvailable cargo	Default publish subscribe subscribe subscribe	Default publish publish publish publish	Default publish subscribe subscribe subscribe

The attribute privilegeToDeleteObject of class Serving is published for reasons having to do with the transfer of responsibility for modeling the Serving instances. The attribute privilege-ToDeleteObject is automatically published by every federate for every class. We'll discuss that later. The attribute position is published by all three federates because they will all update it at various points in the course of the federation execution. The attribute type is published only by Production. Production is the only federate that will update its value (when the Serving instance is registered). All the Boat objects are modeled by the Transport federate and remain its responsibility, so only the Transport federate need publish those attributes.

The Production federate doesn't subscribe to any Serving attributes because it registers all the Serving instances in the federation execution.[4] The Transport and Consumption federates don't subscribe to the Serving position attribute because Serving positions would be redundant, given the positions of the Boats that carry them. (This is a matter of this federation's design.) However, the Production and Consumption federates need all the attributes of Boat instances. And the Consumption federate subscribes to the type attribute of Servings because its diners use the type to decide whether they want a particular Serving.

Table 4-2 lists the interaction publications needed for our initial restaurant federation. The Consumption federate sends the interaction SimulationEnds when it detects that a sufficient number of Servings have been consumed. Therefore it must publish the interaction class. The other federates subscribe the class so that they will receive the interaction.

Table 4-2   Interaction Publications and Subscriptions in Restaurant Federation

	Production	Transport	Consumption
SimulationEnds	subscribe	subscribe	publish

4.5   SHARING DATA: MORE DETAILS

In the preceding section we introduced the fundamental ideas of sharing data between federates, avoiding the details as much as possible. Now we must tackle the details if we're actually to use the declaration and object management groups of services. We won't exhaust the subject in this section, but we'll give enough information to allow you to write code for the initial restaurant federation.

4.5.1   THE PLOT THUS FAR

We'll begin by summarizing key terms:

- An instance of an object class is created when a federate *registers* the instance with the RTI.
- Other federates that have subscribed to some of the attributes are notified of the registration; they are said to *discover* the object.

---

4.   The privilegeToDeleteObject attribute need not be subscribed because its value does not change. It is used to transfer responsibility for modeling an instance attribute from one federate to another.

- When a federate supplies a new value for an attribute, it is said to *update* its value.
- Subscribers of that attribute are notified of the new value; they are said to *reflect* the new value.
- When a federate signals the RTI to take an instance out of the federation execution, it is said to *delete* it.
- Subscribing federates are informed of the deletion; they are said to *remove* the instance.
- The federate that originates an interaction is said to *send* it.
- Subscribers of that class of interaction are notified that the interaction has been sent; they are said to *receive* it.
- The attributes of an object class, considered as a class, are called *class attributes*.
- The attributes of a specific object instance are called *instance attributes*.

4.5.2   PUBLISHERS PRODUCE DATA

By producing data we mean:

- Registering (creating instances of) objects
- Updating values of attributes of those instances
- Sending interactions

4.5.2.1   Declare Intent to Produce Data

Before a federate can produce any data, the federate must declare its intent to publish. In the case of objects, the federate makes its declaration by invoking the PUBLISH OBJECT CLASS service. The federate supplies the object class and the set of class attributes it wishes to publish. The attributes must be among the *available attributes* of that class, that is, attributes declared in the FOM for that class or any of its superclasses. The federate needn't publish all available attributes for a class; as we'll see later, one federate might publish certain of the available attributes, while another federate might publish others. More than one federate can publish the same class attribute.

To invoke PUBLISH OBJECT CLASS with one of the APIs, the federate will need an "object class handle" whose programming-language type is defined as part of the API. (Handle types are usually small integers.) The federate must ascertain the handle beforehand using the support service GET OBJECT CLASS HANDLE. That service takes as a parameter the "object class name," which is simply the name as defined in the FED. (The fact that FED names are case-insensitive applies here, as with all the support services.) Because the federate will have many uses for the class handle, it's convenient for the federate to invoke GET OBJECT CLASS HANDLE once shortly after joining the federation, and to store the handle. The handle doesn't change during the execution.

Similarly, the handle of each attribute must be ascertained with GET ATTRIBUTE HANDLE. (The class handle must be supplied for that call.) The form of the "set of attributes" to be supplied to PUBLISH OBJECT CLASS depends on the API; there is usually a programming-language type or class to represent such a set. Because the federate will need the set repeatedly for updating the attribute values, the set can be formed once and saved.

A federate typically doesn't change its publications during a federation execution. But a federate may do so at any time by invoking PUBLISH OBJECT CLASS again for the same object class. The set of attributes given with the subsequent call replaces the set for that class. If an attribute was being published previously and is not included in the subsequent set, its publication is ended. A federate can drop its publication of an object class by invoking PUBLISH OBJECT CLASS with an empty set of attributes. A federate can drop its publication of a particular class as well by invoking UNPUBLISH OBJECT CLASS.

Federates must also indicate what interactions they intend to send. They do this by publishing those interaction classes, by invoking PUBLISH INTERACTION CLASS. To invoke this service, the federate must have the handle of the interaction class. The federate can retrieve the class handle by invoking GET INTERACTION CLASS HANDLE with the class name from the FED. Note that federates publish interaction classes, not parameters.

4.5.2.2   Register Objects

Once a federate has declared its intent to publish some attributes of an object class, it is free to begin registering instances of that class. A registration informs the RTI of the existence of a new instance of a certain class. It does not provide values for any of the instance attributes. A federate may register a new instance whenever it likes, as object instances may come and go throughout a federation execution. A federate typically registers a new instance when it creates the simulated entity that the instance represents. Thus the Transport federate, which has a known set of Boat objects, will register all the Boats at the outset of the federation execution. By contrast, the Production federate is creating and registering Serving instances from time to time throughout the federation execution.

An instance is known to the RTI both by an instance name and by an instance handle. The name takes the form of a string of characters. The handle takes the form of a small integer. A federate may choose a name, or may allow the RTI to assign a name.[5] Registration of an instance establishes a correspondence between a handle and a name; names must be unique throughout a federation execution.

Why would you want to choose a name for an instance, rather than allowing the RTI to assign one? You would choose names if the names had a particular meaning in your domain of application or if the names existed before the federation execution for some reason.

You register an instance with the service REGISTER OBJECT INSTANCE. You supply the class of the instance (in the usual form of an object class handle). You may supply an instance name, in which case it must be unique. (If you don't supply a name, the RTI will assign one, which can be retrieved later with the support service GET OBJECT INSTANCE NAME.) Registration returns an object instance handle.

---

5. The RTI chooses names that begin with the string "HLA"; your names must avoid this prefix.

The returned handle is unique between the RTI and the registering federate. The registering federate may use the handle to represent the instance in all *its* subsequent calls to the RTI. The handle is not meaningful across the federation; one federate cannot pass a handle to another federate (perhaps through an interaction) and expect the receiving federate to use the handle to refer to the same instance. The object instance name is meaningful across the federation execution and can be usefully passed from one federate to another. A federate receiving such an object name must use the support service GET OBJECT INSTANCE HANDLE to discover the correct handle in its context. Note that Boats designate the Servings they carry by name, not by handle.

4.5.2.3　　Update Attribute Values

A federate updates the values of attributes with UPDATE ATTRIBUTE VALUES. Not surprisingly, the federate must supply the object handle of the instance whose attributes are being updated, and a set of new values in the form of pairs of attribute handles and corresponding values. The federate may supply a federate time, if the federation is using the time management services of the RTI. If the federate specifies a simulation time for the update, it will get back an "event retraction handle." This handle is used by federates performing optimistic time management, which may be required to retract events.

The service also takes a "user-supplied tag." This tag is a sequence of bytes (in the typical API) which the RTI will deliver with the new attribute values to any federate that reflects (receives the new values of) the attributes. What is it for? It can be used for any purpose the federation designers conceive. It shouldn't, as a matter of good design, be used as a substitute for attribute updates, but it can be used to signal some context or condition that is interesting about the particular update. The tag may be omitted.

The federate must have previously declared its intent to publish all the attributes it attempts to update. It need not update all its published attributes at the same time. However, the RTI guarantees that all attributes updated together—that is, in a single invocation of UPDATE ATTRIBUTE VALUES—and which have the same transportation and ordering types, will be delivered together in one invocation of REFLECT ATTRIBUTE VALUES † on each reflecting federate.

Serving objects are an example of different attributes being updated at different times. The position attribute will be updated fairly frequently as a Serving moves from a chef to a boat and is carried around the canal. The type attribute for a Serving is updated once after the Serving is registered but need not be updated again.[6]

Serving objects also provide an example of an aggregate attribute. The attribute position must contain several components since the layout of our restaurant has at least two dimensions. As written, our design implies that the position attribute is an aggregate containing several coordinates. Position might also have been modeled as individual coordinates with the same transportation and ordering types. If the publishers of the position attribute agree always to update all

---

6. This ought to raise in your mind the question: How would a federate that missed the initial update of the type attribute get a value for it? We discuss this later in this chapter.

the coordinates together, the RTI guarantees that all the coordinates will be delivered together to the reflecting federates.

Recall from our earlier discussion of data types that the RTI has no notion of types of attributes or parameters. The federation designers must ensure that federates interpret attribute and parameter values coming from the RTI consistently.

4.5.2.4   Send Interactions

A federate sends an interaction with the service SEND INTERACTION. The federate supplies the class of the interaction and a set of parameters. The parameters are represented as pairs of parameter handles and values. The handles, in a manner similar to attribute handles, are retrieved using the support service GET PARAMETER HANDLE. The values are sequences of bytes, like attribute values.

The federate must have previously declared its intent to publish the interaction class. Because publication of interactions occurs per class, there is no need for parameters to be published individually.

It is not necessary that all the parameters defined for the interaction class be supplied on a SEND INTERACTION invocation. Whether it makes sense for some of the parameters to be omitted depends on the federation design. All the parameters specified in one SEND INTERACTION invocation will be received together by receiving federates. (Recall that the ordering and transportation types are specified for an entire interaction class, not for individual parameters, so the possibility of a group of parameters arriving separately doesn't arise.)

The other parameters to the SEND INTERACTION invocation are like those of UPDATE ATTRIBUTE VALUES. The SEND INTERACTION may specify a logical time, in which case the sending of the interaction becomes an event subject to the rules of time management, just like the update of attribute values. In that case, the invocation will return an event retraction handle. The SEND INTERACTION can also take a user-supplied tag.

In the restaurant federation, the Consumption federate will send SimulationEnds interactions. The Production and Transport federates will receive SimulationEnds.

4.5.2.5   Delete Objects

Federates that register objects have a responsibility to delete object instances that are no longer needed in the simulation, and for which they retain responsibility. The notion of "responsibility" will be made clearer when we discuss ownership management. For now, we chiefly want to make the point that the lifecycle of an object instance includes its removal from the federation. This occurs when the responsible federate resigns from the federation, or when the federate invokes DELETE OBJECT INSTANCE explicitly. In either case, the federates that are subscribed to all or some of the attributes of that object class will have REMOVE OBJECT INSTANCE † invoked on them by the RTI for each deleted instance.

The invocation may have a logical time attached, in which case the deletion is subject to the rules for time management. And, in that case, the invocation will return an event retraction handle.

The invocation may also take a user-supplied tag, like the tags on other services. The tag might be used, by convention of the federation design, to indicate the reason for the deletion.

In the initial restaurant federation, the Consumption federate will delete Serving objects when it is done with them. Boat objects will not be deleted until the federation execution finishes, so they will be deleted as a side-effect of the resignation of the Transport federate.

Once an instance has been deleted, the RTI becomes unaware of its existence; a further attempt to update any of its attributes, or to delete it, will cause an exception.

4.5.3   SUBSCRIBERS CONSUME DATA

By consuming data, we mean:

- Discovering objects
- Reflecting new attribute values
- Receiving interactions

4.5.3.1   Declare Interests

To discover objects of a certain class or to receive values for instance attributes, a federate must first subscribe to the desired class attributes. To receive interactions of a certain class, a federate must subscribe to that class of interactions.

A federate subscribes to object class attributes as attributes rather than the class. A federate may subscribe to only some of the attributes of an object class; it need not subscribe to all in a class. The federate will receive updates only for attributes to which it has subscribed. A federate subscribes to one or more attributes of an object class by invoking SUBSCRIBE OBJECT CLASS ATTRIBUTES on the RTI. To do this, the federate must specify the object class of the attributes and the set of attributes of that class to be subscribed.[7] The attributes must be among the available attributes for the object class, that is, the attributes declared in the FED for that object class or any of its superclasses. If the federate wishes to subscribe to attributes of several object classes, the federate must invoke SUBSCRIBE OBJECT CLASS ATTRIBUTES once for each object class.

The object class and attributes are specified by handles, which can be retrieved from the RTI by invoking the support services GET OBJECT CLASS HANDLE and GET ATTRIBUTE HANDLE. The former service takes an object class name; the latter takes an object class handle and attribute name. These names are the names from the FED and are case-insensitive. As before, the handles don't change values once the federation has begun execution, so the handles can be retrieved once and remembered for later use.

A federate typically doesn't change its subscriptions to attributes after it first subscribes. But a federate may do so at any time by invoking SUBSCRIBE OBJECT CLASS ATTRIBUTES again for the same object class. The set of attributes given with the subsequent call replaces the set for that class. If an attribute had been subscribed previously and is not included in the subsequent

---

7. The service also calls for an optional "passive subscription indicator." This is used only by data loggers. We'll discuss it further later; it can be ignored for now.

set, its subscription is ended. A federate can drop its subscription for an object class by invoking SUBSCRIBE OBJECT CLASS ATTRIBUTES with an empty set of attributes. A federate can drop its subscriptions as well by invoking UNSUBSCRIBE OBJECT CLASS.

A federate subscribes to a class of interactions by invoking SUBSCRIBE INTERACTION CLASS on the RTI. Interactions are subscribed by interaction class, not by parameter. Otherwise, the process is analogous to attribute subscriptions.[8] There is a support service, GET INTERACTION CLASS HANDLE, for retrieving the necessary interaction class handle.

As with attributes, a federate doesn't typically change its subscriptions to interactions after they're first made. However, it is free to do so at any time. A federate can drop its subscription to a class of interactions with the service UNSUBSCRIBE INTERACTION CLASS.

4.5.3.2   Discover Objects

A federate discovers that an object instance has been registered when the RTI calls it with DIS-COVER OBJECT INSTANCE †. With the invocation the RTI supplies an object instance handle and object name for the newly discovered instance, and the object class handle of the class of which this is an instance. The instance handle is meaningful only between the federate and the RTI. If the federate wished to send the identity of this instance to some other federate, it would need to retrieve the corresponding instance name, with the support service GET OBJECT INSTANCE NAME, and send the name. The class handle, like all handles for information from the FED, is valid across the federation execution.

As we've said before, a federate will discover instances only of classes to which it has sub-scribed (at least) some of the attributes. A federate will not discover objects whose attributes it has not subscribed, and it won't discover objects until it has subscribed attributes.

The discovery of an instance should be the occasion for the federate to set aside any neces-sary storage for the instance. The discovery does not supply values for any of the instance attributes; these will come later when the publishing federate updates attribute values.

In the restaurant federation, subscribers of Serving instances will discover those instances as the Production federate registers them. Both the Transport and Consumption federates will have DISCOVER OBJECT INSTANCE † invoked on them by the RTI each time the Production feder-ate registers another Serving. This will occur from time to time throughout the federation execu-tion.

4.5.3.3   Reflect Attribute Values

New values for attributes arrive at a subscribing federate when the RTI invokes REFLECT ATTRIBUTE VALUES † on it. The invocation will specify the instance that these values pertain to—a set of pairs of attribute handles and attribute values, and the usual additional information.

The new attribute values replace old values the federate may have had for those attributes. The value, as we described it earlier, is a sequence of bytes that the federate must interpret according to the conventions for the federation.

---

8.   Interaction subscriptions also have a "passive subscription indicator."

The federate will receive values only for attributes to which it has subscribed. But it may not receive values in each REFLECT ATTRIBUTE VALUES † call for all its subscribed attributes. The updating federate may not have chosen to update all attributes together, or the subscribed attributes may differ in transportation or ordering. In deciding what attributes to include in a particular invocation of REFLECT ATTRIBUTE VALUES †, the RTI will segregate the values to be delivered by transportation and ordering types, so that all attributes delivered in one reflect invocation have the same transportation and ordering type.

The "usual additional information" will include a logical time, if the original update had a time associated with it and the rules of time management call for it. If the update has a time, it will also have an event retraction handle. If the original update had a user-supplied tag, the tag will be included with the reflect call.

4.5.3.4   Receive Interactions

The analog of reflecting new attribute values is receiving an interaction. A federate subscribed to an interaction class receives an interaction when the RTI invokes RECEIVE INTERACTION † on it. The invocation carries the class of the interaction and values for all the parameters that were supplied when the interaction was sent. Each parameter is specified, as with attributes in a reflect call, by the parameter handle and a value. The value, as with an attribute, is a sequence of bytes that must be interpreted according to the conventions for the federation.

If the interaction had a time associated with it when it was sent, and the rules of time management prescribe it, the RECEIVE INTERACTION † invocation will carry a logical time and an event retraction handle. There may be a user-supplied tag.

An interaction is sent as a unit. The interaction, not the individual parameters, has a transportation and ordering, so the interaction, unlike an attribute update, is never split up. All the parameters supplied by the sender are received in the one RECEIVE INTERACTION † invocation.

4.5.3.5   Remove Objects

When an object instance is deleted from the federation, federates that have discovered the object are informed of the deletion by being called by the RTI with REMOVE OBJECT INSTANCE †. The deletion can occur because the federate responsible for the instance deleted it with DELETE OBJECT INSTANCE, or because the responsible federate resigned from the federation.

A federate receiving REMOVE OBJECT INSTANCE † for an instance is free to discard resources associated with the instance. It will receive no more updates for the attributes of that instance.

The object instance handle supplied with the invocation is valid for the federate receiving the call. The tag supplied when the instance was deleted, if any, is supplied with this call. If the deletion had a logical time attached to it, the REMOVE OBJECT INSTANCE † call will supply the time and an event retraction handle.

4.5.4   ADVICE FROM THE RTI

We know that the RTI uses subscription information to limit the data sent to federates. The RTI also uses subscriptions to advise federates whether they should produce data in the first place. This goes for class attributes and interactions. Well-behaved federates listen to advice and accept instruction. Let's consider attributes first.

4.5.4.1   The RTI Will Tell You If a Class Is Interesting

The Transport federate publishes the attributes of the Boat class using PUBLISH OBJECT CLASS. If the Production or Consumption federates have already subscribed to any of those attributes, the RTI will call the Transport federate back immediately by invoking START REGISTRATION FOR OBJECT CLASS † on it, supplying the handle for the Boat class. That informs the Transport federate of the following:

- Some other federate has subscribed to at least one of the attributes it has just published.
- Therefore, if the Transport federate registers instances of that class, some other federate will discover those instances.
- Furthermore, if the Transport federate updates the values of any of those attributes, some other federate will reflect the value of at least one of the attributes.

The Transport federate is free to register instances and update attribute values before getting the START REGISTRATION FOR OBJECT CLASS †, but nobody will be listening. (But note that the fact that instances have been registered is not lost; a federate subscribing to the class later will discover all extant instances of the class at that point.) When one of the other federates subscribes to any of the attributes later, the Transport federate receives START REGISTRATION FOR OBJECT CLASS † at that point.

If a federate is publishing attributes that are subscribed to by at least one other federate and all the subscribers drop their subscriptions to all class attributes the federate is publishing, the publishing federate will receive STOP REGISTRATION FOR OBJECT CLASS † from the RTI. At that point, the publisher may as well stop registering objects of that class and sending updates of attribute values because there is no federate to discover the objects or reflect the values.[9]

Federates receive these advisories by default. Because good advice is often annoying (and the best advice is the most annoying), the RTI provides a way for a federate to be spared these advisories. If a federate invokes DISABLE CLASS RELEVANCE ADVISORY SWITCH on the RTI, the RTI will no longer send START REGISTRATION FOR OBJECT CLASS † or STOP REGISTRATION FOR OBJECT CLASS † to the federate for any object class. If the federate requires these advisories once again, the federate can invoke ENABLE CLASS RELEVANCE ADVISORY SWITCH.

So far we've discussed advisories for attributes. There are similar advisories for interactions. If a federate publishes an interaction class and at least one other federate is subscribed to the class, the publisher will receive TURN INTERACTIONS ON † from the RTI. If no federates are subscribed to the interaction class when the federate publishes it, the federate will receive TURN INTERACTIONS ON † later if (and when) another federate subscribes to the class. The publisher is

---

9. Once again, the RTI does not lose track of the registration of the current instances of that class, or of any instances that are registered after the publishing federate has been told to rest on its oars. Another federate subscribing later to attributes of that class will discover all the relevant instances at that point.

welcome to send interactions of the class before receiving TURN INTERACTIONS ON †, but the RTI will do nothing with them. If a federate has received TURN INTERACTIONS ON † and later all the subscribers drop their subscriptions to the class, the publisher will receive TURN INTERAC- TIONS OFF † from the RTI. A federate can suppress interaction advisories by invoking DISABLE INTERACTION RELEVANCE ADVISORY SWITCH.

You'll recall the passive subscription indicator on SUBSCRIBE OBJECT CLASS ATTRIBUTES and SUBSCRIBE INTERACTION CLASS. Thus far, all the subscriptions we've mentioned are "active," that is, the passive subscription indicator is false. The purpose of passive subscriptions is to allow the unobtrusive monitoring of data. A federation may wish to incorporate a data log- ging federate that subscribes to attributes and interactions and records them without affecting the federation execution. It would be undesirable if the logger's subscriptions triggered advisories to publishing federates. Suppose, for instance, that a federate is publishing a class of interactions and no other federate is subscribed, so the publisher has received TURN INTERACTIONS OFF †. The publisher should not receive TURN INTERACTIONS ON † merely because the logger has sub- scribed to the interaction. If the logger subscribes passively, this will not happen. The RTI does not consider passive subscriptions in determining whether to send advisories to publishing fed- erates.

The passive subscription indicator is handled differently by the various APIs. The C++ API represents the passive subscription indicator as a boolean parameter with a default value. If the subscription call supplies no value, the subscription is active. Java and OMG IDL do not have a notion of default parameter values. Therefore the service is represented by two methods, `subscribeObjectClassAttributes()` and `subscribeObjectClassAttributesPass- ively()`.

4.5.4.2   The RTI Can Tell You If an Instance Is Interesting

The foregoing advisories have to do with object and interaction classes. The RTI can also tell a federate if a particular instance attribute is interesting, so that the federate can control updates by instance and attribute.

The RTI does not do this by default. For a federate to get the RTI's advice about instance attributes, it must invoke ENABLE ATTRIBUTE RELEVANCE ADVISORY SWITCH. This support ser- vice tells the RTI that the federate wants advice about individual instance attributes. There's no fine-grain control over the advisories: a federate that enables this switch gets advisories about all instance attributes.

The advisories come in the form of callbacks from the RTI: TURN UPDATES ON FOR OBJECT INSTANCE † and TURN UPDATES OFF FOR OBJECT INSTANCE †. They both supply an instance handle and a set of attribute handles. The former callback means that the indicated attributes of the indicated instance are required somewhere in the federate, and that the federate should begin updating those instance attributes according to the federation design. The latter callback means there is no need for updates of the indicated instance attributes, and the federa- tion may cease its updates.

As with the class-based advisories, these are advisories. The federate is free to update attributes that the RTI says are not needed.

Try Declaration and Object Management with the Test Federate

We've covered a great many RTI services that you can experiment with using the test federate. Here are some suggestions. Start an RTI executive and two copies of the test federate. Using one test federate, create a federation execution (we'll assume it's the usual restaurant_1) and join each test federate to the federation execution.

You'll need some object class handles and attribute handles to proceed further. You may find it useful to print a copy of the FED file (<CD>\config\restaurant_1.fed) to write down the handles as you use the test federate to discover them. For the sake of a specific example, we'll work with the attributes position and type of object class Serving.

Get the object class handle for Serving by invoking GET OBJECT CLASS HANDLE on one of the test federates ("Support | Object classes & attributes | 10.2 Get object class handle…"). You supply the fully qualified name of the class (ObjectRoot.Restaurant.Serving) in the dialog box. The Test Federate will display a message like "10.2 Handle 3 for object class ObjectRoot.Restaurant.Serving" in its log area. Make a note of the handle.

Now get the attribute handles for the position and type attributes of class Serving. Invoke GET ATTRIBUTE HANDLE ("Support | Object classes & attributes | 10.4 Get attribute handle…"), supplying the previously discovered class handle and the name of the attribute ("position"). The Test Federate will display a message like "10.4 Handle 100 for attribute position, class 3" in its log area. Repeat this for the type attribute.

Subscribe one of the test federates to these class attributes by invoking SUBSCRIBE OBJECT CLASS ATTRIBUTES ("Decl | Subscribe | 5.6 Subscribe object class attributes…"). You supply the object class handle and the set of attributes. Assuming the test federate reported handles 100 and 101 for the attributes, you type the set as "100, 101." The test federate will log something like "5.6 Subscribed class 3 HashSet(100, 101)."

Now publish these class attributes in the other test federate. Invoke PUBLISH OBJECT CLASS ("Decl | Publish | 5.2 Publish object class…") using the object class handle and attribute handles you discovered earlier. (Recall that handles of FED entities are meaningful across a federation.) The federate will log something like "5.2 Published class 3 HashSet(100, 101)" and will immediately log a callback from the RTI: "†(5.10)start RegistrationForObjectClass:3." (The display font renders the dagger as a box.) The callback is the class advisory generated because you'd previously subscribed to the attributes in the other test federate. You might experiment with unsubscribing and then resubscribing the attributes to see the advisories generated by the RTI.

You are now ready to register an instance of class Serving. In the publishing federate, invoke REGISTER OBJECT INSTANCE ("Obj | Register | 6.2 Register object instance…"), supplying the Serving class handle. The federate logs something like "6.2 Registered instance 103 of class 3," which tells you the object instance handle for your new instance. You can discover the instance name the RTI assigned by invoking GET OBJECT INSTANCE NAME ("Support | Object instances | 10.11 Get object instance name..."). Because the RTI assigned the name, it will begin with "HLA" and is probably something predictable like "HLA103." If you attempt to register an object instance in the subscribing federate, the RTI will throw an ObjectClassNotPublished exception.

You are now ready to update one or more of the attribute values of your instance. Because we have not discussed time management, we'll perform a "receive order" update that is independent of logical time. Invoke UPDATE ATTRIBUTE VALUES at the publishing federate ("Obj | Update attributes | 6.4 Update attribute values RO..."). The resulting dialog requires the object *instance* handle and then alternating pairs of attribute handles and values. For the handles, supply the attribute handles for position and type. For the values, supply some text. The test federate, by convention of its design, converts these ASCII characters into a sequence of bytes to supply to the RTI. Type some other text (if you wish) into the field for the user-supplied tag. When you press the "OK" button on the dialog, the Test Federate invokes the service on the RTI. The subscribing federate should immediately log a callback that looks something like the following:

†(6.7)reflectAttributeValues of obj 103, tag: first attr: 100 value: positionvalue attr: 101 value: typevalue

The value you supplied (if any) for the user-supplied tag appears in the top line; the values you supplied for each of the attributes appear in subsequent lines.

As a final exercise, we delete the object instance. In the publishing federate, invoke DELETE OBJECT INSTANCE ("Obj | Delete | 6.8 Delete object instance..."), supplying the object instance handle and, if you wish, a tag. The publishing federate will log the service invocation, and the subscribing federate will log a REMOVE OBJECT INSTANCE †callback: "†(6.11)removeObjectInstance; object:103, tag: bye."

You should now be able to perform similar experiments with interactions. The interaction class defined in our FED, SimulationEnds, carries no parameters. You simply won't supply any parameter handle or value when you send the interaction.

Java Code for Declaration and Object Management

Federate code for declaration or object management must follow the pattern of calls described earlier. We'll describe the calls made by a publishing federate. The federate must obtain object class and attributes handles:

```
int ServingClassHandle = rti.getObjectClassHandle(
   "ObjectRoot.Restaurant.Serving");
int positionHandle = rti.getAttributeHandle(
   "position",
   ServingClassHandle);
```

```
int typeHandle = rti.getAttributeHandle(
  "type",
  ServingClassHandle);
```

The sets of attributes required by many RTI services are represented in the Java by an implementation of the interface `AttributeHandleSet`. This interface is part of the standard Java API. The federate obtains an empty set from an instance of `AttributeHandleSetFactory`, also defined as part of the API. The means of obtaining a factory reference may vary with the RTI implementation; in the case of the Pitch Portable RTI, the means is similar to obtaining an `RTIambassador` reference:

```
hla.rti.AttributeHandleSetFactory ahFactory =
  RTI.attributeHandleSetFactory();
```

The federate uses the factory reference to obtain an empty set, and uses methods defined on `AttributeHandleSet` to add handles to the set:

```
hla.rti.AttributeHandleSet servingAttributes = ahFactory.create();
try {
  servingAttributes.add(positionHandle);
  servingAttributes.add(typeHandle);
}
catch (hla.rti.AttributeNotDefined e) {
  ...
}
```
The federate can now publish these attributes:
```
try {
  rti.publishObjectClass(
    ServingClassHandle,
    servingAttributes);
}
catch (hla.rti.RTIexception e) {
  ...
}
```

If the RTI calls back the federate with an advisory, that will take the form of an invocation of the method `startRegistrationForObjectClass()` on the implementation of `hla.rti.FederateAmbassador` that the federate supplied when it joined the federation.

The federate is now allowed to register object instances:

```
int myServingInstance;
try {
  myServingInstance = rti.registerObjectInstance
  (ServingClassHandle);
```

```
}
catch (hla.rti.RTIexception e) {
  ...
}
```

The federate can update attribute values. In the Java API, an attribute value is represented as an array of `byte`. We've said that the federation designers must choose some way of encoding values of attributes for transmission through the RTI. In the sample implementation, encoding conventions for a given attribute in the FED are embodied in methods on a Java class defined for the attribute. Thus the position attribute is represented in the sample implementation by a federation-specific Java class `Position`. This class has an `encode()` method that returns an instance of `byte[]` suitable for passing to the RTI. The class has a constructor that takes `byte[]` as a parameter which serves to decode attribute values received from the RTI.

The `updateAttributeValues()` method on `RTIambassador` uses an auxiliary class, `hla.rti.SuppliedAttributes`, which is defined in the API. `SuppliedAttributes` holds pairs of attribute handles and values to be supplied for the `updateAttributeValues()` call. It is similar to `AttributeHandleSet` in several ways. Like `AttributeHandleSet`, it is actually an interface. Secondly, a federate gets an empty instance by calling a factory object. Finally, in the Pitch Portable RTI, one uses an implementation-specific call to acquire the reference to the factory object. An example is as follows:

```
Position somePosition:
hla.rti.SuppliedAttributesFactory saFactory =
  RTI.suppliedAttributesFactory();
hla.rti.SuppliedAttributes sa = saFactory.create(1);
sa.add(positionHandle, somePosition.encode());
try {
  rti.updateAttributeValues(
    myServingInstance,
    sa,
    (new String("a user-supplied tag")).getBytes());
}
catch (hla.rti.RTIexception e) {
  ...
}
```

When a subscribing federate reflects attribute values, the callback will take the form of an invocation of the method `reflectAttributeValues()` on the instance of `hla.rti.FederateAmbassador` that the federate supplied when it joined.

4.5.5   WHAT INFORMATION DOES THE RTI STORE?

We've alluded to the fact that the RTI remembers some things about objects and not others. It's time to be more explicit about what the RTI does and does not store. The fundamentals are these:

- The RTI remembers each federate's publications and subscriptions.
- The RTI remembers the registration of an object instance.
- The RTI need *not* store values for any attributes after they are delivered.
- The RTI need *not* remember interactions after they are delivered.

Let's explore the consequences of each of these rules.

4.5.5.1   The RTI Remembers Publications and Subscriptions

The RTI's memory of publications and subscriptions means that it always applies them to the production and consumption of data. A federate that tries to produce data (register an instance, update attributes, send an interaction) that it hasn't previously agreed to publish will receive an exception from the RTI. Also, a federate's consumption of data is always limited by its subscriptions. The RTI will not let a federate discover an instance, reflect attribute values, or receive an interaction without the corresponding subscriptions.

4.5.5.2   The RTI Remembers Registration of Object Instances

Because the RTI remembers the registration of object instances, a late-subscribing federate will always discover the appropriate objects. Suppose one federate publishes a class of objects and registers several instances of the class. Suppose a second federate then subscribes to attributes of that class. After the subscription, the RTI will call the second federate repeatedly so that it discovers all the registered instances of the class. A federate that subscribes to attributes of a class is assured that the RTI will inform it of all registered instances. The subscribing federate will miss none.

4.5.5.3   The RTI Is Not a Repository of Attribute Values

The RTI need not store values for any instance attributes after they are delivered. While a subscribing federate is guaranteed that the RTI will inform it of all registered instances, it has no guarantee that it will ever receive values for the attributes. Suppose one federate publishes attributes of a certain object class, registers some instances, and updates some attributes of those instances. Suppose then a second federate subscribes to some of the same attributes. The RTI will cause the second federate to discover all the registered instances, but it will provide no previous updates to the values. Any updates after the second federate has subscribed will be reflected to it, but the updates occurring before the subscription will never be seen.

In the restaurant federation, the position attribute of Serving objects will be updated fairly frequently, and the subscribers (Transport and Consumption federates) will receive all those updates. However, the Production federate will only update the type attribute once after each Serving is registered. If the Consumption federate is not subscribed to the type attribute before the Production federate updated it, it will never reflect a value for it.

This is evidently unsatisfactory. What can we do? There are three choices: (1) ensure that all publications and subscriptions occur before any attribute values are updated, (2) assume that (or design the federation such that) producers update attributes regularly, or (3) use RTI mechanisms for late retrieval of an attribute value.

The first approach, ensuring that publications and subscriptions occur before attribute updates is not universally applicable, but is helpful in some cases. We could take this approach in the restaurant federation because once the federates have announced their publications and subscriptions they don't change. We would need a means of synchronizing the publications and subscriptions across the federation. A mechanism for this exists in the RTI. We'll discuss this more in Chapter 5, "Synchronizing the Federation." This is just one of several reasons why it is helpful to have phases in a federation execution.

The second solution depends on the behavior of producers. If a late-subscribing federate is sure that some producer will update all the interesting attributes frequently enough, it can simply wait for an update. In the restaurant federation, this is adequate for the position attribute of Serving and the position attribute of Boats. It is not adequate for the type attribute and it's probably not adequate for the spaceAvailable and cargo attributes of Boats.

4.5.5.4   The Recommended Way To Ensure Values

The problem remaining is how does a late-subscribing federate retrieve a value for an attribute when it has no guarantee that the producer will update it? The RTI doesn't remember the answer, but it knows who to ask. A federate needing values for attributes of an instance that it has discovered can invoke REQUEST ATTRIBUTE VALUE UPDATE on the RTI. The requesting federate can specify an instance handle, in which case the request is specific to the named instance, or an object class handle, in which case the request pertains to all discovered instances of the class. The effect, from the requesting federate's point of view, is that it will be called back with REFLECT ATTRIBUTE VALUES † calls that provide the desired values.

Here's what happens to bring this about. When the requesting federate invokes REQUEST ATTRIBUTE VALUE UPDATE, the RTI knows what federate owns[10] each instance attribute being requested. Remember that the request may be for attributes of several instances, if the request named an object class. The RTI calls each owning federate with PROVIDE ATTRIBUTE VALUE UPDATE †, giving the instance handle and attribute handles of the desired instance attributes. If a federate owns several instances of a class (a likely condition), the federate will receive one call for each instance. The federate should respond to each call by invoking UPDATE ATTRIBUTE VALUES on the RTI, providing at least the desired attribute values. These UPDATE ATTRIBUTE VALUES calls cause REFLECT ATTRIBUTE VALUES † calls to subscribing federates in the usual way. Figure 4-7[11] summarizes the steps in this process, assuming a single federate owns all the instance attributes being requested.

---

10. Recall that HLA rules 5 and 8 say that every instance attribute is "owned" by no more than one federate, and that the owner is responsible for updating that instance attribute.

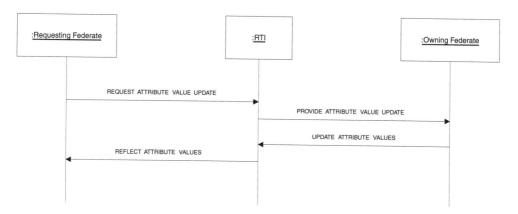

FIGURE 4-7   Protocol for Request Attribute Value Update.

In the restaurant federation, this mechanism could be used in the following way. The Consumption federate will discover Serving instances for whose attributes it needs initial values. It could, if it wished, assume that the position attribute will be updated soon in the course of the federation execution. It cannot assume that about the type attribute. If the Consumption federate has not finished its subscriptions before the Production federate produces its sole update of type, the Consumption federate will miss it. To avoid this, the Consumption federate can, each time it discovers a new instance of Serving, invoke REQUEST ATTRIBUTE VALUE UPDATE, requesting the type attribute for the new instance. The Production federate must be prepared to respond to the consequent PROVIDE ATTRIBUTE VALUE UPDATE † calls from the RTI, by updating the type attribute.

If two federates request an update of an attribute, and the updating federate responds to each request with an update, each subscribing federate will receive two reflect calls. The redundant updates ensure that each federate will receive at least one update after its request.

A federate should not assume that a "new" value reflected for an instance attribute will differ from a previous value. The same value might be reflected multiple times owing to updates requested by other federates. For the same reason, a federate should not assume that reflection of attributes is an event significant in itself.

A federate that employs REQUEST ATTRIBUTE VALUE UPDATE should not assume that it will receive REFLECT ATTRIBUTE VALUES † that match its request exactly. The providing federate is required to update at least the attributes requested, but may update additional attributes.

11. The figure is an instance of a UML sequence diagram [UML 1997]. Time, or at least causality, flows from top to bottom. The boxes at the top represent the objects between which messages are sent. The names are underlined and prefixed with a colon to emphasize that they represent instances rather than classes. The messages passing between federates and the RTI are HLA service calls. Note that in this and all similar diagrams, no messages pass directly between two federates. The RTI mediates all communication.

4.5.5.5   Responding to Requests Is Good Design

A purpose of the HLA is to foster creation of reusable simulations. If a simulation (potential federate) assumes a pattern of updates for attributes it consumes (for instance, that attributes will be updated frequently), the component is less reusable. Reusing it in a new federation whose members don't fulfill the assumption creates a problem. It's good design practice for a federate not to assume an update, but to request initial values from the RTI when it discovers a new object. Then it can place itself in a fully defined state.

Equally as important, any HLA federate should respond properly to PROVIDE ATTRIBUTE VALUE UPDATE †. This makes it more likely that the federate will play well when moved to another federation. It removes the federation design restriction that otherwise lurks in the federate.

4.5.5.6   The RTI Retains No Memory of Delivered Interactions

The RTI does not remember interactions after they are delivered. An interaction of a certain class that is sent before a federate subscribes to that class will never be received by the new subscriber. This is not surprising. It's just another thing to consider in the design of a federation. If a federate is allowed to join (and subscribe) in the middle of the action, what does it mean for the simulation that the federate will begin to receive interactions? Will the newly joined federate be able to interpret the interactions meaningfully?

4.6   OWNERSHIP: RESPONSIBILITY AND COOPERATION IN MODELING AN ENTITY

We describe in this section the HLA's mechanisms for assigning responsibility for modeling an entity to a federate, and the mechanisms for transferring and sharing that responsibility.

4.6.1   RESPONSIBILITY FOR MODELING IS REFLECTED IN OWNERSHIP

We've spoken thus far somewhat loosely about "responsibility for modeling an entity" and "responsibility for updating an attribute." In the HLA, "modeling an entity" means updating one or more of its attributes, so that's what we'll discuss from here on.

- Clearly, for an attribute to be updated, some member of the federation has to do it, and it is good for the federation designers to have thought out which federates are responsible for what updates.
- Just as clearly, you can't have more than one federate attempting to update the same instance attribute at the same time.
- It is very useful to allow responsibility for updates to pass from one federate to another. (Servings pass from Production federate to Transport federate to Consumption federate.)
- It's also useful for the modeling of a single entity to be shared by several federates in cooperation. Although the restaurant federation contains no example of this in its first version, we'll give an example later.

Ownership management services are designed to tackle all these problems. The reason for a set of services designed explicitly for the purpose is that the ownership services ensure unambiguous behavior in the face of network and computing latencies. Other groups of services in the RTI do not have this property. For instance, there is no way, using just the declaration and object management services, to ensure that all publications and subscriptions occur in a federation before any attribute updates. In a truly distributed environment, network and computing latencies eventually will frustrate any design based on just those services. The ownership services, on the other hand, are designed so that the RTI can guarantee their unambiguous operation regardless of latencies, even in a fully distributed environment.

4.6.1.1   Every Instance Attribute Has Its Owner

Here are the key ideas; these implement the notions in HLA rules 5 and 8:

- In the HLA, every instance attribute is *owned* by some federate, or is *unowned*.
- An instance attribute effectively comes into existence when its instance is registered.
- Instance attributes remain in existence, and are owned or are unowned, until their instance is deleted.
- The federate that owns an instance attribute is responsible for updating its value as necessary. Only the federate that owns an instance attribute can update its value. A corollary of this idea is that a federate must be publishing the corresponding class attribute if it is to own an instance attribute.
- An instance attribute is never owned by more than one federate at a time.
- Ownership of an attribute can be transferred unambiguously from one federate to another.
- Ownership of an instance attribute cannot be gained or lost by a federate without its consent.
- Not all attributes of a given instance must be owned by the same federate.

The ownership management services of the RTI exist to enforce these conditions and to allow manipulation of ownership.

Here are two key terms:

- When a federate becomes the owner of an instance attribute, we say the federate *acquires* ownership.
- When a federate gives up ownership, we say the federate *divests* ownership.

Ownership begins with the federate that registers an instance: when a federate registers an instance, it owns all the attributes. More precisely, it owns all the attributes it has agreed to publish. If a federate announces it will publish only some of the attributes of a class, it is still allowed to register instances of that class. It will be given ownership of the attributes of the instance that it is publishing; the other attributes of that instance are unowned, lying *in limbo*, as it were, with the RTI. (We'll see later that another federate can ask to acquire ownership of those instance attributes.)

A federate that acquires ownership of an instance attribute retains ownership until it divests itself of the attribute, either by relinquishing it through one of the transfer mechanisms, or by resigning from the federation.

4.6.1.2   Ownership Transfer in the Restaurant Federation

Ownership transfer plays a key role in the restaurant federation. Although for Boat instances, ownership of the instance attributes remains with the original federate, attributes of the Serving instances are transferred among federates. The transfer of Serving attributes is a key part of the design. The evolution of ownership of Serving attributes is summarized in Figure 4-8. The life of a Serving instance progresses from left to right. The occurrences that are significant for ownership are labeled at the bottom. The owner(s) of each of the three instance attributes are shown as bars.

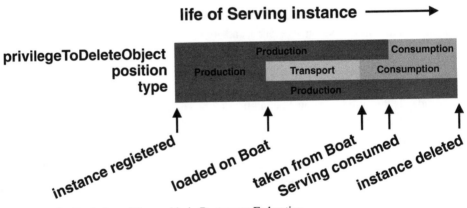

FIGURE 4-8   Evolution of Ownership in Restaurant Federation.

The responsibility for modeling Serving instances, and ownership of their attributes, lies initially with the Production federate that registers them. Responsibility for modeling the position attribute passes to the Transport federate when the Serving is loaded onto a Boat. The transfer of responsibility is marked by transfer of ownership of the position attribute from the Production to the Transport federate. The Transport federate, which is moving the Boats along on the canal, can update the Serving's position attribute. Responsibility for modeling position passes from the Transport federate to the Consumption federate when the Serving is taken off a Boat by a diner. Again, the transfer of responsibility is marked by the transfer of ownership of the instance attribute to the Consumption federate. Ownership of privilegeToDeleteObject remains with the Production federate until just before the instance is deleted by the Consumption federate. As we'll see, the Consumption federate must own privilegeToDeleteObject before it can delete the instance. The type attribute remains with the Production federate throughout the life of the instance.

As with publications and subscriptions, the evolution of ownership is an important matter for federation design. It is another part of translating the federation's "conceptual model" into responsibilities for specific federates. Something not captured by Figure 4-8 is the mechanism used for each transfer of ownership, which we'll discuss next.

4.6.1.3 Ownership Can Be Transferred Several Ways

There are several ways ownership can be transferred. The mechanisms can be grouped as follows:

- Abdication of responsibility: the federate resigns or ceases publishing an attribute, and the affected instance attributes become unowned.
- Negotiated: the RTI mediates an exchange between the current and prospective owners. The negotiation may be initiated either by the current owner ("pushing" ownership) or by the prospective owner ("pulling" ownership).
- Unobtrusive: the federate asks to acquire an instance attribute if it is unowned or if its owner has already announced a desire to divest itself of the attribute.

The restaurant federation makes use of all these categories.

Ownership May Be Divested Unconditionally A federate can always divest itself unconditionally. The result is always that the instance attribute becomes unowned and eligible for acquisition by another federate.

One means of unconditional divestiture is for the federate to cease publishing the attribute. The federate can do this by invoking UNPUBLISH OBJECT CLASS or by invoking PUBLISH OBJECT CLASS with a set of attributes that does not include a previously published attribute. In either case, the effect is on all instances of the class. Because the initial publications in the restaurant federation don't change, this way of divesting ownership doesn't apply to our example.

Another means of unconditional divestiture is resignation. The federate can invoke RESIGN FEDERATION EXECUTION with a directive to release ownership of all the instance attributes it owns. The federate can also direct the RTI to delete all the objects for which it owns privilege-ToDeleteObject.

The restaurant federation uses this mechanism. Executions of the restaurant federation are assumed to come to a well-defined end. At some point, things have gone far enough, and all the federates can cease functioning and resign the federation. As a matter of good design, the federates should do something with the instances that exist and the instance attributes they own, specifically delete all the instances they are responsible for and release ownership of all instance attributes they own. The easiest means of accomplishing this is for the federates to resign with the directive that tells the RTI to do both those things in that order.

A Federate Can Offer to Acquire The negotiated forms of ownership transfer allow the negotiation to be started from either end: from the acquiring end, known as "pulling," or from the divesting end, known as "pushing." Let's discuss "pulling" first.

A federate that wishes to acquire ownership of certain instance attributes asks the RTI. The federate need not know what federate, if any, presently owns the attributes. If any of the attributes are unowned, the RTI grants ownership immediately. Otherwise, the RTI goes to each federate that owns one or more of the attributes and asks the federate to release the requested attributes that it owns. When the owning federate releases the attributes, the RTI notifies the requestor that it has gained ownership of those attributes.

The federate requesting to acquire ownership invokes ATTRIBUTE OWNERSHIP ACQUISITION on the RTI, specifying the instance attributes it desires by the instance handle and set of attribute handles. As the current owner(s) of the requested attributes releases them, the RTI will call the original requestor back with ATTRIBUTE OWNERSHIP ACQUISITION NOTIFICATION †, specifying which attributes the requestor now owns. If the requested attributes are owned by several different federates, the requestor may get several callbacks as attributes are released in groups.

On the owner's side, the request to release attributes comes in the form of a callback REQUEST ATTRIBUTE OWNERSHIP RELEASE † from the RTI. The owning federate decides which, if any, attributes it will divest. It responds by invoking ATTRIBUTE OWNERSHIP RELEASE RESPONSE on the RTI, specifying the attributes it is releasing. From the moment this service call completes, the responding federate no longer owns those attributes, and may no longer update them. (Note that the owning federate is not divested of attributes involuntarily: the owning federate must agree to divest.) This is diagrammed in Figure 4-9.

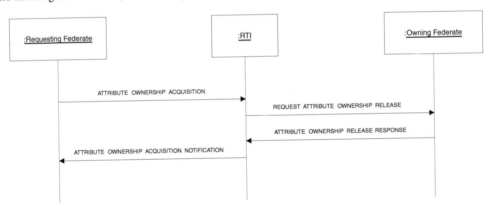

FIGURE 4-9   A Federate can request to acquire.

How is this mechanism used in the restaurant federation? It is used to transfer ownership of a Serving instance's privilegeToDeleteObject from the Production federate to the Consumption federate.

Here's the protocol. When the Consumption federate has finished modeling the consumption of a Serving, it will delete the Serving. It must first acquire ownership of privilegeToDeleteObject for the instance (for reasons we'll discuss later). The Transport federate invokes ATTRIBUTE OWNERSHIP ACQUISITION, giving the Serving instance handle and the attribute handle for the privilegeToDeleteObject class attribute. Because the Production federate owns this attribute, it will get the callback REQUEST ATTRIBUTE OWNERSHIP RELEASE †, requesting release of privilegeToDeleteObject for the Serving instance. The Production federate, being the good federation player that it is, invokes ATTRIBUTE OWNERSHIP RELEASE RESPONSE immediately, naming the requested attribute. It has ceased at that point to own it. The RTI will then invoke ATTRIBUTE OWNERSHIP ACQUISITION NOTIFICATION † on the Transport federate, which from that point on owns the attribute.

A Federate Can Offer to Divest A negotiated transfer of ownership can be initiated from the other direction: a federate can offer to divest instance attributes. Where the offer to acquire is "pulling," this is "pushing." The procedure is a kind of dual of the one we've just presented. The divesting federate informs the RTI it wishes to divest certain instance attributes. The RTI informs all other federates that are publishing the attributes (and hence are eligible to acquire ownership) that the instance attributes are available. Any federate can signal the RTI that it wishes to acquire some or all of the offered attributes. The RTI will notify the acquiring federate of its good fortune, and the RTI will notify the divesting federate that it is divested of those attributes. This protocol is diagrammed in Figure 4-10.

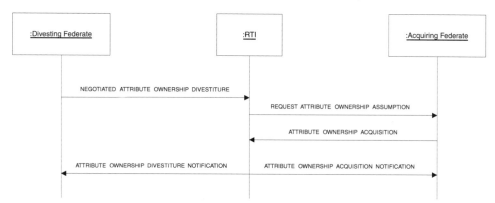

FIGURE 4-10 A Federate Can Offer to Divest.

The services involved are as follows. The divesting federate makes its offer to divest by invoking NEGOTIATED ATTRIBUTE OWNERSHIP DIVESTITURE, providing the usual instance handle and set of attribute handles. The service also can take a user-supplied tag, which might be used to indicate the reason for the divestiture. The RTI then invokes REQUEST ATTRIBUTE OWNERSHIP ASSUMPTION † on the eligible federates, specifying the instance and attribute handles and the tag supplied with the offer to divest. A federate that wishes to acquire some or all of the offered attributes invokes ATTRIBUTE OWNERSHIP ACQUISITION or ATTRIBUTE OWNERSHIP ACQUISITION IF AVAILABLE on the RTI, specifying which of the instance attributes it desires. Note that ownership has not changed hands to this point. The RTI then sets about informing the divesting and acquiring federates: the RTI invokes ATTRIBUTE OWNERSHIP DIVESTITURE NOTIFICATION † on the divesting federate, at which point it must cease updating the attributes; and the RTI invokes ATTRIBUTE OWNERSHIP ACQUISITION NOTIFICATION † on the acquiring federate, at which point the acquiring federate is responsible for updating the attributes. The divesting federate may get multiple callbacks of ATTRIBUTE OWNERSHIP DIVESTITURE NOTIFICATION † as several federates respond by acquiring various subsets of the offered attributes.

We'll use the negotiated divestiture protocol twice in the restaurant federation: once to transfer a Serving from a chef to a Boat, and again to transfer a Serving from a Boat to a diner. We'll describe these uses briefly here to illustrate the services; we'll revisit them in more detail when we explore the sample implementation of the federation.

Let's discuss loading a Boat first. Loading a Boat consists in transferring ownership of the position attribute of a Serving instance from Production to Transport. When the attribute's ownership is transferred, the Serving becomes attached to the Boat: its instance name becomes the value of the Boat's cargo attribute, and the Serving's position is from then on updated to be the same as the Boat's position.

When the Production federate perceives that an empty Boat has come within reach and decides that it wishes to load a Serving that the chef has made onto the Boat, it invokes NEGOTIATED ATTRIBUTE OWNERSHIP DIVESTITURE, providing the Serving's instance handle and the attribute handle for position. The Production federate places the name of the Boat that it wishes to load in the user-supplied tag. Because the Transport federate is publishing the position attribute of Serving, it receives REQUEST ATTRIBUTE OWNERSHIP ASSUMPTION †. If the Transport federate decides that it will accept the Serving, it invokes ATTRIBUTE OWNERSHIP ACQUISITION IF AVAILABLE, naming the proffered Serving instance. Because the attribute has been offered for divestiture, the transfer takes place immediately. The RTI will invoke ATTRIBUTE OWNERSHIP DIVESTITURE NOTIFICATION † on the Production federate, relieving it of the responsibility of modeling that instance's position, and ATTRIBUTE OWNERSHIP ACQUISITION NOTIFICATION † on the Transport federate, completing the transfer of the attribute.

We'll discuss the transfer of a Serving from a Boat to a diner later.

Negotiations Can Be Canceled   In the preceding discussion of transferring a Serving from a chef to a Boat, the decision of whether to accept a Serving is made by the Transport federate. The Production federate announces its desire to load a Boat with NEGOTIATED ATTRIBUTE OWNERSHIP DIVESTITURE and the Transport federate decides whether to respond. Why might the Transport federate decline the offer? One reason is that the Boat might not actually be empty by the time the offer is received. If a number of chefs are next to each other, the same Boat might come within reach of them all and they might all offer to load the same Boat. The Transport federate might respond to one request and load the Boat, only to have another request for the same Boat arrive afterward.

The ability to cancel a negotiation is exercised here. If the Transport federate determines that a request to load a Boat cannot be fulfilled, it does nothing. The Production side has an offer outstanding. It will remain outstanding indefinitely unless the Production federate does something.

The ownership services are designed to allow such a situation to be resolved. An initiating federate may elect, after waiting for some period, to cancel its offer either to acquire or divest attributes. In the divestiture case, the initiating federate can invoke CANCEL NEGOTIATED

ATTRIBUTE OWNERSHIP DIVESTITURE, which immediately suspends the transaction. In the restaurant federation, the Production federate watches the Boat of its desire sail out of reach. If this occurs before the Production federate has received ATTRIBUTE OWNERSHIP DIVESTITURE NOTIFICATION †, it will invoke CANCEL NEGOTIATED ATTRIBUTE OWNERSHIP DIVESTITURE, canceling its offer.

The astute reader will notice the possibility of a race condition. After all, as we so tirelessly keep saying, this is a distributed system, and the designer cannot count on things happening instantaneously. It is possible that the Transport federate has been slow in accepting the offer. Thus the RTI's notification of the completion, in the form of an ATTRIBUTE OWNERSHIP DIVESTITURE NOTIFICATION † callback, may be on its way as the Production federate decides to cancel. What then? The RTI will throw the Production federate an exception to the effect that it does not own the attribute. The Production federate can then assume that the divestiture notification is on the way and can be acted on in due course.

This brings us to an important point. *The RTI always ensures that ownership transfers are resolved unambiguously.* It may be inconvenient to be thrown an exception, but that sometimes is life in a distributed, concurrent world. The complexity we're revealing here is inherent in distributed systems; the HLA furnishes the mechanisms to manage the complexity reliably.

In fact, the reason the restaurant federation uses ownership mechanisms to model the transfer of Servings from chef to Boat to diner is that they are unambiguous in the face of uncertainty. You might invent a protocol of interactions to accomplish this (in fact we did for the first draft of the federation) but you then take on the burden of reliability. A better solution is to buy reliability from your RTI provider.

To cancel an acquisition, the initiating federate invokes CANCEL ATTRIBUTE OWNERSHIP ACQUISITION. The RTI will respond either with CONFIRM ATTRIBUTE OWNERSHIP ACQUISITION CANCELLATION †, which cancels the transaction, or with ATTRIBUTE OWNERSHIP ACQUISITION NOTIFICATION †, if a resolution of the transaction was already on the way.

Cancellation of any of the ownership transactions may cause the RTI to respond with both CONFIRM ATTRIBUTE OWNERSHIP ACQUISITION CANCELLATION † and ATTRIBUTE OWNERSHIP ACQUISITION NOTIFICATION † for disjoint sets of attributes. This may occur if another federate was in the midst of divesting or acquiring some but not all the attributes originally requested. In any event, all the originally requested attributes will be accounted for.

Ownership May Be Acquired Unobtrusively The "pulling" acquisition protocol described earlier is obtrusive, in that the RTI will actively solicit release of desired attributes from their current owners. There is another style of acquisition that does not involve this solicitation. Instead, the initiating federate will be given ownership only of the requested attributes that: (1) are unowned; or (2) are presently being offered for divestiture by their owning federate. In no case does the RTI call back an owning federate, unless the federate has already offered to divest some of the attributes.

Here are the specifics. The initiating federate invokes ATTRIBUTE OWNERSHIP ACQUISITION IF AVAILABLE, giving the usual instance and attribute handles. The RTI eventually will call back

the initiator with (possibly multiple) invocations of ATTRIBUTE OWNERSHIP ACQUISITION
NOTIFICATION † or ATTRIBUTE OWNERSHIP UNAVAILABLE †, such that the callbacks account for
all the attributes requested. The RTI will report an attribute as unavailable (include it in a
ATTRIBUTE OWNERSHIP UNAVAILABLE † callback) only if the attribute is presently owned by
some federate, and that federate does not have a request pending to release it (has included it in
a NEGOTIATED ATTRIBUTE OWNERSHIP DIVESTITURE invocation to which the RTI has not yet
responded). This is diagrammed in Figure 4-11. In (a), the ownership transfer succeeds because
the attribute(s) had been made available for acquisition previously. In (b), the ownership transfer
fails because the attribute(s) is owned by some federate and is not available for acquisition.
Notice that in both cases the RTI decides whether the transfer will succeed or fail without invoking services on any federate.

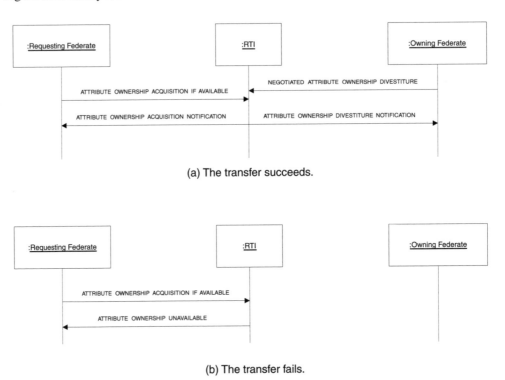

(a) The transfer succeeds.

(b) The transfer fails.

FIGURE 4-11   Unobtrusive Acquisition.

We use this protocol as part of transferring a Serving from a Boat to a diner. When the
Transport federate loads a Serving, it takes the position attribute of the Serving instance and
makes it available for acquisition by invoking NEGOTIATED ATTRIBUTE OWNERSHIP DIVESTI-
TURE. When the Consumption federate spies a loaded Boat within reach of a diner, and decides
to take the Serving, it invokes ATTRIBUTE OWNERSHIP ACQUISITION IF AVAILABLE for the posi-

tion attribute of the Serving instance on the Boat. In the normal case, the RTI transfers owner-ship immediately, calling back the Transport federate with ATTRIBUTE OWNERSHIP DIVESTITURE NOTIFICATION † and the Production federate with ATTRIBUTE OWNERSHIP ACQUISITION NOTIFICATION †.

The usefulness of ATTRIBUTE OWNERSHIP ACQUISITION IF AVAILABLE appears in the case of contention. As with transferring from a chef to a Boat, there is the possibility of a race wherein several diners are interested in the same Serving, all perceiving it to be available. Some lucky diner will actually get the Serving. The others will be called back with ATTRIBUTE OWNER-SHIP UNAVAILABLE †. The design of the ATTRIBUTE OWNERSHIP ACQUISITION IF AVAILABLE ser-vice ensures that no attempt to transfer is left hanging. This contrasts with ATTRIBUTE OWNERSHIP ACQUISITION, which, like NEGOTIATED ATTRIBUTE OWNERSHIP DIVESTITURE, remains outstanding until canceled. And, once again, the Ownership Management services guar-antee that the federation avoids ambiguity.

4.6.2   YOU CAN'T DELETE WHAT YOU DON'T OWN

Ownership management is used to arbitrate not only what federate is responsible for updating each attribute of an instance, but also to arbitrate what federate may delete an instance. An instance cannot be deleted by any arbitrary federate. Recall that each object class inherits the attribute privilegeToDeleteObject from the class ObjectRoot. Because all object classes inherit this attribute, every instance has it. The rule is that a federate may only delete an object if it owns privilegeToDeleteObject for that instance.

When a federate registers an instance of any object, it receives ownership of all the instance attributes of that class that it is publishing at the time. Every federate is deemed (with-out any action on its part) to be publishing privilegeToDeleteObject, so a federate registering an instance becomes the owner of privilegeToDeleteObject for the instance. Ownership of that instance attribute may be transferred through the Ownership Management services just like ownership of any other instance attribute.

In the restaurant federation, the only objects that are deleted before the federation halts are Servings. They are deleted by the Consumption federate when the diner has finished eating them. The Consumption federate must acquire privilegeToDeleteObject for each Serving instance before it can delete it. We described in Section 6.1.3.2 how the Consumption federate acquires ownership as needed.[12]

4.6.3   RESPONSIBILITY FOR MODELING AN OBJECT MAY BE SHARED

You'll have noticed that in the operation of the restaurant federation different instance attributes

---

12. You may have noticed earlier that privilegeToDeleteObject is never subscribed by any federate. The only reason to subscribe an instance attribute is to receive updates of its value or to ensure discovery of instances. The attribute privilegeToDeleteObject is never updated in this example. However, privilegeToDeleteObject can carry values like any other attribute. It could be used, for instance, to convey a reason for deletion of an object.

of a given Serving instance are owned by different federates. This is displayed in Figure 4-8. It is an important aspect of the intended application of ownership management. We use it casually in the restaurant federation, but it becomes central to the extension of the federation discussed in Chapter 7, "Extending the Federation for a New Purpose." To round off our discussion of owner-ship management, we talk briefly here about shared modeling.

One reason ownership is defined in terms of individual attributes of instances, rather than in terms of entire instances, is to support shared or cooperative modeling of entities. The idea is that a federation might together model a single entity, with some aspects of the entity being modeled by one federate and other aspects by another federate.

For example, suppose an object class Aircraft has the following attributes: position; veloc-ity; acceleration; and icingLoad, the weight of ice on the wings of the aircraft. The aircraft's flight dynamics are modeled by a federate specialized to that purpose, while the icing is modeled by a separate federate. The icing federate uses as inputs to its modeling the position and velocity of the aircraft and atmospheric conditions. In this example, the flight dynamics federate pub-lishes the position, velocity, and acceleration attributes. When the flight dynamics federate cre-ates an instance of the Aircraft class, it automatically gains ownership of the attributes (of that instance) that it publishes. The other attributes of the new instance, including icingLoad, initially are unowned. The icing federate subscribes to (at least) the position and velocity attributes of the Aircraft class. Thus the icing federate discovers the instance of Aircraft as it is registered and receives updates of those attributes. The icing federate publishes the icingLoad attribute. When the icing federate discovers a new instance of Aircraft, it attempts to acquire ownership of the icingLoad attribute for that instance. Because the icingLoad attribute is unowned, the RTI grants the icing federate ownership of it immediately. Then the icing federate may update the icing-Load attribute for the instance.

How is the deletion of an instance handled in the case of shared modeling? Some federate owns privilegeToDeleteObject for an instance. (Or no federate owns it, in which case the instance cannot be deleted until some federate acquires ownership of the attribute.) When that federate deletes the instance, every federate that is subscribing to any of the instance attributes will receive REMOVE OBJECT INSTANCE †. In addition, any federate that owns any of the instance attributes will also receive REMOVE OBJECT INSTANCE †. In the example above, the icing federate must be prepared to receive REMOVE OBJECT INSTANCE † for an instance of Aircraft whose icing-Load attribute it owns.

Exploring Ownership Management With the Test Federate

Your grasp of the patterns used with the Ownership Management services will be strengthened by experimenting with them. The test federate is well suited to that purpose. We suggest that you start two or three copies of the test federate and join them to a federation execution. Designate one federate as the publisher and the others as subscribers. Have the publisher publish several attributes of an object class, e.g., position and type of class Serving, and register several instances. Then experiment with the various patterns of ownership transfers. You can check the current ownership of a given instance attribute with the Ownership service QUERY ATTRIBUTE OWNERSHIP ("Own | 7.15 Query attribute ownership..."). That service will return the federate handle of the current owner, or zero if the instance attribute is unowned. Recall that the Test Federate displays its federate handle in its title bar. Federate handles are valid across a federation; you can check ownership of an attribute from any joined federate. You can also check whether an attribute is owned by a given federate by invoking IS ATTRIBUTE OWNED BY FEDERATE ("Own | 7.17 Is attribute owned by federate...") from the federate.

4.7 SUMMARY

With the use of the HLA services described in this chapter, the restaurant federation is complete, in the sense that the federation can run and yield useful results. Although there is more to say about the HLA, the description thus far is complete for the topics covered.

Chapter 5, "Synchronizing the Federation," describes the HLA's services for ordering events in logical time and coordinating the lifecycle of federates. The sample implementation of the restaurant federation that comes on the CD-ROM uses those services. If you are interested in the sample implementation, we suggest you continue through Chapter 5.

Synchronizing the Federation

5.1 BUILDING A FEDERATION: MORE ON THE EXAMPLE

This chapter continues the tutorial on building a federation begun in Chapter 4, "The Sushi Restaurant Federation." We assume you have read that chapter. This chapter discusses three topics:

- Ordering events in the simulation, with a presentation of the time management group of services
- Synchronizing independent federates through the federation lifecycle
- Synchronizing the federation to perceived time

The HLA services described in the previous chapter are sufficient for building a running federation. However, HLA federations typically are distributed systems and are subject to computational and network delays. Although it might be useful for many purposes, the restaurant federation as described to this point cannot be relied on to behave in exactly the same way from one federation execution to another. The common theme of this part is the HLA services and patterns of design that allow a federation to behave reproducibly despite being distributed across a network.

The sample implementation of the restaurant federation that is included on the CD-ROM is an implementation of the federation as described in the previous chapter and in this one. You should read this part before examining the sample implementation.

5.2 TIME MANAGEMENT: EVERYTHING IN ORDER

Time management in the HLA has to do with ensuring that events are delivered to federates in the correct order. With federates running perhaps on different computers with different speeds, ensuring the correct order of events is a significant problem. This section motivates the discussion by describing the problem in more detail, describes the relation of logical time to the problem of ordering events, gives an overview of time management, and then plunges into details.

5.2.1   WHY WE NEED EVENT ORDERING

The goal of this section is to motivate an interest in time management. The purpose of time management is to ensure that events are delivered to federates in the correct order. Many simulations, including distributed simulations, run "in real time," by which their designers mean that there is no explicit management of the order of events. We begin by showing the limitations of that approach.

5.2.1.1   Simulated Time Is Not Wall Clock Time

If we were to run the federation as it is designed thus far, all the federates would run as fast as their processors and networks would allow. We'd experience only a meaningless series of events flitting across our monitors. Obviously, simulation designers don't do that. Instead, a common goal is to have the federation simulation progress at about the rate of the clock on the wall. The Boats appear to go along the canal at the simulated rate, Servings appear at reasonable intervals and diners take reasonable amounts of time to enjoy their food. In rough terms, this is what is meant by a simulation running *in real time*: intervals between events in the simulation equal intervals perceived by an observer.

Notice that we've embraced with this idea a distinction between logical time and wall clock time. *Logical time* is the time as represented by the simulation. *Wall clock time* is the time an observer sees on the clock on the wall. There is no direct relation between them. If the simulation is running in real time, logical time and wall clock time are running at the same *rate* but have different origins. Wall clock time is the time displayed by the observer's wrist-watch, and logical time may be some hypothetical Tuesday in the future.

To run a federation in real time, we must program each federate so it changes state roughly "at the same pace as real time." What do we mean by that? Let's take the Transport federate as an example. Its job is to model the movement of the Boats along the canal surrounding the chefs in the restaurant. The Transport federate is a time-stepped simulation, i.e., it advances logical time in equal steps or increments. Every second of wall clock time (or whatever the time step is), the Transport federate computes the positions of the Boats one second later. The Boats are moving at a constant velocity along the canal, so those computations aren't exactly onerous. For a few dozen Boats, it may take the Transport federate, say, 200 milliseconds (it's a slow machine) to compute the next positions. The Transport federate doesn't want to issue updates for the position attributes until the proper interval of wall clock time has elapsed, so the Transport federate effectively goes to sleep for 800 milliseconds (by the clock on the wall) and then issues the updates. This is diagrammed in Figure 5-1. The diagram shows the progression of logical time as a function of wall clock time for the Transport federate. The federate begins (in the lower left corner) to compute the Boats' positions for the next time step. The federate finishes those computations after 200 milliseconds. Its logical time effectively advances by a second at that point, because it has computed the Boats' state a second beyond its previous logical time. But the federate is early (ahead of the appropriate wall clock time), so it waits for 800 milliseconds, with its logical time remaining constant. After its rest, the federate's wall clock time now corresponds to the federate's logical time, so the federate issues the updates, and the cycle begins again.

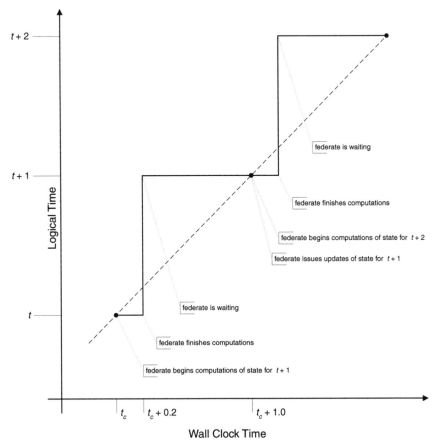

FIGURE 5-1   Time-Stepped Simulation in Real Time.

You can see that the Transport federate's ability to create the illusion of running in real time depends on its ability to compute its state for each time step before too much wall clock time elapses. The federate has one second of wall clock time between steps. If it can finish its computations within the second, all is well: it can simply sleep for the remainder of the step. If the federate cannot finish within a second, perhaps because of other demands on its processor, the illusion breaks down.

An event-driven or next-event simulation [Kiviat 1969] is much the same case, except that its advances in logical time are not uniform. An event-driven simulation is always trying to compute its state at the time of the next event on its queue; the computation must be finished before the corresponding wall clock time arrives. This is illustrated in Figure 5-2. In this diagram, an event-driven simulation attempts to advance time, first by 500 milliseconds, and then by 1.1 seconds. In each case, the federate is able to finish its computations of its state at the next value of logical time before the corresponding wall clock time arrives. It then sleeps varying amounts of time so that it issues updates at the correct points in wall clock time. As with a time-stepped federate, if the necessary state computations cannot be completed on time, the real-time illusion is destroyed.

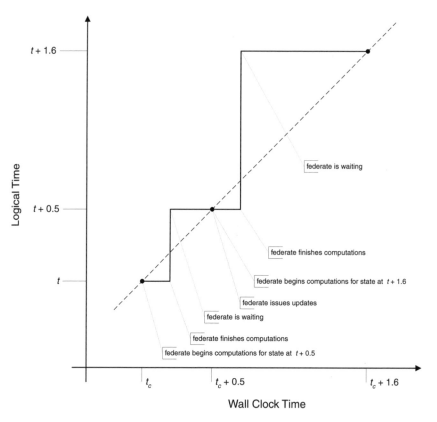

FIGURE 5-2   Event-Driven Simulation in Real Time.

5.2.1.2   We Can't Go Fast With This Scheme
Although we haven't said much about it, some organization is paying for all the work involved in integrating the restaurant federation. (Nobody would do this as a hobby, would they?) With money comes accountability. And that means, inevitably, a vice president arrives for a demo. In a rare visitation of good fortune, the engineers' planning and rehearsals pay off, the networks and computers remain operational, and the demo proceeds smoothly. But one of the engineers is unaware of the principle enunciated by Dilbert's Pointy-Haired Boss, that the higher the rank of the visitor, the less technical the presentation. The engineer mentions the fact that the federates'

processors are, on average, spending 80% of their time sleeping. The vice president condescends to deliver to the development team a vision of bold new restaurant designs explored by repeated federation runs overnight at five times real time. After all, if the processors are spending about 80% of their time waiting, the federation could try to advance logical time five times as fast as wall clock time. The state calculations in each federate would be ready about when the corresponding wall clock time arrived. Each federation execution could simulate five hours of restaurant operation in an hour, allowing five times as many executions overnight.

Nobody on the development team is aware that, in a decisive cost-cutting move, the same vice president has decreed that the system used for the Transport federate will also house the World Wide Web site for the International Brotherhood of Sushi Transporters. Nor are they aware (engineers being considered management and thus not numbered among the brethren) that the Brotherhood has just negotiated a new employment contract, the details of which are on the website. On the first evening of analysis runs, computation of the Boats' state is competing for the processor with thousands of web-literate Sushi Transporter brethren. The state computations are taking several seconds per step, with the result that the water in the canal appears to have been replaced with syrup, because the Transport federate is running far more slowly than the others. The thoughts of the development team turn toward the recruiters who've called recently.

As an alternative to a messy job change, the development team seeks a way to coordinate the attribute updates and other state changes across the federation so they remain properly ordered in logical time. The Consumption federate, whose behavior depends on the modeling of the Boats, must not run ahead of the Boats' arrival, even if the advance of logical time in the Transport federate is impeded. And similarly for the Production federate.

5.2.2   EVENTS IN A DISTRIBUTED SIMULATION MUST BE ORDERED

As we've seen, the order in which events arrive at a federate in a distributed simulation cannot be guaranteed. Latencies in network traffic and processing prevent this. Thus events do not arrive at a federate in the order of cause and effect, and if the simulation is run a second time, the same events may not arrive in the same order as in the first run. The goal of time management services is to allow a federation to ensure that events arrive at each federate in the causally correct order, and that another execution of the same federation will produce the same ordering.

Time management services deal with logical, or simulated, time. Time management services do not create any relationship between federates and real time or wall clock time. A federation using time management services may cause logical time to advance faster than real time, or slower. If one or more of the federates pace their advance of logical time to real time, time management services allow those federates to pace the entire federation. But the time management services themselves have no reference to real time. Nor do they provide any mechanism for determining wall clock values or elapsed-time values. *Time management services coordinate the advance of logical time within the federation and the delivery of time-stamped data.*

Logical time, as understood by the RTI, is abstract. It begins at a defined initial time. It progresses positively. It is well ordered. But it has no units. The designers of a federation must agree on a convention for the meaning of logical time.

The time management services support a variety of time management schemes, including at least the following:

- No explicit time management, as exemplified by the restaurant federation presented thus far
- *Conservative synchronization*, where no federate advances logical time except when it can be guaranteed not to receive any events in its past
- *Optimistic synchronization*, where a federate is free to compute into the future, but may receive events in its past that cause it to roll back to its state at an earlier time
- *Activity scan*, where federates progress through episodes in which they exchange messages at the same time, until they agree to advance logical time together

The time management services even support the construction of federations that mix these strategies. The rest of this section explains how to make the restaurant federation conservatively synchronized, because that is the simplest case of active time management. By a *conservatively synchronized federation*, we mean one in which each federate is conservatively synchronized. In later sections we'll add some bells and whistles to this framework. In Chapter 8, "Advanced Topics," we'll discuss strategies for integrating optimistic and activity-scan federates.

5.2.3   THE FOLLOWING IDEAS APPLY TO ALL HLA TIME MANAGEMENT STRATEGIES

Before plunging into the details of the time management services, it's a good idea to survey the subject. This survey is important to understanding the next section.

5.2.3.1   Each Federate Has a Logical Time

Each federate has a logical time. The purpose of the time management services is to coordinate the advance of logical time of all the federates. The federation has no logical time. Logical time has meaning only with respect to a given federate.

Logical time is abstract. It possesses these properties:

- It has an initial value.
- It is well ordered: given two logical times, the RTI can always say which is greater, or whether they are equal.
- It is always greater than or equal to the initial time.
- It has a value of positive infinity, called the *final time*, which is larger than any other value.

Logical time is not tied to any system of units. Whether a logical time of one in a federation represents a millisecond, a second, or a fortnight, is a matter of federation convention.

5.2.3.2   Each Federate Chooses Its Degree of Involvement

Not all the federates in a federation must be involved in time management. Each federate may choose its degree of participation. The choice is characterized by whether the federate is or is not time-regulating, and is or is not time-constrained. A *time-regulating* federate is one whose advance of logical time regulates the rest of the federation (specifically those federates that are time-constrained). A *time-constrained* federate is one whose advance of logical time is constrained by the rest of the federation (specifically those federates that are time-regulating). The two choices are independent, which gives rise to four possibilities, diagrammed in Figure 5-3.

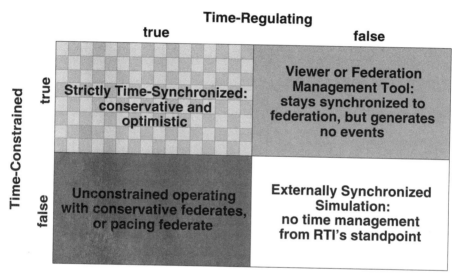

FIGURE 5-3   Choices for Time Management.

- A federate that is neither regulating nor constrained simply isn't participating in time management. This is the default condition for a federate when it joins a federation. All the restaurant federates have been in the default condition to this point.

- A federate that is both constrained and regulating is fully involved in time management; it is fully synchronized. Its logical time cannot run ahead of the rest of the federation, nor can the federation run off without it. We'll modify the restaurant federation so that all its federates are both constrained and regulating.

- A federate that is constrained but not regulating is allowing the rest of the federation to regulate its logical time, but it cannot affect the other federates. This is a useful choice for a data logger or display, or other passive federate. We added such a federate to the restaurant federation when we created the sample implementation.

- A federate that is regulating but not constrained paces the rest of the federation but is not constrained by it. As an example of using this choice, suppose you had a conservatively synchronized federation (all federates both constrained and regulating) which, because of clever programming and new hardware, could run much faster than wall clock time, that is, the logical time of the federates outpaces the clock. If you wanted to retard the federation to wall clock time to be able to visualize the simulation, you could add a federate whose job was simply to advance its logical time at the desired wall clock rate. Such a federate could be regulating but not constrained.

5.2.3.3   The Effects of Time Management Are Seen In Events

In the HLA, the effects of time management are seen in the sending and receiving of events. A federate *sends an event* when it invokes any of the following:

- UPDATE ATTRIBUTE VALUES
- SEND INTERACTION
- DELETE OBJECT INSTANCE

A federate *receives an event* when the RTI invokes any of the following on it.

- REFLECT ATTRIBUTE VALUES †
- RECEIVE INTERACTION †
- REMOVE OBJECT INSTANCE †

Thus sending or receiving an event involves familiar operations of the RTI. Their event character consists of the fact that these operations can carry logical time stamps and their operation can be coordinated by the time management services. Notice that REGISTER OBJECT INSTANCE and DISCOVER OBJECT INSTANCE † are not on either list. Those operations are not involved in time management.

You'll recall from our discussion of the object management services that the sending of an event by one federate can cause multiple events to be received by receiving federates. Specifically, one federate invoking UPDATE ATTRIBUTE VALUES will cause REFLECT ATTRIBUTE VALUES † at all the federates that are subscribed to any of the sent attributes. Similarly, if a federate invokes SEND INTERACTION, all the federates subscribed to that class of interaction will receive a corresponding RECEIVE INTERACTION †. Finally, invoking DELETE OBJECT INSTANCE will cause REMOVE OBJECT INSTANCE † at all the federates that have discovered the object.

The foregoing "event" services, and certain other time management services, are the only operations of the RTI that have temporal significance, that is, are related to logical time. Other services, like the declaration management services (publish and subscribe) and the ownership services, have no temporal significance. They are not related to the passage of logical time. But these services have effects that are felt in logical time. It's up to the federation designers to ensure that declarations and ownership transactions are properly related to logical time. The RTI provides the tools necessary to do this; we'll discuss it particularly in the section on federation lifecycle.

Received events are said to be in either *receive order* (RO) or *time stamp order* (TSO). Only TSO events have temporal significance; only they carry time stamps and have the ordering of their arrival guaranteed by the RTI. Only TSO events have their delivery to the federate controlled by the passage of logical time. RO events are delivered to the receiving federate in the order they are received by the federate, irrespective of the order they were sent (hence the name). A federate cannot deduce anything about the order in which RO events were sent. RO events carry no time stamps; their delivery is unaffected by the progress of logical time.

Whether an event is received as RO or TSO depends both on how it was sent and how it is received. We speak of an event as being sent TSO or RO, and being received as TSO or RO.

Let's discuss the sending side first. Remember that each received event is the result of an originating event sent by some federate. For an event to be sent TSO, the following must be true at the sending federate:

- The federate that sends the originating event must be time-regulating.
- The attributes, in the case of UPDATE ATTRIBUTE VALUES, or the interaction class in the case of SEND INTERACTION, must have the order type TSO.
- The UPDATE ATTRIBUTE VALUES or SEND INTERACTION invocation must include a time stamp; that is, the sending federate must have used the forms of those services that include a time stamp, rather than the forms that omit a time stamp.

If all these conditions are met, the event is sent TSO; otherwise, it is sent RO. Only a time-regulating federate can produce a TSO event, and only if the federate includes a time stamp when it sends the event, and only if the data sent have order type TSO.

Now let's discuss the receiving side. Remember that there may be multiple receivers for a given sender. The order type of a sent event affects all the receivers of the event. For an event to be received as TSO, the following must be true:

- The event must have been sent TSO.
- The receiving federate must be time-constrained.

Only a time-constrained federate can receive an event as TSO. An event sent as TSO will be received as RO by an unconstrained federate.

We said that the ordering of an event depends on the order type of the attributes or interaction involved. How is the order type determined? Attributes and interaction classes have a *preferred order type* that is defined in the FED. That preferred order type can be overridden. A federate may elect to change the order type associated with an instance attribute (attribute of a *specific instance*) by invoking CHANGE ATTRIBUTE ORDER TYPE. The instance attribute retains its new order type until the instance attribute changes ownership, at which point it reverts to its preferred order type, the one in the FED. The preferred order type of an interaction class may be overridden by invoking CHANGE INTERACTION ORDER TYPE.

Here's a fine point in the case of attributes. An invocation of UPDATE ATTRIBUTE VALUES can name attributes with different orderings, for instance, some TSO and some RO. Some

attributes may be sent TSO, and some RO, according to the rules we're setting out. The RTI seg-
regates the attributes by order type, creating separate received events if necessary, so that all
attributes in one received event have the same ordering. The RTI makes several callbacks if necessary to deliver all the attributes. So a single UPDATE ATTRIBUTE VALUES invocation could
result in two RECEIVE INTERACTION † callbacks at a receiver: one with the TSO attributes, and
another with the RO attributes.

5.2.3.4   The RTI Guarantees Delivery of TSO Events In Order

A federate that wishes to operate with conservative synchronization can use the RTI in such a
way that the following are guaranteed:

- TSO events will be delivered to the federate in time-stamp order, irrespective of the order
  in which the originating events were sent.
- No event will be delivered to the federate in its past, that is, with a time stamp less than its
  current logical time.

These guarantees imply the following for the federate:

- Despite the fact that the federate is operating effectively in parallel with other federates,
  and there is no central control of logical time, the federate never has its state invalidated by
  the arrival of events in its past. The federate is allowed to advance its state in logical time
  only when it is safe to do so.

With a slightly different pattern of use, a federate intending to perform optimistic synchronization can also use the RTI to enforce appropriate guarantees. This is discussed in Chapter 8,
"Advanced Topics."

All these guarantees have to do with the order of reception of events. The HLA does not
restrict the order in which a federate sends events. They need not be sent in time-stamp order.

5.2.3.5   Each Federate Specifies a Lookahead

All the time-advance mechanisms in the RTI use a lookahead value. Lookahead is a duration of
logical time that each federate specifies when it becomes time-regulating. In the time advance
schemes we'll use with the restaurant federation, lookahead must be strictly positive. (Among
the advanced topics we'll discuss in Chapter 8 are the uses and consequences of allowing lookahead to be zero, which the HLA also supports.) Lookahead places a restriction on the time-regulating federate; if the federate is at logical time t and has lookahead value l, the RTI will not
allow it to send events with time $t_s < t + l$. That is, the federate must look ahead from its current
logical time, and not send events whose times are less than its current time plus its lookahead.

Why is lookahead necessary? One reason is to avoid deadlock [Fujimoto 1999]. Suppose
there was no lookahead, and suppose you have a set of federates, all of which are time-regulating and time-constrained. At some instant during the federation execution, some federate has the
smallest logical time; let that time be T. This federate could generate events at time T of interest

to any of the other federates. This means the RTI cannot deliver events with times greater than T to those other federates because to do so risks delivering events out of order. And this means that none of the other federates can advance their logical times beyond T because to do so risks having an event delivered in their past. No federate can advance its clock, and the federation is deadlocked.

One means of circumventing this problem is to allow events to be delivered out of time-stamp order. Such optimistic synchronization techniques require the federate to be capable of rolling back its state to an earlier time when it detects an error caused by out-of-order delivery. The RTI supports this approach, and we'll discuss it in Chapter 8.

The other means of circumventing the problem, which we describe now, involves the use of lookahead. If each time-regulating federate in the federation has a positive lookahead, the RTI can allow federates to move their clocks ahead. The RTI knows the logical time and lookahead of all the other time-regulating federates in the federation. From this information, the RTI can compute the earliest time stamp that might accompany any event from any other federate. That lower bound is the latest time to which the RTI can allow the federate to advance its logical time.[1] We've hardly scratched the surface of the theory behind these time management protocols; we suggest you consult [Carothers et al. 1997], [Nicol and Fujimoto 1993], and [Fujimoto 1999] for more information.

The larger the lookahead relative to the time step or granularity of time stamps on events, the more parallelism the federation can achieve. However, a federate's lookahead limits how quickly a federate can produce events (in logical time) in response to events it receives. The choice of lookahead is related intimately to the details of the simulation model in the federate, so the RTI cannot choose it. Lookahead is a property of a federate, not a federation. The following suggestions for the source of a reasonable lookahead are taken from Fujimoto [Fujimoto 1999].[2]

• *How quickly can a model react to an external event?* The Production federate detects that a Boat has moved within range of a chef and may have room for another Serving. If the chefs being modeled by the Production federate require at least 500 milliseconds to decide, after noticing the Boat, whether to try to load a serving, the Production federate can guarantee that it will not schedule an external (affects other federates) event at least 500 milliseconds into the future, and it could adopt a lookahead of 500 milliseconds.

• *How quickly can one model affect another?* Suppose you have two models of computer processes and data packets in different federates. Suppose one modeled process must react to the arrival of a modeled data packet over a network from the other, and there is a minimum time required for the packet to travel over its network. The arrival of the packet can be

---

1. Other federates that are not time-regulating play no part in this computation. Events originating from them cause only RO callbacks at the receiver, so the order of delivery of those events to the receiver is merely the order in which they arrive from other federates through the RTI.
2. We note again that the HLA supports zero lookahead for, for example, "activity scan" federates. See Chapter 8.

scheduled at least as far into the future as the minimum travel time, providing some lookahead.

- *Does the simulation proceed in uniform time steps?* In a time-stepped simulation, the lookahead is usually the size of the step, because the model cannot schedule events into its current
time step, but only into the next step or later.

A federate may change its lookahead during the federation execution. But its lookahead
cannot be reduced instantaneously. The sum at any moment of the federate's logical time and its
lookahead can never be lessened. Other federates' logical times can be advanced to the sum of
this federate's logical time plus lookahead, because they are guaranteed that the federate will
send no events with time stamps less than this value. Thus, if a federate asks to reduce its lookahead by an amount k, the federate's logical time must advance by at least k before the RTI can
grant the request.

5.2.3.6   Each Federate Asks the RTI to Advance Its Logical Time

How does each time-constrained federate advance its logical time? It asks the RTI to grant each
advance it desires. The RTI uses the requests from all time-regulating federates to determine
when to allow time-constrained federates to advance.

This implies two things worth noting. Firstly, if a federate is time-regulating, it should regularly request the RTI to allow it to advance its clock. If the federate is not time-constrained, the
RTI will grant the advance immediately. Secondly, it is the requests to advance that coordinate
the advance of logical time, and not the sending of time-stamped events. Reception of events is
controlled by the advance of logical time, but events do not advance time.

There are five different time advance mechanisms in the RTI. We will only consider two
mechanisms in this section, TIME ADVANCE REQUEST and NEXT EVENT REQUEST. But all the
mechanisms operate on the same cycle we'll describe here.

Regardless of the mechanism chosen, a federate advances time in cycles. In each cycle, the
federate asks to advance its time, and awaits a callback from the RTI granting the advance. The
federate's logical time does not advance on its request, but on the grant from the RTI. The grant
callback carries the time to which the federate has been advanced. (This may not be the time for
which it asked.) The federate's temporal state can be represented by the state machine illustrated
in Figure 5-4.

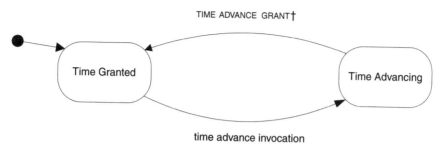

FIGURE 5-4   Time Management States.

The federate begins in the Time Granted state, with a known logical time (and lookahead). In this state, the federate can simulate behavior at its current logical time. The federate is guaranteed that the RTI will not send it an event with a time stamp less than its logical time. The federate can send events with any time stamp at least its logical time plus its lookahead. The federate need not send events in time-stamp order. When the federate believes it is ready to advance its clock, it invokes one of the time advance services on the RTI, specifying the time it wishes to move to.

With the time advance invocation, the federate moves into the Time Advancing state. Its logical time does not change. However, the constraint on time stamps of events it sends does change. The federate may send TSO events with time stamps at least the *time it has requested* plus lookahead. The federate will begin to receive TSO events. (It receives no TSO events in the Time Granted state.) TSO events will be delivered in increasing time-stamp order, until the RTI invokes TIME ADVANCE GRANT † on the federate. The callback carries the federate's new logical time. Depending on which time advance service was invoked earlier, the new logical time may be less than what the federate asked for. As of the callback, the federate's logical time moves to the new value, and the federate enters the Time Granted state again.

The federate will receive TSO events only while in the Time Advancing state. By default, a time-constrained federate receives RO callbacks only in the Time Advancing state. If a time-constrained federate wishes to receive RO callbacks in the Time Granted state as well, it can ask the RTI to deliver RO callbacks by invoking ENABLE ASYNCHRONOUS DELIVERY. A federate that is not time-constrained receives RO callbacks in either state. (Recall that for an unconstrained federate, events that are sent TSO are converted to RO when received.)

5.2.4   MECHANICS OF USING TIME MANAGEMENT

From the federate's perspective, employing time management involves some initial operations, and then repetitions of the advance-grant cycle outlined above.

5.2.4.1   Getting Started

There are no restrictions on the order in which a federate performs publications, subscriptions, object registrations, and time management initializations. These can occur in any order. They can be interleaved throughout a federation execution. However, it is helpful if a federate participating in time management sets its time switches before it subscribes, to ensure the correct relation of events to time. The reason is that a federate will receive no events before it subscribes, and may receive events at any time after it subscribes. To ensure that events intended to be TSO are received as TSO (and not converted to RO), the federate should set its time switches before subscribing. Similarly, if the federate wishes to produce TSO events, it must get its time switches set before sending them. So we recommend the general order:

- Enable time constraint
- Enable time regulation
- Publish and subscribe
- Register initial instances
- Enter normal simulation loop

When a federate joins, it is neither time-regulating nor time-constrained. It is legal to set the time switches in either order. However, if a federate intends to set both, it is useful to set the constraint switch first, because being constrained affects the RTI's behavior while the federate is becoming time-regulating. If a federate is already time-constrained, the process of becoming time-regulating is like a time advance cycle, and TSO messages are received correctly. This is illustrated in Figure 5-5.

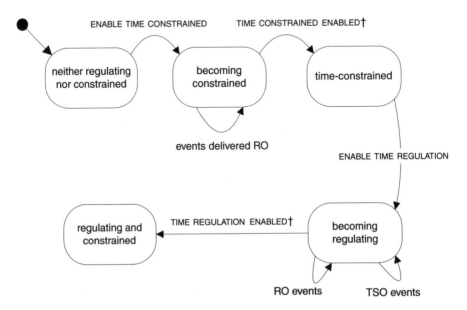

FIGURE 5-5   Setting Time Switches.

To become time-constrained, the federate invokes ENABLE TIME CONSTRAINED. It then waits until the RTI calls it back with TIME CONSTRAINED ENABLED †. The RTI supplies a logical time for the federate with the callback. This logical time has the same significance as a logical time for any time-constrained federate; it represents a guarantee from the RTI that no TSO events will arrive in the federate's past, that is, with time stamps less than the federate's logical time. In fact, it is the federate's new logical time.

Note that the RTI may deliver events to the federate between its invocation of ENABLE TIME CONSTRAINED and its receipt of TIME CONSTRAINED ENABLED †. Because the federate is unconstrained in this interval, all events are delivered to it as RO, including events that may have been sent as TSO, and which may have had time stamps greater than the logical time eventually assigned to the federate. This is one reason that we recommend setting the constraint switch before subscribing to data.

The federate then invokes ENABLE TIME REGULATION, supplying a value for its logical time, and a value for its lookahead. The RTI uses the logical time as advice: it obviously can't allow the federate to assume a time in any time-constrained federate's past. In the absence of other information, the federate can supply the logical time "initial time." If the federate has previously enabled time constraint, it must supply a logical time at least its current logical time, that is, the logical time that was returned by the RTI with TIME CONSTRAINED ENABLED †.

The federate then awaits a TIME REGULATION ENABLED † callback. If the federate has previously enabled time constraint, the federate may receive RO and TSO events from the RTI in the interval before receiving TIME REGULATION ENABLED †. The RTI treats the federate as if it had requested moving its logical time ahead to the time specified with ENABLE TIME REGULATION, that is, as if the federate had moved into the Time Advancing state of the time advance cycle. So the federate must be prepared to receive RO and TSO events in this interval. Of course, if the federate has subscribed to nothing before this point, it will receive no events.

With the receipt of TIME REGULATION ENABLED †, the federate is time-regulating, with an established logical time and lookahead. It can begin to send TSO events (with time stamps at or beyond its logical time plus lookahead). The federate is in the Time Granted state, and may commence normal time cycling. The RTI may return a time with TIME REGULATION ENABLED † beyond what the federate asked for. The RTI cannot grant the federate a logical time that would allow it to send events in the time-constrained federate's past, so it may have to drag the federate up to an appropriate time, delivering, as necessary, all events along the way.

5.2.4.2 Advancing Time

The RTI offers five different services for advancing time. This profusion reflects the RTI's goal of supporting a variety of federate organizations. We'll concentrate in this example on the two that are intended for conservative synchronization. (We'll discuss others in Chapter 8, "Advanced Topics.") All the time advance services embody the basic time advance cycle that was described above. In the following discussion, we assume the federate is time-constrained and time-regulating.

In the basic loop, the federate begins in the Time Granted state. It has a current logical time and lookahead. It requests moving its logical time forward, invoking one of the time advance services (TIME ADVANCE REQUEST (TAR) or NEXT EVENT REQUEST (NER)). The federate enters the Time Advancing state. The RTI then will deliver RO and TSO events. The TSO events will be delivered in order of increasing time stamp. The federate is free to update its internal state to the time of the last-received TSO event. It may produce TSO events, but their time stamps must be at least the last time the federate requested plus lookahead. The federate can produce RO events as it chooses.

Eventually the RTI calls back the federate with TIME ADVANCE GRANT †. The logical time delivered with the callback becomes the federate's new logical time. At that point, the federate enters the Time Granted state. It is free to compute its models at the new time, because the RTI guarantees that the federate has seen all the events from other federates that can have occurred before or at its new logical time. It can produce TSO events whose time stamps are at least its current logical time plus lookahead. It can produce RO events at will. In the Time Granted state it will not receive more TSO events. It will not receive RO events unless it has enabled asynchronous delivery.

5.2.4.3   Time-Stepped Simulation

The simplest approach to managing logical time in a simulation is to advance time in equal steps. If such a federate is using a step s and is at logical time t, it will produce events with time stamps of $t + s, t + 2s, ...$ The federate will use s as its lookahead. A typical pattern is represented in Figure 5-6.

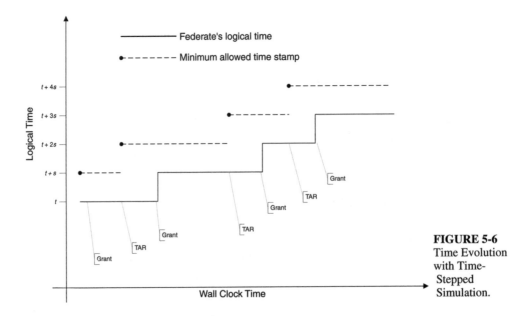

FIGURE 5-6
Time Evolution
with Time-
Stepped
Simulation.

In this diagram, wall clock time proceeds to the right. It is shown without units to emphasize the lack of correlation between wall time and logical time. The diagram shows a time-stepped federate operating with a lookahead equal to its time step. The federate does the usual cycle of TIME ADVANCE REQUEST (labeled "TAR") and TIME ADVANCE GRANT † (labeled "Grant"). The figure shows the evolution of two quantities as the federation execution proceeds. The logical time of the federate is shown with a solid line. Notice that it does not increase until the Grant arrives. The dotted line represents the minimum time stamp the RTI will accept on any event from the federate at each point in wall clock time. The minimum time stamp increases at a TAR because, at the moment the federate has asked to advance its clock, the RTI accepts the request to advance as a promise from the federate not to produce earlier events.

5.2.4.4   How Time Management Coordinates Time-Stepped Federates

We've said that time management coordinates the advance of logical time among all the federates in a federation. More precisely, the RTI prevents time-constrained federates from running off without respect to time-regulating federates. In a conservatively synchronized federation, all federates are regulating and constrained, and thus the federation advances together. We'll give some examples in this section that will make this clearer. The details are worth studying because they will give you the understanding you'll need to design federations correctly and to debug anomalous behavior.

The discussion in this section applies to federates that use TIME ADVANCE REQUEST to advance time, rather than NEXT EVENT REQUEST. It is the service that a federate uses to advance time that determines the RTI's behavior, not the size of the federate's time steps. TIME ADVANCE REQUEST allows the size of the requested advance to vary with each invocation. We assume unvarying step sizes in this section only for simplicity.

The first example is a conservatively synchronized federation of two federates. Both are time-stepped federates that use TIME ADVANCE REQUEST to advance time. The first federate, akin to the Manager federate we'll introduce in the section on federation execution lifecycle, seeks to advance time at regular intervals of wall clock time. It has little other computation to perform. It spends much of its time waiting. The second federate, akin to the Transport federate, has substantial computation to perform, but not so much that it might hold up the Manager. The evolution of logical time in the two federates is shown in Figure 5-7.

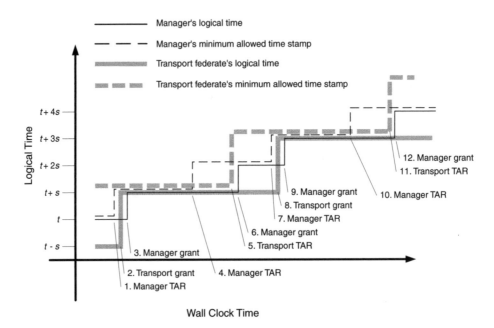

FIGURE 5-7   Time Evolution with Two Federates.

In addition to the logical times of the two federates, there are two other quantities whose evolution is displayed in the figure. These are the minimum allowed time stamp of each federate, that is, the minimum time stamp the RTI will allow each federate to place on an event it sends, as a function of wall clock time. For a federate in the Time Granted state, this minimum is logical time plus lookahead. For a federate in the Time Advancing state, the minimum is requested time plus lookahead. The RTI can always safely grant a federate a time advance to any time less than the smallest time that might appear in any event the federate might receive. For a federation of two regulating federates using TIME ADVANCE REQUEST, one federate's minimum allowed time stamp is a lower bound for the other federate on time stamps on events it might receive.

Let's go through the diagram in detail. We'll see the way in which the two federates control each other's time advances. The Manager federate seeks to advance its logical time in steps of s. In the diagram, it begins with a logical time of t. The Transport federate seeks to advance its time in steps of $2s$. In the diagram it begins with a logical time of $t - s$. Both federates operate with constant lookaheads that are small compared to s. (The small value is chosen for the sake of illustration; as we said earlier, a time-stepped federate might choose its step as its lookahead.)

The behavior illustrated in Figure 5-7 is cyclical. The diagram must begin somewhere, so we've chosen a representative place at the beginning of a cycle, and the initial values are chosen accordingly. The Manager is in the Time Granted state, and the Transport is in the Time Advancing state.

The first interesting occurrence in the diagram, labeled "1. Manager TAR," is the Manager invoking TIME ADVANCE REQUEST. This causes its minimum allowed time stamp to rise immediately. The Manager enters the Time Advancing state. This in turn triggers occurrence 2, a TIME ADVANCE GRANT † to the Transport federate to time $t + s$. The Transport federate had previously requested an advance to $t + s$; the RTI was waiting for the lower bound on time stamps from all other regulating federates to advance beyond this value. Occurrence 1 also triggers occurrence 3, a TIME ADVANCE GRANT † to the Manager. Because the Transport federate's minimum allowed time stamp already exceeded the Manager's requested time, the RTI can grant the advance immediately. That causes the Manager's logical time to rise to $t + s$. Here we see the Transport federate's dependence on the Manager, and the Manager's on the Transport federate.

After this, the Transport federate is busy computing its new state at logical time $t + s$. The Manager remains in the Time Granted state, idling until occurrence 4. (Its purpose is to pace the federation to wall clock time, as we'll explain later.) The Manager then invokes TIME ADVANCE REQUEST, seeking to move to $t + 2s$. This causes its minimum allowed time stamp to rise to its requested time plus lookahead.

Sometime after this, the Transport federate finishes its computations and seeks to advance to $t + 3s$ (occurrence 5), causing its minimum allowed time stamp to rise. This in turn allows the RTI to grant an advance to the Manager (occurrence 6). At this point the federation is in the same relative state it was at the beginning, except that both federates' logical time has progressed by $2s$. Occurrences 7 through 12 duplicate the behavior of 1 through 6.

5.2.4.5   Event-Driven Simulation

In addition to the time-stepped pattern, another typical pattern of time management is the event-driven pattern [Kiviat 1969], [Fujimoto 1999]. The simulation proceeds by processing its next event, that is, the known event with the smallest future logical time. Processing this event generates other events, which are entered on a time-ordered list or queue, or deletes events from the queue. The simulation then goes back to its queue for what is then the next event.

To include such a simulation in an HLA federation, it is necessary to integrate the federate's event queue with events arriving from the rest of the federation. The federation does not maintain a central, combined event queue. Instead, the federate uses the time management services of the RTI to discover events from other federates (external events) that must be combined with events generated by the federate itself (internal events). The federate maintains its internal event queue as if it were operating by itself.

Instead of using TIME ADVANCE REQUEST, as does a time-stepped federate, the event-driven federate uses NEXT EVENT REQUEST to request an advance of its clock. The federate specifies with the request the logical time of the next event on its internal queue. The RTI responds in one of two ways:

- The RTI calls back with TIME ADVANCE GRANT † and the time the federate gave in the NEXT EVENT REQUEST. In this case, the RTI is guaranteeing that there is no event from the rest of the federation before the internal event. The federate's logical time then moves to the time of its next internal event. Therefore the federate is free to remove that event from its queue and process it, perhaps producing other internal or external events.

• The RTI calls back with an external event (REFLECT ATTRIBUTE VALUES †, RECEIVE INTERACTION †, or REMOVE OBJECT INSTANCE †) with a time stamp before the requested time, and then with TIME ADVANCE GRANT † carrying the time of the external event. In this case, the RTI is guaranteeing that there will be no external event before the one just delivered. The federate's logical time moves to the time of the event, and it is free to process that event, perhaps generating external or internal events.

Thus the federate's logical time does not move in even steps, but moves from event time to event time, with its internal events interleaved with external events. The federate's main loop is as follows:

```
while the simulation is running loop:
    examine next event on internal queue;
    invoke NEXT EVENT REQUEST with time of next internal event;
    await and process RO and TSO events and other RTI-initiated
        services;
    await TIME ADVANCE GRANT †;
    logical time moves to the granted time;
    if logical time is at least the time of internal event
        dequeue internal event and process;
end loop;
```

An implementation of this loop must handle two details omitted for simplicity: firstly, RO callbacks may arrive between the NEXT EVENT REQUEST and the TIME ADVANCE GRANT †, and secondly, there may be more than one TSO event delivered with the same time stamp.

What about lookahead? It applies just as it does in the time-stepped case, but its proper value is not as obvious. At any moment in the federation execution, the federate is not allowed to produce events with timestamps less than its logical time plus lookahead. You can use the ideas mentioned earlier to settle on a suitable lookahead. The larger the lookahead relative to the federate's typical increment of time to the next event, the more concurrent will be the federation.

In the NEXT EVENT REQUEST scheme, the RTI sometimes relaxes its restriction on the minimum time stamp allowed from a federate. This is diagrammed in Figure 5-8. Two cycles are diagrammed of request to advance and advance grant. The relaxation is illustrated in the second cycle. The figure shows a single federate with a lookahead of 0.5. The minimum time stamp allowed on an event from the federate begins as 0.5 more than the federate's logical time because its lookahead is 0.5. At the point labeled "NER to $t + 1$," the federate asks to move ahead by 1.0. The minimum time stamp increases by 1.0 at "NER to $t + 1$" because the federate certifies it is ready to move its logical time by that amount. Eventually, at the point labeled "Grant to $t + 1$," the RTI grants an advance by the full amount, and the federate's logical time increases by 1.0. In the next cycle, the federate again requests to move ahead by 1.0. At the point

"Grant to $t + 1.5$," the federate is only granted to $t + 1.5$, because an external event has arrived. The minimum time stamp had moved by 1.0 at "NER to $t + 2$" because the federate certified it was ready to move its logical time by that amount. After the event arrives, the RTI relaxes the minimum allowed time stamp to the federate's new logical time plus lookahead (0.5 less than what the federate was prepared to move to).

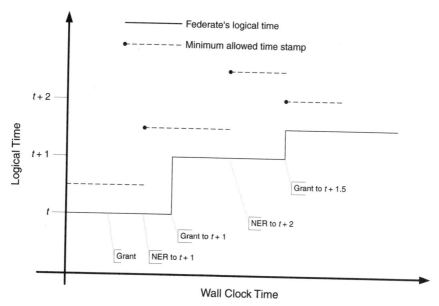

FIGURE 5-8   Time Evolution with Event-Driven Simulation.

The reason for the relaxation is that the RTI must compute the minimum time stamp conservatively. After the federate performs the NER to $t + 2$, the best information the RTI has is that the federate will eventually be granted to $t + 2$. The RTI cannot allow the federate to send events with a timestamp less than $t + 2$ plus lookahead, lest some other federate reply with an event less than the time to which the federate is eventually granted. As soon as the RTI has enough information to grant the federate to a lesser time ($t + 1.5$ in the example), it can also be certain that no events will arrive with timestamps less than $t + 1.5$.

5.2.4.6   How Time Management Coordinates Event-Driven Federates

To illustrate how a federate using NEXT EVENT REQUEST interacts with other federates, we give another illustration similar to our earlier one with two federates using TIME ADVANCE REQUEST. The behavior of a federate using NEXT EVENT REQUEST depends on the arrival of events to the RTI's queues for the federate, so there is an added dimension of variability to any such illustration. To keep things simple, we show two federates:

- One federate is akin to the Manager, as before. It seeks to move its logical time in equal steps using TIME ADVANCE REQUEST. It has little computation to perform, and spends much of its time idling in the Time Granted state.
- The second federate is akin to the Production federate. It is event-driven and advances its logical time using NEXT EVENT REQUEST. It is typically able to complete the computations it must perform for each event it encounters soon enough that it does not retard the Manager. Its progress depends both on the Manager's behavior and the arrival of events.

The example appears in Figure 5-9. As before, we show logical time as a function of wall clock time for each federate. We also show two additional quantities. The first is the minimum allowed time stamp for the Manager, that is, the minimum time the RTI will allow on any time-stamped event sent by the Manager. The second additional quantity is the output time for the Production federate. This *output time* is the greatest lower bound that the RTI can compute on time stamps on events that will come from the federate now or later in the federation execution. For a federate in the Time Granted state, its output time is its logical time plus lookahead.

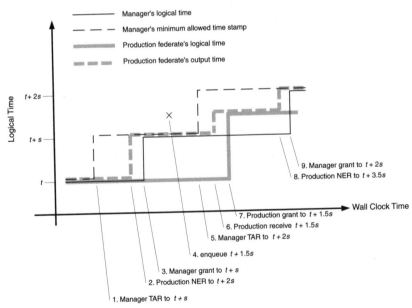

FIGURE 5-9   Time-Stepped and Event-Driven Simulations.

For a federate using TIME ADVANCE REQUEST, its output time equals its minimum allowed time stamp. But this is not the case for federates using NEXT EVENT REQUEST. When a federate uses NEXT EVENT REQUEST, the RTI may relax its minimum allowed time stamp when the federate receives a grant because an event arrives. Suppose other federates had been allowed to advance their logical time on the basis of the minimum allowed time stamp. After the minimum allowed time stamp was relaxed, the federate might be free to send events that would arrive in the other federates' past. So the RTI cannot use the minimum allowed time stamp as the basis for advancing other federates' clocks. Instead the RTI uses an output time for the federate. The RTI performs a running computation for each federate of the minimum output time of all other time-regulating federates. This minimum is called the *lower bound on the time stamp* or *LBTS*. The LBTS for each federate represents, at each moment in the federation execution, the smallest time stamp that might be received by the federate now or later in the federation execution. A federate can discover its RTI-calculated LBTS at any moment by invoking QUERY LBTS.

One way the output time can be computed for a federate in the Time Advancing state using NEXT EVENT REQUEST is as the minimum, at each point in wall clock time, of the following:

- The federate's requested time plus its lookahead
- The time stamp of the earliest event that the RTI has queued to deliver to the federate, if any
- The federate's LBTS

For a federation of two constrained and regulating federates, each federate's LBTS is the other federate's output time.

Let us turn to Figure 5-9. The Manager federate seeks to advance its clock in steps of s; the Production federate seeks to advance at each point by $2s$. Both federates have lookaheads that are small compared to s for the sake of illustration. As the diagram begins, both federates are in the Time Granted state with logical time t. There are no events queued for delivery to the Production federate.

The first occurrence is labeled "1. Manager TAR to $t + s$." The Manager invokes TIME ADVANCE REQUEST, seeking to advance to $t + s$. Its minimum allowed time stamp (and output time) rises to $t + s + lookahead$. The Production federate's output time does not rise because it is in the Time Granted state.

At the second occurrence, the Production federate invokes NEXT EVENT REQUEST to $t + 2s$. It enters the Time Advancing state. Its output time rises to $t + s + lookahead$, the minimum of its LBTS and its requested time (there are no events in its queue). This causes occurrence 3, a TIME ADVANCE GRANT † to the Manager. The grant occurs now, because the Production federate's output time is the Manager's LBTS. This illustrates the fact that the Production federate regulates the Manager. The Production federate has not advanced yet because the Manager regulates the Production federate, and the Manager has not advanced far enough yet.

In occurrence 4, the Manager federate sends an event with a time stamp of $t + 1.5s$. The event goes in the Production federate's queue. Its output time does not rise, because its LBTS is smaller than the event's time stamp.

At occurrence 5, the Manager requests an advance to $t + 2s$, causing several things to happen.

- Its output time rises to $t + 2s + lookahead$, which also raises the LBTS of the Production federate.

- The output time of the Production federate thus rises to the time stamp of the event in its queue, since that is smaller than its LBTS.
- This causes occurrence 6: the Production federate receives the event in its queue.
- The increase of LBTS of the Production federate also causes occurrence 7: the Production federate receives a grant to $t + 1.5s$.

This illustrates the Production federate's advance being regulated by the arrival of events and the behavior of the Manager. Occurrences 5, 6, and 7 are shown in Figure 5-9 slightly separated in wall clock time. This is for clarity in the figure. Their actual separation in wall clock time depends on the speed of computation of the RTI implementation. In any case, occurrences 6 and 7 occur after 5 because 6 and 7 depend on 5.

At occurrence 8, the Production federate asks to advance to $t + 3.5s$. With no events in its queue, the Production federate's output time rises to its LBTS. That in turn allows occurrence 9, a grant to the Manager.

To sum up, you've seen how two time-regulating and time-constrained federates control each other's advance of time. Neither can run off without the other. The details of the evolution differ, depending on the time advance service that each federate uses and the events exchanged, but the notions of output time and LBTS apply in all cases. The examples presented here can be extended to any number of federates, limited only by your patience and the number of shaded lines you can distinguish.

Experimenting With Time Management

The test federate is an ideal tool for experimenting with Time Management. You can join multiple copies of the Test Federate to a federation, cause them all to become time-constrained and time-regulating, and then experiment with advancing time.

We recommend that you begin by verifying the scenarios in Figure 5-7 and Figure 5-9. After you have joined two copies of the Test Federate, choose one federate and invoke ENABLE TIME CONSTRAINED ("Time | Switches | 8.5 Enable time constrained"). The test federate should quickly log a callback for TIME CONSTRAINED ENABLED † ("† (8.6)timeConstrainedEnabled, time: time<0.0>"). Then invoke ENABLE TIME REGULATION ("Time | Switches | 8.2 Enable time regulation..."). In the resulting dialog, you must specify a logical time, which should be the time the federate got back with TIME CONSTRAINED ENABLED †, and a lookahead. The lookahead can be a fraction, for instance, 0.1. The RTI should call back quickly with TIME REGULATION ENABLED † ("† (8.3)timeRegulationEnabled, time: time<0.0>").

Repeat this process with the other federate. You are now ready to advance time with, for instance, TIME ADVANCE REQUEST ("Time | Time advance | 8.8 Time advance request...").

If you are going to experiment with NEXT EVENT REQUEST, you will need to send TSO events to make your experimentation interesting. One way to do this with the restaurant federation is to send updates for, say, the position attribute of a Serving instance. When you have joined all the copies you wish of the test federate and have enabled time constraint and regulation on each, then perform the necessary publications and subscriptions on the position attribute. Then register an instance. You are then ready to send a TSO update of the position attribute's value. The TSO version of UPDATE ATTRIBUTE VALUES is invoked with "Obj | Update attributes | 6.4 Update attribute values TSO…"

5.3 FEDERATION EXECUTION LIFECYCLE: COORDINATING INDEPENDENT FEDERATES

We've alluded several times to problems of initialization, getting a federation execution started in a controlled way. It's time to generalize the problem to the federation's lifecycle, including initialization and shutdown. We must be clear at the outset that coordination is a practical problem in distributed systems made up of independent components. Components that otherwise act independently must be made to coordinate activities related to the distributed system's lifecycle. In the HLA, the system is a federation and the components are federates. Managing the lifecycle is not a problem inherent in the HLA; we'll use RTI services to solve the problem.

The HLA does not demand a particular policy of initialization or of phases of federation execution. The RTI services are designed to accommodate federates joining and resigning throughout the execution. The RTI will behave in a defined, predictable way, which is useful for some applications. In the case of the conservatively synchronized federation we've discussed so far, it's easier to introduce phased initialization and shutdown. We give you a general approach that you can adapt as it suits your problem, and we introduce the RTI mechanisms that support this and similar approaches.

5.3.1 THE PROBLEM EXEMPLIFIED: EVERYBODY STARTING TOGETHER

If you were to run the restaurant federation as described to this point, each federate would perform its own initialization and begin to advance time. The federates are not coordinated. There is no control over the order in which federates join, or over the speed at which they get through their initialization and begin advancing time. This causes problems with time synchronization and inconvenience in obtaining initial values.

The initial values problem is a mere nuisance which can be solved by use of RTI services. A subscribing federate will not miss any objects even if the subscriber performs its subscriptions after publishing federates have announced their publications and have instantiated and updated all their initial objects. The RTI sees to that. But the subscriber may have missed some initial updates. The subscriber must laboriously ask for initial values with REQUEST ATTRIBUTE VALUE UPDATE. It would be simpler if the subscribing federate could be guaranteed that it will complete its subscriptions before publishers begin updating.

The difficulty with time synchronization may be more significant. If one of the federates begins advancing time before another federate can set its time-regulating switch, the first federate will march off unconstrained by the second. The second federate can become time-regulating eventually and synchronization can be achieved, but at a later time. This process is not reproducible because the order of joining and initialization is not guaranteed. Thus the reproducibility of the federation execution, which is often a goal of conservative time management, is lost. The solution is a guarantee that all federates have joined and have set their time switches before any federate begins to advance.

5.3.2   PHASED EXECUTION

The solution to these problems requires: (1) a means of global synchronization across a federation, and (2) a way to know that all expected federates have joined the federation. The RTI furnishes both mechanisms.

Recall that we recommended the following order in which each federate should perform initialization:

1. Enable time constraint.
2. Enable time regulation.
3. Publish and subscribe.
4. Register initial instances.
5. Enter normal simulation loop.

As we've described the problems above, the two desirable points of synchronization are before step four and before step five. Synchronization before step four makes life simpler for the federation designers because they know, before a federate begins registering and updating its initial instances, that all federates have joined and have finished their publications and subscriptions. Thus no subscribing federate misses initial attribute updates. Synchronization before step five is to aid reproducibility. The reproducibility of a federation is facilitated if the federation designer can ensure that all federates have joined and have set their time switches before any federate requests to advance time. Because of the order we've given of the other steps, this means synchronizing when all federates are ready to advance time.

Thus we suggest the following phases of execution, which cover both initialization and shutdown:

1. *Preliminaries*: Each federate joins, sets time switches, performs publications and subscriptions.
2. *Populating*: Each federate registers and updates (furnishes initial values for) initial instances.
3. *Running*: Each federate advances logical time in normal operation.
4. *Post-processing:* Each federate ceases to advance time and performs post-processing required after the federation execution. This phase guarantees that each federate can finish processing messages that remain outstanding with the federation still intact.
5. *Resigning*: Each federate resigns from the federation and shuts down.

5.3.3   SYNCHRONIZATION POINTS

To synchronize the federation execution at the beginning of a phase, we'll use a *synchronization point*, as defined in the federation management services.

5.3.3.1   The General Idea

The lifecycle of a synchronization point is as follows:

- A federate registers a synchronization point. That defines the synchronization point to the federation and registers it with the RTI.
- The RTI announces the newly registered synchronization point to each federate. We say that the synchronization point is now *awaiting synchronization*.
- As each federate "achieves the synchronization point," it tells the RTI. The meaning of "achieves the synchronization point" is up to the federation designers. It should depend on reaching some unambiguous state.
- When all federates have achieved the synchronization point, the RTI informs each federate that the federation is synchronized at the point.
- After informing all the federates, the RTI removes the synchronization point from its registry. The synchronization point is no longer awaiting synchronization.

You could designate a federate and a set of interactions that would duplicate this behavior, but it would be tedious and error-prone and it would erect another barrier to understanding your federation. Better to use this standard mechanism. Note that none of these operations carries a logical time with it. Like publication and subscription, the synchronization point mechanism operates without respect to the time management services.

There can be several synchronization points awaiting synchronization at a time. Synchronization points are distinguished by labels supplied when the point is registered.

What happens if a federate joins while there are one or more synchronization points awaiting synchronization? Each synchronization point has a *synchronization set*, the set of federates that must achieve the synchronization point to cause the RTI to conclude that the federation is synchronized at that point. The synchronization set for a synchronization point is defined initially as the set of federates that are joined when the point is registered. If another federate joins before the other federates have achieved the synchronization point, the new federate is added to the synchronization set of each point awaiting synchronization, and the federate has each point awaiting synchronization announced to it. This is important for our use of synchronization points. It means that it does not matter whether federates join before or after the synchronization points are registered. Federates joining after the registrations are included in the RTI's decision that the federation is synchronized.

If a federate resigns while synchronization points are awaiting synchronization, the resigning federate is removed from the synchronization sets. Its resignation does not prevent the remaining federates from achieving synchronization.

When a federate registers a synchronization point, it may specify the initial synchronization set. If the federate does not specify the synchronization set, the set is (as described above) the set of currently joined federates. If it does specify the synchronization set, it need not include itself in the set. If a federate in a specified set resigns before the federation is synchronized, the federate is removed from the set. If a federate joins while a synchronization point is awaiting synchronization with a specified set, the new federate is not added to the synchronization set, and the synchronization point is not announced to it.

Like other aspects of the HLA, the federation synchronization mechanism can be employed in many different ways. The designers of a federation must decide what, if any, synchronization points the federation will define. The definition of each synchronization point must include its label and the condition upon which each federate will decide it has reached the synchronization point. And the designers must decide which federate will register the synchronization point and ensure that the registration occurs before the point is to be reached.

5.3.3.2   The Precise Services

The precise services to be used are as follows.

- A federate registers a synchronization point by invoking REGISTER FEDERATION SYNCHRONIZATION POINT. The federate supplies a label in the form of a string. The label must differ from any current synchronization point. The federate can also supply a user-supplied tag, which will be delivered when the synchronization point is announced. The tag may be used for any purpose of the federation designers. It might carry an indication of context or a parameter of a sort. The registrar may specify an initial synchronization set for the synchronization point. The registering federate will be called back with CONFIRM SYNCHRONIZATION POINT REGISTRATION †. The callback indicates whether the registration succeeded. (Failure occurs if the supplied label was already attached to a synchronization point awaiting synchronization at the time of registration.)
- Each other federate in the synchronization set (including the registrar if the registrar is in the synchronization set) is called by the RTI with ANNOUNCE SYNCHRONIZATION POINT †. The callback carries the label and the tag supplied by the registrar.
- A federate informs the RTI it has achieved a synchronization point by invoking SYNCHRONIZATION POINT ACHIEVED, specifying the label.
- The RTI eventually calls back all the federates in the synchronization set with FEDERATION SYNCHRONIZED †.

5.3.3.3   How We Use Synchronization Points

To define the beginning of the populating phase, some federate registers the synchronization point ReadyToPopulate. In the initialization policy we're describing here, for a federate to achieve ReadyToPopulate means that it is ready to enter the populating phase. The RTI announces the registration of ReadyToPopulate to each federate. As each federate finishes the preliminaries phase, it tells the RTI it has achieved ReadyToPopulate. When all federates have

achieved ReadyToPopulate, the RTI announces to each federate that the federation is synchronized at ReadyToPopulate.

When each federate hears that the federation has reached ReadyToPopulate, it begins the
work of the populating phase. Meanwhile, some federate registers another synchronization
point, ReadyToRun.[3] The meaning we attach to ReadyToRun is that the federate achieving it has
finished the populating phase and is ready to advance time. When each federate hears that the
federation is synchronized at ReadyToRun, it enters the running phase and begins to advance
time. We describe the subsequent phases below.

5.3.4   KNOWING WHEN EVERYONE HAS JOINED: INTRODUCTION TO THE MOM

We've talked about the use of synchronization points to define phases of execution, but the
phases we've defined depend as well on knowing that all the expected federates have joined. To
be sure that all interested federates receive the initial updates of the initial objects, we must be
sure that all interested federates have joined and performed their subscriptions. To ensure that no
federate is left behind in time management, we must ensure that all federates have joined and
have set their time switches before any federate begins advancing time.

We'll meet this requirement in this initialization policy by postulating a member of the
federation that will not achieve ReadyToPopulate until: (1) the federate itself has finished the
preliminaries phase, and (2) it knows that all the other expected federates have joined the federation execution. We'll call this federate the Manager federate. The Manager federate could be a
separate federate whose sole purpose in the federation is to perform this synchronization function. However, the Manager federate need not be a separate federate; it could be any federate to
which these functions are added. In the spirit of building reusable simulation components that
can be combined for various purposes, we'll talk in terms of a separate Manager federate.

We haven't yet said how the Manager federate knows when the other federates have
joined. There are various ways you could accomplish this. The mechanism designed for the purpose is the MOM.

The idea behind the MOM is: Why not use the RTI to carry management information
about the federation execution in the same way the RTI carries simulation data? Distributed simulations are distributed computer applications, subject to all the ills of any other distributed
application. Their successful execution requires management of the communications, computers, and software that constitute the application. As long as we have a sophisticated mechanism
for passing data and interactions around the simulation—the RTI—we might as well use it for
management data and operations, as well as for simulation data.

The FOM defines the data to be handled by the RTI in a federation execution. All the simulation entities and interactions represented in a federation are defined in its FOM. The entities

---

3. The definitions of the RTI synchronization services allow all the synchronization points for the federation lifecycle to be registered at the outset. There is no need to wait for the first to be achieved before the
second is registered, etc. The Manager federate, to be introduced below, is the logical candidate for registering the synchronization points.

and interactions associated with managing the federation execution are likewise defined in the MOM. The MOM definitions are part of the HLA Interface Specification and are thus supported by every RTI. They must be included in every FOM. If you look in the FED for the restaurant federation, you'll find an object class Manager and an interaction class Manager. They are direct subclasses of ObjectRoot and InteractionRoot, respectively. The Manager classes are the roots of the MOM hierarchies for objects and interactions.[4]

The MOM includes objects and interactions. The objects convey information about the state of each federate and the federation as a whole. The RTI itself populates and updates the MOM objects. The MOM interactions allow a management federate to control certain aspects of the RTI's behavior and to change some parts of the state of a federate. We'll defer discussion of most of the MOM to Chapter 8, "Advanced Topics"; for now, we'll concentrate on solving the problem of knowing what federates have joined.

This is actually rather simple. The MOM defines a Federate object class;[5] the RTI automatically registers and updates an instance of Federate for each federate that joins the federation execution. For the Management federate to know what federates have joined, it need only subscribe to some attributes of class Federate. It will then discover an instance of Federate as each federate joins.

For our present purpose it hardly matters what attributes of Federate the Management federate subscribes; it only need subscribe to one. The Management federate might wish to subscribe a great many attributes in order to display them. In that case, the federate may wish to use the MOM interaction Manager.Federate.Adjust.SetTiming to cause the RTI to update the Federate attributes periodically. The RTI does not update MOM attributes otherwise.

5.3.5   KNOWING WHEN TO QUIT

We need some way to indicate the end of the running phase. In a conservatively synchronized simulation, the first thought that comes to mind is to declare an ending time that all federates should seek to reach. There are two difficulties with this approach. The first is that all federates must seek to advance to exactly the ending time, or some might get stuck short of the goal. The second problem is that a suitable ending time may not be known in advance. The "end" of the simulation may consist in achieving some condition irrespective of the time it is reached.

In the restaurant federation, we shall define the ending condition to be that so many Servings are consumed. The Consumption federate will be responsible for determining this. It will send the interaction SimulationEnds when the condition is fulfilled. The other federates will receive the interaction. They will move into the post-processing phase.

---

4. The MOM is abbreviated in the display of the restaurant FED. It is discussed further in Chapter 8. The complete MOM is given in the interface specification.
5. The fully qualified name is ObjectRoot.Manager.Federate.

Note that we have made another decision about the design of our federation. We have chosen to employ an interaction to signal the end of the running phase. This is another example of a decision that must be reached by the federation designers.[6]

5.3.6   EACH FEDERATE HAS RESPONSIBILITIES

Let's summarize the duties of each federate in the federation lifecycle scheme. We present the federate's actions as a sequence of items, and then display the same behavior as a UML statechart immediately following.

- The federate joins the federation. It is in the preliminaries phase. It enables time constraint and time regulation. It performs its publications and subscriptions. It awaits announcement of the synchronization point ReadyToPopulate. It informs the RTI it has achieved ReadyToPopulate. (If the federate tells the RTI it has achieved ReadyToPopulate before the synchronization point is announced, the RTI will throw an exception. So the federate must wait for the announcement. This ensures that the Manager has joined and will be included in the synchronization set.)

- When the federate hears that the federation is synchronized at ReadyToPopulate, it enters the populating phase. The federate registers its initial instances and performs initial updates on all its attributes. It informs the RTI it has achieved ReadyToRun.

- When the federate hears that the federation is synchronized at ReadyToRun, it enters the running phase. It begins its normal time advance cycle. Eventually it receives an interaction announcing the end of the running phase.

- When the federate hears that the running phase is over, either by a interaction or a synchronization point, it enters the postprocessing phase. The federation remains intact as the federate processes events through the end of the Running phase. The federate performs whatever postprocessing is necessary. It informs the RTI it has achieved ReadyToResign.

- When the federate hears that the federation is synchronized at ReadyToResign, it enters the Resigning phase. It may resign.

The preceding is depicted in the UML statechart in Figure 5-10.

---

6.   We used an interaction to signal the end in part because we wanted an example of using an interaction. The synchronization point mechanism is an alternative. Some federate, probably the Manager, registers the synchronization point. Those federates having no opinion about the ending condition achieve the synchronization point immediately. In the case of the restaurant federation, these are the Manager, Production, and Transport federates. The Consumption federate achieves the point upon fulfilling the ending condition, and all federates are notified that the federation is synchronized. This approach has two advantages over the interaction scheme. The first is stylistic. The synchronization point parallels the use of other synchronization points in the federation lifecycle. The second is substantive. The synchronization point scheme can be extended to handle the case where the ending condition is the conjunction of conditions sensed by multiple federates.

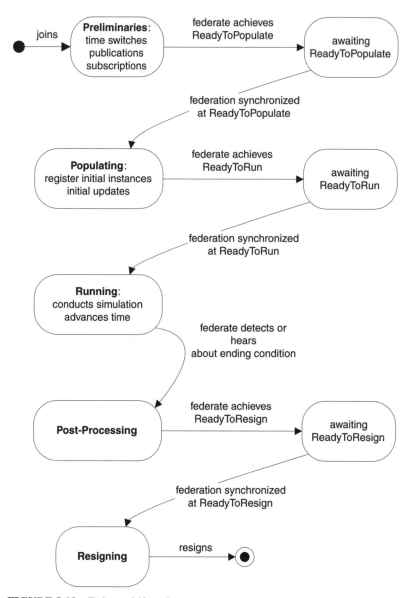

FIGURE 5-10 Federate Lifecycle.

5.3.7   MANAGER FEDERATE COMBINES USE OF SYNCHRONIZATION AND MOM

Let's summarize the duties of the Manager federate in our federation lifecycle scheme.

- The Manager federate joins the federation. It is in the preliminaries phase. It immediately registers the synchronization points ReadyToPopulate, ReadyToRun, and ReadyToResign. The Manager federate enables time constraint and time regulation. The Manager federate doesn't need to know about objects or interactions specific to the restaurant federation. Its only subscription is to the attribute FederateHandle (or some other attribute) of class ObjectRoot.Manager.Federate.[7] It will need to know how many other federates to expect. When it detects that the proper number of federates have joined, it informs the RTI it has achieved ReadyToPopulate.
- When the Manager federate hears that the federation is synchronized at ReadyToPopulate, it enters the populating phase. Having nothing to do in this phase, it informs the RTI it has achieved ReadyToRun.
- When the Manager federate hears that the federation is synchronized at ReadyToRun, it enters the running phase. It advances its logical time until the Running phase ends.
- When the Manager hears that the running phase is over, it enters the postprocessing phase. Having nothing to do in this phase, it informs the RTI it has achieved ReadyToResign.
- When the Manager federate hears that the federation is synchronized at ReadyToResign, it enters the resigning phase. It may then resign.

The foregoing is depicted in the UML statechart in Figure 5-11. The federate statechart had states populating, running, postprocessing, and resigning that do not appear in the Manager statechart. They do not appear because the Manager has nothing to do in those states, and moves immediately to perform the next action.

---

7. Because we'd like to use the Manager federate in another federation, it's a good thing that it does not need any federation-specific information.

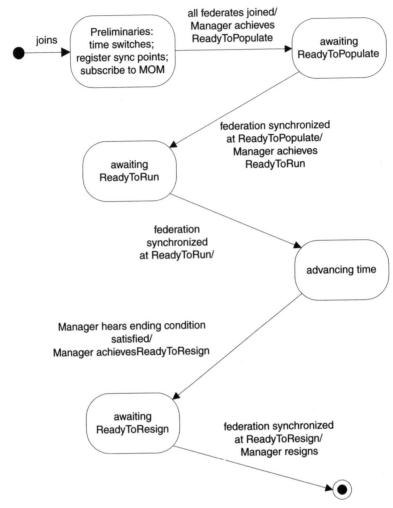

FIGURE 5-11   Manager Lifecycle.

5.3.8   SUMMARY OF THE FEDERATION LIFECYCLE

Achieving the full benefits of time management requires that a federation execution be started and stopped in a controlled way. The RTI offers the mechanisms to accomplish this, chiefly the federation synchronization point and the MOM. These mechanisms can support a range of policies; in this section we've set out a design that exemplifies the main points and should serve for most federations. The main features of our design include the following:

- Definitions of synchronization points to control entry into each phase
- Use of the MOM to discover when a federate joins
- A Manager federate that registers synchronization points and notices when all federates have joined
- Robustness in the face of network or processing latencies

5.4 REQUIREMENTS CREEP SETS IN: THE DEMO RETURNS

The restaurant federation development team has applied time management services to the restaurant federation and has implemented the lifecycle coordination protocol we outlined in the preceding section. The result is that they can conduct federation executions all night long as fast as the processors and networks will allow. And they're able to repeat runs when questions are asked about the results. So they've satisfied (for now) the analytical requirements they were given.

But their success with the earlier demonstration has bred more requests. The vice president wants to bring visitors in and show the effects of various adjustments to the federation. So the requirement to run in real time hasn't gone away.

Furthermore, the vice president is concerned about visitors' attention span. There are several parts of the simulation that the visitors will find interesting, but they last only a brief while, and they are separated by many minutes of tedium. While the vice president enjoys a remarkable attention span, no one wants the visitors, like the Emperor in *Amadeus*, to respond merely that the simulation had "too many events." To the development team, this means an ability to execute a federation as fast as possible to an interesting part of the scenario, run the federation for a while at wall clock rate, and then run as fast as possible to the next interesting part.

5.4.1 SYNCHRONIZING THE FEDERATION TO PERCEIVED TIME

Fundamentally, the new requirements for the demo amount to this: the ability to pace the execution of the federation to the progress of wall clock time, and to change the ratio of the rate of progress of logical time to that of wall clock time, all while maintaining causal correctness.

The federation, as a result of its adaptation for analytical work, is entirely conservatively synchronized. A consequence is that the federation can always be paced by a time-regulating federate. Recall in the earlier discussion of TAR and NER in two-federate federations that we showed how the federates depended on each other to advance their clocks. If a time-regulating federate stops advancing its logical time, the entire federation stops rather quickly. If a time-regulating federate advances its logical time only as the corresponding wall clock time arrives, the rest of the federation will be paced to the same rate. To say this another way:

- The RTI holds all the federates together in logical time.
- One federate maintains the desired rate of progress with respect to wall clock time.
- Therefore all the federates proceed at the desired rate.

We're making an important assumption, namely, that the federation can run faster than wall clock time. If the federation (and each federate) cannot run faster than wall clock time in the first place, nothing in the RTI can speed it up.

Our approach, therefore, will be to add pacing behavior to one of the federates. Because this functionality is independent of the fact that we're modeling a restaurant, it is advisable to add the behavior to the Manager federate we've already defined. Then we may be able to use these functions in another federation. (This is why, in the earlier discussion of TAR and NER, we labeled one of the federates the Manager and the other the Transport or Production federate, respectively.)

The modifications are fairly simple. When the Manager federate enters the running phase, it will advance its clock in suitable time steps of s (where "suitable" remains to be defined). The Manager's behavior in logical time is exemplified in Figure 5-12.

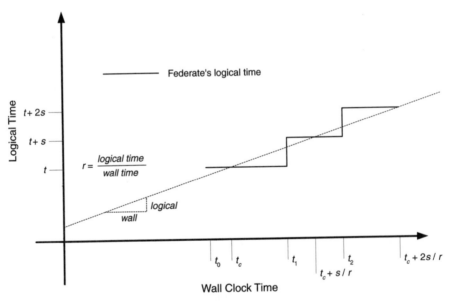

FIGURE 5-12   Manager Pacing the Federation.

Suppose the federation is to run at a (dimensionless) rate of r seconds of logical time per second of wall clock time. Suppose the Manager federate was previously granted to (logical) time t at wall clock time t_0. The Manager federate requests at wall clock time t_c to advance logical time to $t + s$. When the request is granted at wall clock time t_1, the Manager sleeps for an interval of (wall clock time) $t_c + s/r - t_1$. At that point (wall clock time $t_c + s/r$), the Manager requests to advance logical time to $t + s$. When that request is granted at wall clock time t_2, the Manager sleeps until wall clock time $t_c + s/r$ (that is, for an interval of $t_c + s/r - t_2$), at which point it requests to advance logical time to $t + 3s$.

What is the Manager doing between requesting advance of logical time and getting the grant? In the diagram above, these are the intervals $(t_c, t_1]$ and $(t_c + s / r, t_2]$. The Manager is waiting to be granted its requested advance, which means it is waiting for the rest of the federation to advance time. The assumption that the federation can compute faster than wall clock time ensures that $t_1 < t_c + s / r$ and $t_2 < t_c + 2s / r$.

Here is pseudocode for the Manager's time advance. Let logicalTime hold Manager's logical time, S hold the step size, and let R hold the rate as above.

```
loop
    let timeBeforeAdvanceRequest be current wall clock time;
    invoke TIME ADVANCE REQUEST to logicalTime;
    await TIME ADVANCE GRANT;
    let timeAtGrant be current wall clock time;
    sleep for timeBeforeAdvanceRequest + S/R - timeAtGrant;
    increment timeBeforeAdvanceRequest by S;
    increment logicalTime by S;
end loop;
```

Let's summarize this discussion. The important thing is that the Manager's requests to advance occur at exact intervals. The Manager's grants can come irregularly; the Manager sleeps for varying amounts of time to ensure the regularity of its requests to advance. It is these requests that allow the rest of the federation to advance, by affecting the Manager's output time, and thus the LBTS of the other federates. During each cycle the Manager must get its grant before it is due to request the next advance; otherwise it will be late. The Manager will get its grant in time if the rest of the federation is finishing its computations before the cycle completes. This is the same thing as saying the federation is capable of running faster than wall clock time.

What is a suitable value of s, the step size in logical time? Suitability is a trade-off between two things.

- As s decreases, the load of computation and communication needed to coordinate logical time goes up.
- The Manager's logical time as a function of wall clock time advances in stair-step fashion from the ideal of the straight line defined by r. As s increases, the size of the deviation from the line increases.

The Manager federate should have a control to allow the rate to be varied. It should also have a control that causes it to stop advancing its clock, effectively setting its rate to zero.

5.4.2 VIEWING THE RESTAURANT FEDERATION'S BEHAVIOR

An execution of the restaurant federation that was designed for a demonstration would include some means of visualizing the behavior of the federation. Each federate might include a visual representation of its model. The federation might have a special federate designed to create an overall picture. The purpose of this section is to discuss briefly the strategy for designing such a Viewer federate in a conservatively time-managed federation. The chief tasks of the Viewer are as follows:

- Getting all the data it requires
- Staying synchronized in time without affecting the rest of the federation
- Translating data updates to display updates

5.4.2.1   The Viewer Gets the Data It Requires

The publish-and-subscribe functions of the RTI make it easy for the Viewer to get all the data it needs. In the case of the restaurant federation, the Viewer will subscribe to attributes of the Boat and Serving classes. The Viewer federate need not concern itself with what federate is generating what data.

5.4.2.2   The Viewer Remains Synchronized With the Rest of the Federation

The Viewer's logical time must be constrained by the rest of the federation. It should not run ahead, nor should it lag behind. But the Viewer should not impede the progress of logical time for other federates. From our previous discussion, you might expect that the solution is for the Viewer to be time-constrained but not time-regulating. As a time-constrained federate, the Viewer will not be allowed to advance its logical time until it is safe to do so. But if the Viewer is late in advancing its clock, it will not impede the rest of the federation.

5.4.2.3   The Viewer Translates Data Updates to Display Updates

This task of the Viewer is complicated by the fact that data may arrive in a pattern that doesn't match the desired display updates. This is not a problem peculiar to HLA federations; it's a problem common to all systems that display time-varying data. There are three questions the designer must consider:

What time advance service will the Viewer use? The Viewer can advance its time in steps, using TIME ADVANCE REQUEST, or it can advance from one event to the next, using NEXT EVENT REQUEST. In either case, data is delivered to the display in time-stamp order. If the display uses NEXT EVENT REQUEST, it must complete a time-advance-grant cycle for each update of data. The display can lower the number of advance-grant cycles it must compute by advancing its time in steps (using TIME ADVANCE REQUEST) that are large compared to the average inter-arrival times of the data.

What triggers the Viewer to update its display? The Viewer can use the grant callback to trigger an update, or some other means. The advantage of using the grant callback is that its meaning in logical time is well defined. If the Viewer is advancing time in equal steps with TIME ADVANCE REQUEST, the grants will come at regular intervals. If the Viewer wishes to update its display with the arrival of each new value, it can still use the grant. If it advances logical time with NEXT EVENT REQUEST, it will receive a grant when all updates at a given logical time have arrived. Alternatively, the Viewer can advance with TIME ADVANCE REQUEST and use the REFLECT ATTRIBUTE VALUES † to trigger display updates.

How will the Viewer resolve the difference in time between data updates and display updates? Unless the Viewer updates its display each time it reflects new data, there will be some disparity between the logical time of the new data and the logical time of the display update. If displayed objects are moving, the disparity causes some error in the displayed position. Figure 5-13 depicts the evolution of a Viewer that advances logical time in equal steps. The Viewer updates its display shortly after receiving each TIME ADVANCE GRANT †. The Viewer receives REFLECT ATTRIBUTE VALUES † at various points in wall clock time. Because we assume the federation is staying up with wall clock time, all REFLECT ATTRIBUTE VALUES † arrive in wall clock time before their corresponding logical time, so they lie above the line denoting logical time equal to wall clock time. The new values arriving within one time advance cycle are candidates for extrapolation to the logical time the complete display update is performed. In a conservatively synchronized federation, the REFLECT ATTRIBUTE VALUES † carries a time stamp that can be used as the basis of the extrapolation.

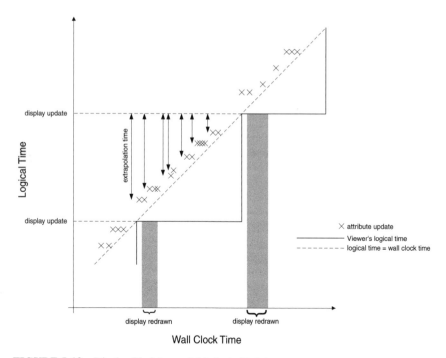

FIGURE 5-13   Display Updates and Attribute Updates.

5.4.3   TRIPLING THE SIZE OF THE RESTAURANT

Once again, the federation development team is a victim of their own success. Their success in modeling the restaurant, and their timely, compelling demonstrations to visiting decision-makers have led to an interest in building the world's largest sushi boat restaurant. Modeling this proposed behemoth will require far more of everything: chefs, Boats, Servings, and diners. The processors at each federate site are inadequate and cannot be replaced with faster ones. How to handle the increased load?

One approach, in the absence of faster processors, is more processors. The point of this section is that the HLA supports replication of identical federates straightforwardly. However, it does so at the cost of increased communication. This limits the scalability of the replication approach.

5.4.3.1   The HLA Supports Replication of Federates

Thus far we've had one federate of each type: Production, Transport, and Consumption. The RTI is capable of supporting and integrating multiple federates of each type. Thus, instead of one Production federate, we might have two or three, each modeling a disjoint set of chefs, and producing a disjoint set of Serving objects.

Each category of RTI service supports replicated federates. The subscribers to Serving attributes cannot tell, nor do they care, which of the several Production federates is responsible for updating attributes of a given Serving instance. As each Production federate registers a Serving instance, it will be given ownership of the attributes. When one of the Transport federates seeks to acquire ownership, the RTI will route the divestiture requests to the correct Production federate. The Time Management services, likewise, do not require each federate to be aware of the others: the RTI is responsible for knowing what time-regulating federates constrain each clock. Again, the federation synchronization services that underlie our lifecycle coordination protocol do not require a federate to know what other federates are participating. The only change in that protocol is that the Manager federate must know the number of federates expected to join.

Replication of federates does require a new mechanism to ensure the correct division of labor. Multiple Production federates must each know which chefs they are to model. Likewise, each Boat becomes the responsibility of one of the Transport replicates. Strictly speaking, this is not a concern of the RTI, but it is a concern of the federation developers. The RTI can be used to pass configuration data from a central source to each of the replicated federates.

5.4.3.2   This Approach May Not Scale Up Indefinitely

Expanding the capacity of a federation by replicating its federates cannot be pursued indefinitely. Adding federates is only one dimension along which a federation may be expanded. Another is number of objects. When expansion along these and other dimensions will exhaust network or computing resources depends greatly on the RTI implementation used. Implementations may differ widely in their ability to scale up and to scale along different dimensions.

5.5 SUMMARY

The theme of this part of the book has been the HLA mechanisms that allow a federation to behave reproducibly despite computational and network delays. The federation as described in this part can produce the same results each time it is run. It is implemented in the sample code. The implementation is described in Chapter 6, "A Sample Implementation." There are still some important aspects of the HLA to be discussed:

- The HLA supports extension of an existing federation. See Chapter 7, "Extending the Federation for a New Purpose."
- All the HLA service groups have been discussed except data distribution management; that group is discussed in Chapter 8, "Advanced Topics."
- There is more to say about time management (zero lookahead, optimistic federates), federation management (save and restore), and the MOM. See Chapter 8.

CHAPTER 6

A Sample Implementation

6.1 INTRODUCTION

In this chapter we present a sample implementation of the restaurant federation. The software, both as Java source and as class files, is on the CD-ROM. We include this implementation for the following reasons:

- To show the use of the HLA
- To furnish an example of an organization of a federate, with some variations
- To give a starting point for applications of your own

Although the discussion here involves details of the Java language and platform, you should find it accessible if you're a programmer but are unfamiliar with Java. We assume that you have read Chapters 4 and 5. You may also wish to read the programming notes (on the CD-ROM) on the Pitch RTI about programming with the RTI in Java.

You can run the federation with the RTI provided on your PC or other Java platform. See the CD-ROM for system requirements. You may modify the source code of the sample implementation for your own applications.

Typographic conventions are as follows. In roman font, Boat is an HLA object class. In monospaced font, `Boat` is a Java class. Names of HLA object classes are capitalized. The Production federate's model of a chef is written in lower case but the HLA object class Chef is capitalized. Likewise, diner is the Consumption federate's model but Diner is the HLA object class.

6.2 EXACTLY WHAT IS IMPLEMENTED

This sample implements the basic restaurant federation as developed in the preceding chapters, with some changes described below. A Viewer federate has been added so you can see the federation in operation.

The restaurant federation FOM has been extended to make the Viewer more useful. The extended object class hierarchy appears in Figure 6-1. Chef and Diner classes have been added to the restaurant FOM in the restaurant federation so the Production and Consumption federates can publish the position and current state of their internal models of chefs and diners. This data, which is not otherwise needed for the restaurant federation, allows the Viewer federate to display the position and state of Chefs and Diners.

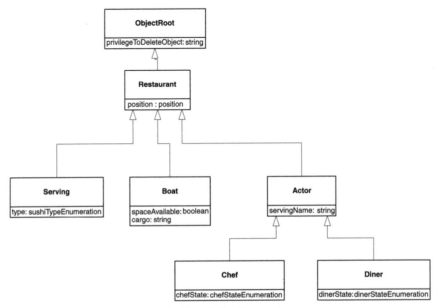

FIGURE 6-1   Object Classes in the Sample Implementation.

The Actor class serves as a place to define the servingName attribute defined in common for Chefs and Diners, ensuring that the attribute has the same type for both classes. The attributes chefState and dinerState are both conceptually enumerations and will both be represented in Java as `ints`. They are distinguished, however, because the enumeration values are different. Their enumeration values also differ from those of attribute type of class Serving. The extended FED for the sample implementation is presented in Figure 6-2.

```
(FED
(Federation restaurant_1)    ;; we choose this tag
  (FEDversion v1.3)           ;; required; specifies RTI spec version
  (spaces                     ;; we define no routing spaces
  )
  (objects
    (class ObjectRoot          ;; required
      (attribute privilegeToDeleteObject reliable timestamp)
      (class RTIprivate)
      (class Restaurant
        (attribute position reliable timestamp)
        (class Serving
          (Attribute type reliable timestamp)
        )
        (class Boat
          (attribute spaceAvailable reliable timestamp)
          (attribute cargo reliable timestamp)
        )
        (class Actor
          (attribute servingName reliable timestamp)
          (class Chef
            (attribute chefState reliable timestamp)
          )
          (class Diner
            (attribute dinerState reliable timestamp)
          )
        )
      )
      ;; Manager class and subclasses are required
      (class Manager....
    )                          ;; end ObjectRoot
  )                            ;; end objects
  (interactions
    (class InteractionRoot reliable timestamp
      (class TransferAccepted reliable timestamp
        (parameter servingName)
      )
      (class RTIprivate reliable timestamp)
      (class Manager reliable receive
        (class SimulationEnds reliable receive)
      )
    )                 ;; end InteractionRoot
  )                   ;; end interactions
)                     ;; end FED
```

FIGURE 6-2 FED for Sample Implementation.

The interaction class SimulationEnds appears as it did in Chapter 4, "The Sushi Restaurant Federation." Another interaction class has been added called TransferAccepted (a direct subclass of InteractionRoot) whose purpose will be explained later.

The attribute publications and subscriptions for the sample implementation are presented in Table 6-1. They are unchanged from those in Chapter 4, except that the Viewer's subscriptions are added, and the Production and Consumption federates now publish the Chef and Diner classes, respectively. The Viewer uses passive subscriptions because it is merely a passive observer of the federation execution.

Table 6-1 Attribute Publications and Subscriptions in Sample Implementation

	Production	Transport	Consumption	Viewer
Serving privilegeToDeleteObject publish type	default publish publish publish	default publish publish	default publish publish subscribe	default publish passive subscribe passive subscribe
Boat privilegeToDeleteObject position spaceAvailable cargo	default publish subscribe subscribe subscribe	default publish publish publish publish	default publish subscribe subscribe subscribe	default publish passive subscribe passive subscribe passive subscribe
Chef privilegeToDeleteObject position chefState servingName	default publish publish publish publish	default publish	default publish	default publish passive subscribe passive subscribe passive subscribe
Diner privilegeToDeleteObject position dinerState servingName	default publish	default publish	default publish publish publish publish	default publish passive subscribe passive subscribe passive subscribe

The interaction class subscriptions and publications are presented in Table 6-2. Those for SimulationEnds are unchanged from Chapter 4. The Transport federate publishes TransferAccepted because the interaction is sent to signal a Boat's acceptance of a Serving. The Production federate subscribes because the interaction affects the state of the Chef trying to load the Serving.

Table 6-2 Interaction Class Publications and Subscriptions in Sample Implementation

	Manager	Production	Transport	Consumption	Viewer
SimulationEnds	subscribe	subscribe	subscribe	publish	subscribe
TransferAccepted		subscribe	publish		

6.3 RUNNING THE SAMPLE IMPLEMENTATION

File paths on the CD-ROM are in Windows format, using the symbol `<CD>` to represent the drive letter of the CD-ROM. The top-level directories are listed in Table 6-3. The source files under `<CD>\src` are arranged hierarchically in packages, as are the class files under `<CD>\bin`. All the documents included on the CD are under `<CD>\doc`.

Table 6-3   Top-Level Directories on CD

Directory	Contents
`<CD>\bin`	Class files for sample implementation and test federate
`<CD>\config`	Configuration data needed to run sample implementation and test federate, including FED files, .props files and images
`<CD>\doc`	All documents
`<CD>\lib`	Java archives needed to run RTI, sample implementation and test federate.
`<CD>\src`	Java source for sample implementation and test federate.

The code is arranged in Java packages as described in Table 6-4. The Manager code is kept separate from the restaurant code to make it easier to use with a different federation.

Table 6-4   Java Packages for Sample Implementation

Package Name	Contents
`org.mitre.hla.book.manager`	Manager federate
`org.mitre.hla.book.restaurant`	Classes used by all restaurant federates
`org.mitre.hla.book.restaurant.production`	Production federate
`org.mitre.hla.book.restaurant.transport`	Transport federate
`org.mitre.hla.book.restaurant.consumption`	Consumption federate
`org.mitre.hla.book.restaurant.viewer`	Viewer federate

For non-programmers: Ensure you have an RTI executive running on the computer you'll use for the sample implementation. Start the federation by running the batch file `<CD>\rest&view.bat`.

For programmers: After starting an RTI executive, start a Manager with:

```
java -classpath <classpath> <options> org.mitre.hla.book.manager.Manager
```

The classpath must contain the Pitch RTI archive, the sample implementation class files, the JGL and Swing archives. The *options* are the same as for the test federate. Start the other federates similarly:

```
java -classpath <classpath> < options>
org.mitre.hla.book.restaurant.production.Production
```

```
java -classpath <classpath> <options>
org.mitre.hla.book.restaurant.transport.Transport
```

```
java -classpath <classpath> <options>
org.mitre.hla.book.consumption.Consumption
```

```
java -classpath <classpath> <options>
org.mitre.hla.book.restaurant.viewer.Viewer
```

6.4   TYPES COMMON TO ALL FEDERATES

The package `org.mitre.hla.book.restaurant` contains classes relevant to the restaurant federation that are used by all the restaurant federates. The class `RestaurantNames` defines manifest constants for names that appear in the FED, such as names of HLA object classes and attributes.

The classes `Boat`, `Chef`, `Diner` and `Serving` are used by the federates to store data related to HLA instances of the corresponding HLA object class. These classes have fields (instance variables) for each HLA attribute and additional fields that are required for the federates' housekeeping. A Java instance typically is constructed to correspond to an HLA object instance when the HLA object is registered or discovered. The Java instance reference is discarded when the corresponding HLA object instance is deleted or removed.

Notice that there are two Java fields corresponding to each HLA class attribute. One field (for instance, `_position` in class `Boat`) contains the value of the instance attribute. The other field (`_positionState`) stores the state of the attribute. These attribute state fields take values defined in the class `AttributeState`. Their purpose is to "keep the books" as to whether:

- The federate owns the instance attribute and its value inside the federate is consistent with the last value sent with UPDATE ATTRIBUTE VALUES.
- The federate owns the instance attribute and its value inside the federate is inconsistent with the last updated value; the value should be updated.
- The federate is reflecting the instance attribute.
- The attribute is in a transient state after discovery (no values have been reflected for the HLA instance that has been discovered).

The classes `Chef` and `Diner` define the enumeration values for the attributes `chefState` and `dinerState`, respectively. The kinds of sushi that may be made in a federation execution are configuration data read at federation execution time. This determines valid values for the attribute `_type` of class `Serving`.

The class `Position` represents the attribute of the same name. Because this attribute is a complex type, the Java class serves to define its data members. It also contains `encode()` and `decode()` methods that define a uniform encoding of attribute values for this attribute. Recall that the FED does not define the types or encodings of attribute values; the encodings must be decided by the federation designers. This class embodies our decision for this federation. It uses printable characters to allow the use of a Test Federate to examine and inject attribute values for debugging the federation.

As defined for this implementation of the restaurant federation, a position attribute contains two fields: an angle and an offset. This is depicted in Figure 6-3. The restaurant is circular, so that position can be defined as an angle and a radial offset from the boats' canal. Thus the offset is an enumeration type that indicates if the position is inside the canal (with the chefs), on the canal (with the boats) or outside the canal (with the diners). Angles are represented (the federation designers must agree to something) as degrees, construed as counter-clockwise from east.

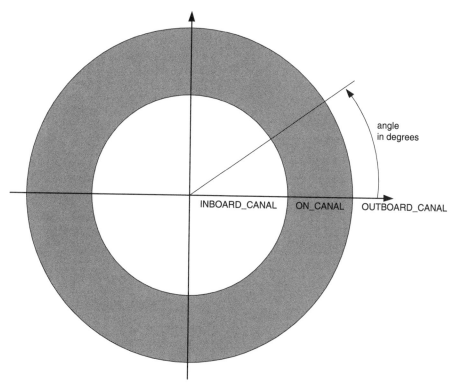

FIGURE 6-3 Coordinate System for Positions.

Other attributes, such as `servingName`, `chefState`, and `spaceAvailable`, are represented as common Java types (`String`, `int`, and `boolean`, respectively). The classes `InstanceName`, `IntegerAttribute`, and `SpaceAvailable` serve as homes for static methods for encoding values of these attributes.

At the beginning of Chapter 4, we asserted that the Production, Transport, and Consumption federates had been developed independently and had different internal structures and data representations. This may be the case when simulations are integrated using the HLA. For the sake of clarity in the sample code, all the federates use common data representations and internal structures.

6.5   STRUCTURE OF THE PRODUCTION FEDERATE

The Production federate is described in some detail because the Transport and Consumption federates have identical structures. The Manager and Viewer federates are somewhat different; the differences are described later.

6.5.1   THE FEDERATE'S USER INTERFACE

The user interface of the Production federate is depicted in Figure 6-4. The main window is split into a chef table and a log area. The chef table contains a tabular display of the state of the chefs the federate is modeling. The log area displays messages written by the federate. The "Clear Log" button may be used to clear the log area. Above the main window are displayed the federate's current logical time and its time state (advancing or granted).

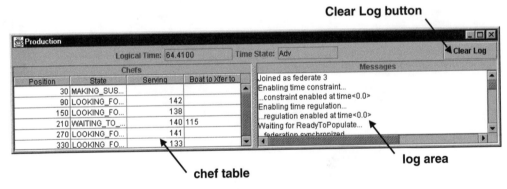

FIGURE 6-4   Production Federate User Interface.

The tabular data depicts the following:

- The angular position of the chef along the canal
- The chef's state (as described in Section 6.5.5)

- The object instance handle of the Serving the chef has prepared (and is trying to put on a Boat)

- The instance handle of the Boat the chef is trying to load

6.5.2 GETTING CONFIGURATION DATA

The Production federate, like all the sample federates, uses the `java.util.Properties` mechanism to obtain configuration data. It uses `Properties` from two sources, the command line and the properties file. The federate has four properties whose values may be supplied at the command line:

- `RTI_HOST` is the name of the host that is running the RTI executive. It defaults to the host on which the federate is running.

- `RTI_PORT` is the TCP port number on which the federate should contact the RTI executive. It defaults to 8989, which is the RTI executive's default setting.

- `CONFIG` is the URL in which the federate should look for the properties file. This URL is also the path prefixed to the FED URL passed eventually to the RTI upon invocation of `RTIambassador.createFederationExecution()`. It defaults to a file-type URL that is composed of two concatenated parts. The first part is the directory in which the federate has started (the Java "user directory"). The second part is a file separator and `config`.[1] Thus, if you start the federate from a Windows directory `C:\my_rti_installation`, `CONFIG will default to file:///C:/my_rti_installation/config.`

- `FEDEX` is the name of the federation execution. It defaults to `restaurant_1`.

All these defaults can be overridden on the command line in the usual manner for Java.

The Production federate reads more properties from a properties file. The federate expects to find the file in the same directory as the FED file, and expects it to have the name *<federation execution name>*`.props`. All the federates read from the same file. See `<CD>\config\restaurant_1.props` for an example.

6.5.3 NOTABLE OBJECTS

The notable objects in the Production federate are depicted in Figure 6-5. The top-level object in the Production federate is an instance of class `Production`. It contains the `main()` method. This object holds the references to the notable data structures and to the other notable objects. All the calls to `RTIambassador` occur in its code.

---

1. When the RTI executive executes the `createFederationExecution`, the path is interpreted relative to its own user directory. If the RTI is run from a different place than the federates (this will not be the case if your run them off the CD-ROM), you'll need to use an actual URL and have the files served by an HTTP server.

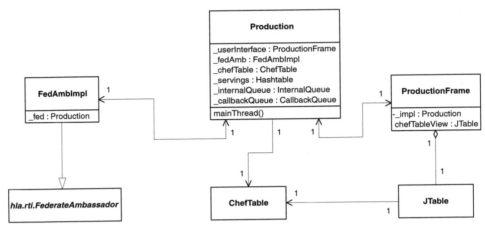

FIGURE 6-5 Notable Objects in Production Federate.

The Production instance creates an instance of ProductionFrame, which contains all the user interface code. The intent of the design is that there be no user interface code outside ProductionFrame (and its subsidiaries), so that no packages that support user interfaces, such as javax.swing, need be imported into any other classes. Likewise, ProductionFrame does not import hla.rti.

The Production instance also creates an instance of FedAmbImpl, an implementation of hla.rti.FederateAmbassador, which is passed to the RTI when the federate joins. Callbacks from the RTI are invoked on FedAmbImpl, which in turn calls methods on the Production instance. The code for FedAmbImpl is such that all callbacks result in messages displayed in the Production log area, except where FedAmbImpl methods have been rewritten for a specific service. Thus any callbacks not expected by the design of the Production federate will cause messages in the log area.

The notable data structures in the Production instance are _chefTable and _servings. The former holds the state of the modeled chefs (and HLA Chef instances); the later holds the state of HLA Serving instances created by the federate. Because the _chefTable also acts as the model for the chef table in the user interface, its reference is passed to the ProductionFrame instance.

The Production instance has two other structures that it does not expose to other objects, and which are important to its functioning. One is an instance InternalQueue, which holds "internal events," that is, events generated by the chef models and of interest only to the Production federate. The other structure is an instance (_callbackQueue) of CallbackQueue. Typically, each time the RTI calls back the federate, the callback results in an instance of Production.Callback being placed on _callbackQueue. The main thread of the federate dequeues the Callback instance in the time-advance loop and processes it. The callback

ANNOUNCE SYNCHRONIZATION POINT † is handled outside the callback queue because these occur when the main thread is not in its time-advance loop.

6.5.4   THREADS OF EXECUTION

Java supports multi-threading as a language and platform. The RTI implementation included with this book is multi-threaded, in the sense that RTI-initiated services occur in a separate thread of control from any held by the federate. Consequently, all the federates in the sample implementation are multi-threaded.

The notable threads in the Production federate are depicted in Figure 6-6. The "main" thread is started when the federate begins execution. The user interface thread is started by the Swing code and responds to user's inputs. A callback thread comes from the RTI each time the RTI invokes a service on the federate. The design assumes there may be more than one user interface thread or more than one callback thread.

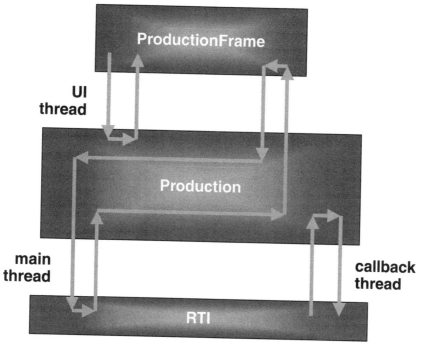

FIGURE 6-6   Notable Threads of Control in Production Federate.

Two concerns arise from the presence of multiple threads in the federate. One is that those data structures that will be acted on by multiple threads must be synchronized to ensure they remain in consistent states. Two examples of synchronized objects in the Production object are _chefTable, which is visited by the user interface and main threads, and _callbackQueue, which is visited by the main thread and callback threads. The other concern is coordination of activities between threads, particularly between the main thread and callback threads. The main thread often must wait for the arrival of callbacks from the RTI. The sample includes barrier and queue classes, built on Java's thread coordination primitives, for coordinating the main thread and callbacks.

The objects _chefTable and _callbackQueue in the Production instance are vulnerable to simultaneous access by several threads. The _chefTable object serves as the model or data store behind a tabular display of chef information in the user interface; thus the user interface thread will invoke methods on it. Code in the Production instance that processes callbacks, running in the main thread, will also access the _chefTable to update it. We use the Java modifier synchronized on all the methods of _chefTable to ensure that only one method runs in an instance at a time, thus ensuring the internal consistency of the object's state. The _callbackQueue object is also vulnerable to access from several threads. Production.Callback instances are placed on the queue by code running in callback threads from the RTI. Simultaneously, the federate's main thread is dequeing Production.Callback instances. The _callbackQueue object is therefore synchronized.

The main thread must coordinate its activities with other threads, particularly with callback threads from the RTI. Barriers and a queue are used to effect this coordination. The barriers and queue use the Java wait() primitive to put the main thread to sleep until some condition is true. The barriers and queue serve to encapsulate the check on the waiting condition and to store data associated with the condition in a thread-safe way.

A simple example of the employment of a barrier occurs early in the main thread. The main thread's code is in the mainThread() method of the Production instance. After acquiring some configuration data, ensuring that the federation execution has been created, and joining the federation execution, the main thread enables time constraint by invoking ENABLE TIME CONSTRAINED with the Java method _rti.enableTimeConstrained(). There is nothing for the main thread to do then until the RTI calls back with TIME CONSTRAINED ENABLED †. The callback appears in the federate code as a thread from the RTI invoking the method timeConstrainedEnabled() on the FedAmbImpl instance. The main thread must do something until the callback arrives. It could spin in a loop waiting for a variable to change state (the variable would be changed by code executed by the callback thread) but this would waste computation. Instead, the main thread, before it calls enableTimeConstrained(), creates a Barrier instance and installs it in the FedAmbImpl. The main thread then executes barrier.await(), effectively putting itself to sleep until the callback thread changes the barrier's state and awakens the main thread. This barrier object device is used wherever the main thread invokes an RTI service and must wait until a corresponding callback arrives.[2]

The barrier is a simple example of a thread-coordinating object. There is a simple discussion of the design of such objects in [Campione and Walrath 1996]. A deeper discussion of concurrency is available in [Lea 1996].

The _callbackQueue allows the main thread to deal with callbacks one at a time and it coordinates the main thread and callback threads. While the federate is advancing time, it will receive callbacks of several different kinds from the RTI that have significance for its modeling of the chefs' behavior. As the chefs' states evolve, the main thread must deal with those callbacks one at a time. The _callbackQueue is a structure whereby various callback threads can queue callbacks for later handling. The _callbackQueue imposes an order on the callbacks as they are enqueued. The _callbackQueue coordinates threads as follows. Its dequeue() method causes the main thread to wait until a Production.Callback instance is available to be dequeued.

Another consequence of the queue mechanism is that no significant processing occurs in response to a callback in the RTI callback thread that delivered it. In particular, no reentrant calls are made back into the RTI from the RTI's own thread. RTI implementations are not required to tolerate such reentrancy. Thus the sample implementation is portable to another RTI in an important way.

We should mention a final thread-related matter. The Swing components used to build the user interface are, unfortunately, not thread-safe. Their behavior is unpredictable if they are accessed by threads other than the system-spawned user interface thread. The main thread must be able to post messages to the log area. The code to do this is in ViewerFrame.post(). That code does not add to the log area text directly, but creates an object, which when executed by the user interface thread will add the intended text. The code uses SwingUtilities.invokeAnd-Wait() to ask the Swing executive to execute the object in its thread. This idiom comes from the Swing documentation.

6.5.5   STATE OF THE CHEFS

Each chef modeled by the Production federate has an entry in the _chefTable. Each chef is modeled as a state machine whose statechart is presented in Figure 6-7.

2.   There is a weakness in the federate's design that the reader is invited to amend. The code as it stands relies on correct behavior of the RTI and the other federates. While the main thread is awaiting the TIME CONSTRAINED ENABLED † callback, it is in a state where it expects no other callbacks, and the code as presented may not deal correctly with an unexpected callback. A solution is to define a state for the main thread, based on what set of callbacks is expected at any given point, and use that state to reject the unexpected callback.

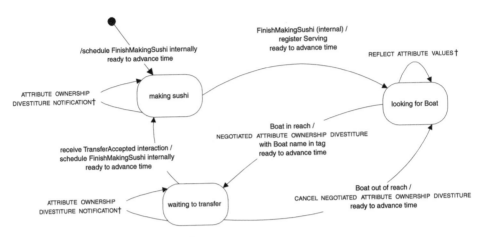

FIGURE 6-7   State of Modeled Chef.

Each chef begins life in the "making sushi" state. (See method makeChefs() of Produc-tion.) At the time the chef is created, a FinishMakingSushiEvent is placed on the internal event queue. An instance of the HLA object class Chef is registered and its attributes updated for the benefit of the Viewer federate. When the internal event is dequeued and dispatched, an instance of the HLA object class Serving is registered, and the chef moves into the "looking for Boat" state. The chef is now waiting for an empty Boat to come within reach.

The Production federate perceives the motion of Boats as their position attributes are updated. Therefore the triggering event labeled "Boat within reach" occurs when all the follow-ing are true:

- The RTI invokes REFLECT ATTRIBUTE VALUES † for a Boat position attribute.
- The Boat is not loaded.
- The Boat is computed to be within reach of a chef that is in the "looking for Boat" state.

The chef attempts to load the Boat. The federate invokes NEGOTIATED ATTRIBUTE OWNERSHIP DIVESTITURE for the position attribute of the Serving instance it wishes to load. It places the HLA object instance name of the desired Boat in the user-supplied tag of the invocation. The chef moves into the "waiting to transfer" state.

The Transport federate must decide (it may have competing offers for the same Boat) whether to accept the transfer. It will accept or decline ownership of the offered attribute. If the Transport federate accepts ownership, it sends the interaction TransferAccepted, including as a parameter the HLA object instance name of the accepted Serving. If the Transport federate declines ownership, it does nothing.

Thus the Production federate receives the TransferAccepted interaction to signal transfer of the Serving to the Boat. The federate moves the chef back into the "making sushi" state, scheduling another internal FinishMakingSushiEvent. The federate also receives ATTRIBUTE

OWNERSHIP DIVESTITURE NOTIFICATION †, indicating it no longer has ownership of the Serving's position attribute. That callback may come before or after the interaction is received. It does not affect the chef's state, and is thus shown as a self-loop on the "waiting to transfer" and "making sushi" states. The callback is the occasion for the federate to update the state of the position attribute in the _servings data structure, from AttributeState.OWNED to AttributeState.REFLECTED. Until the actual transfer of ownership, the Production federate remains responsible for updating the attribute.

If the Transport federate declines the offered attribute, the Production federate will hear nothing from the RTI. The Production federate instead will notice, when the position of the desired Boat is updated (on another REFLECT ATTRIBUTE VALUES † callback), that the Boat is now out of reach of the chef and the chef is still waiting to transfer. The Production federate invokes CANCEL NEGOTIATED ATTRIBUTE OWNERSHIP DIVESTITURE and moves the chef back into the "looking for Boat" state.

The interaction TransferAccepted may seem redundant for the transfer of ownership of the Serving's position. The ATTRIBUTE OWNERSHIP DIVESTITURE NOTIFICATION † callback marks the actual transfer of ownership. The use of the interaction accomplishes two things. First, it makes the transfer event visible to another federate. The ownership transfer transaction is private between the affected federates: a third federate that needs to observe the transfer event gets no indication of it from the RTI. The second purpose of the interaction is to tie the event to logical time. The ownership transfer services are not related to logical time. If all legal transitions out of the "waiting to transfer" state were independent of logical time, the federate could await callbacks in that state without advancing logical time. (There is an example of this in the Consumption federate.) But because one of the transitions from "waiting to transfer" is an HLA event, all the transitions must be.

6.5.6   EVENTS: OBJECTS, QUEUES, AND THE MAIN LOOP

The chef state machine changes state in response to internal events or callbacks from the RTI. There is a queue for internal events and another for callbacks. The callback queue is synchronized because callback threads are adding events to it, while the main thread is removing them. The internal queue is used only by the main thread and thus need not be synchronized.

Callbacks are queued and processed as Java objects, instances of Production.Callback. Callback is an inner class of Production. It represents a general RTI callback that may not carry a logical time. There is an extension of Callback called ExternalEvent for those RTI callbacks that do carry a logical time. Callback and ExternalEvent are abstract classes; the various kinds of RTI callbacks are represented by extensions of one or the other, depending on whether the callback carries a time. Thus GrantEvent and ReflectAttributeValuesEvent extend ExternalEvent, while AttributeOwnershipDivestitureNotificationCallback extends Callback. The Production federate defines both ReceiveInteractionCallback and ReceiveInteractionEvent because it receives interactions with and without time stamps.

The processing required to respond to each kind of callback is contained in each subclass's `dispatch()` method. All these classes are inner classes of `Production`, so the dispatch methods operate in the context of the `Production` class. The `dispatch()` method of each class returns a `boolean`, which is `true` only in the case that the event corresponds to a TIME ADVANCE GRANT †. For each class of callback there is a method on Production to queue an instance of the callback class; these methods are called by the callback handlers in `FedAmbImpl`.

Internal events are likewise represented as instances of subclasses of an abstract class `InternalEvent`. There is only one such class, `FinishMakingSushiEvent`. Internal events must be processed separately from external events because internal events can be processed only when the federate's logical time has advanced to the time of the event.

6.5.7   THE MAIN THREAD

The main thread of control for the federate executes in `Production.main()`, the constructor for `Production`, and `Production.mainThread()`. The `main()` method loads properties, constructs an instance of `Production` and calls `mainThread()` on it.

The constructor for `Production` constructs all the major objects mentioned above. It also performs all the initialization required to use the RTI. Code specific to this implementation of the RTI is contained here; no code outside the constructor should require modification if the federate were moved to another RTI implementation.

The code in `mainThread()` implements the federate lifecycle protocol and the time advance loop. This code is nearly identical in the Production, Transport, Consumption, and Viewer federates, except for the time advance service used. Production and Consumption use NEXT EVENT REQUEST. The Transport and Viewer federates use TIME ADVANCE REQUEST. The Manager federate contains a slight variation on the `mainThread()` code.

Any exception occurring in the main thread will be caught at the end of `mainThread()`, causing a log entry "Exception in main thread:" and a stack trace. This includes exceptions generated by the federate's calls into the RTI. Exceptions that are generated by federate code in callback threads must be detected through the RTI's callback exception logging. The federation code as supplied causes no exceptions, unless the federate cannot find the RTI executive or a file that it needs.

Just before the federate enters its time advance loop, it invokes ENABLE ASYNCHRONOUS DELIVERY. This directs the RTI to deliver receive-order callbacks (like the SimulationEnds interaction) while the federate is in either the time advance or time granted states. This is especially important in the Manager federate, because otherwise the Manager will never have the REMOVE OBJECT INSTANCE † callbacks delivered to it (for Manager.Federate instances) that inform it that federates have resigned.

The time advance loop consists of inner and outer loops. After an advance has been requested, the inner loop awaits and dispatches callbacks, until it detects a TIME ADVANCE GRANT †. The outer loop then updates the federate's internal state at the newly granted time, including checking its internal queue. It then loops to request another time advance. Receipt of the SimulationEnds interaction changes the state of the `boolean` variable `_simulationEnds-Received` and causes departure of the inner and outer time loops.

Recall that a property of advancing time with NEXT EVENT REQUEST is that the RTI eventually will grant the federate to exactly the logical time it requests. This is important for the Production and Consumption federates because they generate internal events that should be dispatched at the correct times. Those federates seek to advance to the time of their next internal event. The RTI will deliver each external event (callback with time stamp) that occurs in the meantime, and will grant an advance to the event time after it delivers each external event. By contrast, the Transport federate advances time in equal steps, updating its Boats at each time step.

6.5.8   CALLBACKS NOT HANDLED THROUGH THE CALLBACK QUEUE

All RTI-initiated services or callbacks are handled through the callback queue. This lessens the chances of data structures inadvertently being subjected to multiple threads. It also lessens the likelihood of inadvertent reentrant calls to the RTI, that is, calls made from the RTI's callback thread.

The service ANNOUNCE SYNCHRONIZATION POINT † gets special treatment. This callback occurs outside the callback dispatching loop. It causes the method `Production.recordSynchronizationPointAnnouncement()` to be executed, recording (by lowering a corresponding `Barrier`) the announcement of the synchronization point. To get past a synchronization point, the federate must first wait for the synchronization point to be announced. Then it must declare that it has achieved the synchronization point. Then it must await the RTI's declaration that the federation is synchronized at the point. The announcement barriers (one for each expected point) are created at the outset; as the Manager federate registers the points, the Production federate records the announcements to ensure that each point has been announced before it declares it has achieved it. The code appears early in `mainThread()`.

6.5.9   TIME ADVANCE

The Production federate, like all the federates, is time-constrained and time-regulating. It seeks to advance time via NEXT EVENT REQUEST. As described in Chapter 5, "Synchronizing the Federation," this federate always seeks to advance its time to the time of the next internal event on its internal queue. When it is granted to that time, it dispatches any internal events at that time. When no internal events are pending (the queue is empty), the federate seeks to advance to the final time, the greatest defined time.

The choice of lookahead for the Production federate is determined by the need to respond to internal and external events. The Production federate schedules an internal event to complete manufacture of a Serving. If the Production federate chooses a lookahead smaller than the smallest possible manufacture time, it will not be able to generate events at the time when a Serving is manufactured. The other constraint on lookahead is the need to respond to an external event with an attribute update. When the federate receives the interaction TransferAccepted, it changes the state of the target Chef instance and updates its servingName and chefState attributes. The time stamp on those updates can be no less than the time of the interaction plus the federate's lookahead. Thus the choice of lookahead for this federate is constrained by two modeling concerns: (1) the minimum manufacture time, and (2) the allowable interval between a Serving being loaded on a Boat and the Chef's state being updated. The lookahead is set by the property `Production.lookahead`. You may wish to experiment with different values.

6.5.10   UPDATING PUBLISHED ATTRIBUTES

The Production federate updates values for several attributes as the federation execution progresses. It changes its internal value of attributes for Chef and Serving instances as it processes various callbacks in the advancing state. The federate only performs an external update, by invoking UPDATE ATTRIBUTE VALUES, when it is in the time granted state, for the following reason. The federate uses NEXT EVENT REQUEST to advance time. As discussed in Chapter 5 (see Figure 5-8), it can invoke UPDATE ATTRIBUTE VALUES at its logical time plus lookahead only when it is in the granted state. Therefore the federate defers external updates until it receives a grant to a new logical time. When the federate changes the internal value of an attribute while processing a callback, it changes the attribute's associated attribute state to `Attribute-State.OWNED_INCONSISTENT`. Each time the federate is granted to a new logical time, the `Production` instance executes `updateChefs()` and `updateServings()` to invoke UPDATE ATTRIBUTE VALUES for any inconsistent attributes. The attribute state for updated attributes is then set back to `AttributeState.OWNED_CONSISTENT`.

There is a side effect of deferring and batching external updates, which, though it makes no difference to the Production federate's behavior, would be beneficial for a more complex federate. In a complex federate, different attributes of the same instance might have their internal values changed in different places in the federate's code. Rather than produce piecemeal updates, all the required external updates for an instance are performed together.

The Consumption federate uses the same mechanism for the same reason. The Transport federate does not need this mechanism. The Transport federate updates its Boats' state in response to a grant, so it need not defer external updates.

6.5.11   SUMMARY

This completes the sketch of the structure of the Production federate. The other federates have very similar structures; indeed the code will look quite familiar once you've studied the Production federate. The following sections will describe the other federates as they differ from the Production federate.

The federate may seem to contain a great deal of machinery. It really contains only the minimum machinery needed for any component to function reliably in a distributed environment. The modeling aspects of all the restaurant federates have been kept as simple as possible so as not to detract from their real purpose of exemplifying operations with the RTI. Given the small amount of modeling code, the event-handling machinery constitutes a disproportionate fraction of the federate's code. The RTI is, in a sense, hard for a small program to interact with and easy for a large one. Given the machinery presented here, you will find it easy to add new features. This machinery is easy to adapt to a new federate, as the authors did once the Production federate was built.

6.6   THE TRANSPORT FEDERATE

The description of the Production federate applies to the Transport federate, except for the evolution of the state of the Boat objects. Accordingly, we'll describe that in some detail.

6.6.1   THE FEDERATE'S USER INTERFACE

The Transport federate's user interface appears in Figure 6-8. It is identical to that of the Production federate, except that the tabular data refers to the Boats modeled by the federate, rather than chefs.

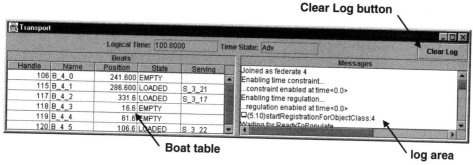

FIGURE 6-8   User Interface of the Transport Federate.

Each row represents one Boat. The columns in the table display the following:

• The object instance handle of the Boat instance

• The object instance name

• Its angular position along the canal

• Its state

• The name of the Serving instance it is carrying, if any

6.6.2   STATE OF THE BOATS

The Transport federate models the sushi boats in the canal. Each Boat is modeled as a state machine that is depicted in Figure 6-9.

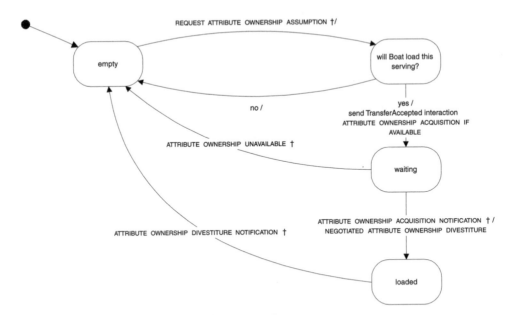

FIGURE 6-9   State of the Boat Instance.

Each Boat is in the "empty" state when it is created. Its spaceAvailable attribute has the value true. The Transport federate moves each Boat along the canal, updating its position attribute. When an empty Boat passes within reach of a chef with a Serving waiting to be loaded, the Production federate will attempt to transfer ownership of the Serving's position attribute. The Transport federate will receive REQUEST ATTRIBUTE OWNERSHIP ASSUMPTION † for the position attribute of the Serving. The Boat's object instance name will be given in the user-supplied tag delivered with the callback. That is how the Transport federate knows that this Boat instance is the object of desire of the Production federate, and not some other. The Boat moves to the "will Boat load this serving?" state.

The Transport federate must then decide if it will accept this Serving. If the Transport federate declines the offer, it does nothing and the Boat instance returns to the "empty" state. The Production federate will determine it has been rejected when the Boat moves out of reach of the chef. If the Transport federate accepts the offered Serving, it sends the interaction TransferAccepted, naming the Serving in the servingName parameter, and it invokes ATTRIBUTE OWNERSHIP ACQUISITION IF AVAILABLE for the position attribute of the offered Serving instance. The Boat moves to the "waiting" state. In the code, the decision state ("will Boat load this Serving?") does not actually appear, because the decision is made in the course of dispatching the REQUEST ATTRIBUTE OWNERSHIP ASSUMPTION † callback.

In the "waiting" state the Transport federate awaits positive notification that it has acquired ownership of the attribute. If for some reason the Production federate fails to divest ownership, the Transport federate will receive ATTRIBUTE OWNERSHIP UNAVAILABLE † and will return the Boat to the "empty" state. The Production federate would have to delete the instance unexpectedly to cause this, since it has previously offered to divest the attribute. If the Production federate behaves as expected, the Transport federate will receive ATTRIBUTE OWNERSHIP ACQUISITION NOTIFICATION † and the Transport federate will move the Boat to the "loaded" state. The Transport federate updates the spaceAvailable and servingName attributes of the Boat to reflect its newly acquired load. It also updates the position attribute of the Serving, exercising its newly acquired right to do so, to show that the Serving is now on the canal. Finally, the Transport federate invokes NEGOTIATED ATTRIBUTE OWNERSHIP DIVESTITURE on the position attribute of the Serving. This is the beginning of the protocol to transfer the Serving to a diner.

That protocol is completed when a diner seeks to transfer the Serving by acquiring ownership of its position attribute. The Transport federate receives ATTRIBUTE OWNERSHIP DIVESTITURE NOTIFICATION † for the instance attribute; it moves the previously loaded Boat to the "empty" state and updates its spaceAvailable and servingName attributes.

In this state machine, all the triggering events are callbacks from the RTI. You will find inner classes in `Transport` for each kind of callback: `RequestAttributeOwnership-AssumptionCallback`, `AttributeOwnershipUnavailableCallback`, `Attribute-OwnershipAcquisitionNotificationCallback`, and `AttributeOwnershipDivestitureNotificationCallback`. These all extend the abstract class `Transport.Callback`. The only event (callback with a time stamp) that the Transport federate receives is TIME ADVANCE GRANT †.

6.6.3   TIME ADVANCE

The Transport federate is time-stepped. It uses TIME ADVANCE REQUEST to move its logical time forward in equal steps. The size of the step is the property `Transport.advanceInterval`. The transfers of Servings on and off Boats occur at the times defined by the time steps.

The Transport federate's lookahead (the property `Transport.lookahead`) might be set to its time step. However its lookahead also constrains the interval between a change in a Boat's state, which occurs at a time step, and the federate's update of the Boat's state. The update can be sent no earlier than logical time plus lookahead. The lookahead also constrains the interval between the federate receiving an offer to load one of its Boats and the federate's response with the TransferAccepted interaction.

6.7   THE CONSUMPTION FEDERATE

The Consumption federate models diners that consume Servings. It registers and updates Diner objects for the benefit of the Viewer.

6.7.1   THE FEDERATE'S USER INTERFACE

The user interface for the Consumption federate is presented in Figure 6-10.

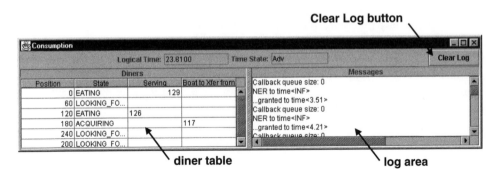

FIGURE 6-10   Consumption Federate User Interface.

The diner table displays the following information:

- The diner's angular position
- The diner's state
- The object instance handle of the Serving being consumed by the diner, if any
- The object instance handle of the Boat a diner is trying to unload, if any

6.7.2   STATE OF THE DINERS

The Consumption federate models each diner as a state machine, as presented in Figure 6-11.

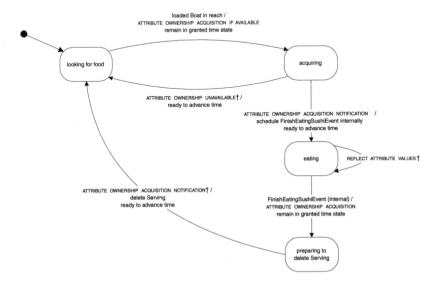

FIGURE 6-11   State of Modeled Diner.

Each diner begins in the "looking for food" state. When a loaded Boat passes within reach of the diner (the triggering event is a REFLECT ATTRIBUTE VALUES † for the position attribute of the Boat), the Consumption federate invokes ATTRIBUTE OWNERSHIP ACQUISITION IF AVAILABLE, attempting to acquire ownership of the position attribute of the Serving the Boat is carrying. Because the Transport federate has previously offered to divest the attribute, the RTI will reply with ATTRIBUTE OWNERSHIP ACQUISITION NOTIFICATION †. The Consumption federate will schedule an internal event `FinishEatingSushiEvent`, and the diner moves to the "eating" state. If somehow the Serving instance has been deleted, the Consumption federate will instead receive ATTRIBUTE OWNERSHIP UNAVAILABLE † and the diner will be returned to the "looking for food" state.

While the diner is in the "eating" state, the federate will receive REFLECT ATTRIBUTE VALUES † events as the Boats move. The diner remains in the "eating" state until the internal `FinishEatingSushiEvent` event is dispatched.

When the internal event `FinishEatingSushiEvent` is dispatched, it is time for the Serving instance to be deleted. However, before the Consumption federate can delete the instance, it must acquire ownership of the instance's privilegeToDeleteObject attribute. To accomplish this, the federate invokes ATTRIBUTE OWNERSHIP ACQUISITION for the attribute and places the diner in the "preparing to delete Serving" state. When the federate receives ATTRIBUTE OWNERSHIP ACQUISITION NOTIFICATION † for the privilegeToDeleteObject attribute, it marks the Serving instance for deletion and returns the diner to the "looking for food" state.

The Consumption federate updates the object instance of Diner that corresponds to each diner as the diner changes state. It updates the dinerState and servingName attributes. This allows the Viewer federate to display the state changes.

The Consumption federate does not invoke UPDATE ATTRIBUTE VALUES for every change in the dinerState attribute. The federate performs an external update only on transitions into the "looking for food" and "eating" states. The other states are significant to the federate but not to the Viewer. The federate performs external updates only on the transitions that occur at distinct logical times.

6.7.3   TIME ADVANCE

The Consumption federate advances time with NEXT EVENT REQUEST. Like the Production federate, it seeks to advance to the time of its next internal event. If no internal event is scheduled it seeks to advance to the final time. If all the federate's diners are in the states "acquiring" or "preparing to delete Serving," then there is neither an internal event scheduled, nor is there the prospect of an external event (callback with time stamp) arriving. The federate does not advance logical time in this condition, but continues to process other callbacks until one of the diner's state changes. This is the reason for the addition in this federate's code of another inner time advance loop after a grant has been received.

Considerations for lookahead, the property `Consumption.lookahead`, are similar to those for the Production federate. Lookahead cannot exceed the minimum consumption time.

Lookahead also constrains how quickly the federate can update a diner's state after a Serving has been acquired or deleted.

6.8   THE MANAGER FEDERATE

The Manager federate differs in a few respects from the Production, Transport, and Consumption federates. We'll discuss the differences in its user interface and its main thread.

6.8.1   THE FEDERATE'S USER INTERFACE

The Manager federate's user interface is depicted in Figure 6-12.

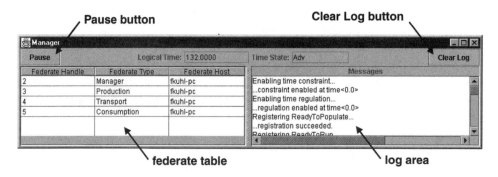

FIGURE 6-12   Manager Federate's User Interface.

In addition to the now familiar user interface controls, the Manager sports a pause button. Toggling the pause button causes the Manager federate to cease to advance logical time, thereby pausing the entire federation. When the pause button is toggled off, the Manager resumes its advance.

The federate table displays the following:

• The federate's federate handle
• The federate's type, as specified when it joined the federation
• The host the federate is running on

6.8.2   THE FEDERATE'S MAIN THREAD

The Manager federate's main thread is similar to the Production federate's, with a few differences that reflect its particular function.

The code for the main thread is in `Manager.mainThread()`. The code begins as usual by attempting to create the federation execution. The federate then joins the federation and enables time regulation and time constraint. The Manager federate then registers all the synchronization points used by the federation. After it registers each synchronization point, it awaits receipt of

SYNCHRONIZATION POINT REGISTRATION SUCCEEDED † from the RTI. The federate ignores the ANNOUNCE SYNCHRONIZATION POINT † that it, like the other federates, receives from the RTI.

The federate then subscribes the attributes of Manager.Federate that it will display and the interaction SimulationEnds. It then awaits discovery of the expected number of Manager.Federate objects, corresponding to the proper number of federates joining the federation. The number it expects is a property, `Manager.numberOfFederatesToAwait`. You can watch the federates join as the federate table acquires rows. (But the vagaries of updates to the Java user interface may cause the table to lag substantially behind.)

The federate then steps through achievement of the synchronization points ReadyToPopulate and ReadyToRun. With achievement of ReadyToRun, the federate begins advancing time. The Manager federates, like the other federates, begins at logical time zero. The size of its time steps is the property `Manager.advanceInterval`. Its lookahead is the property `Manager.lookahead`.

The Manager federate paces the rest of the federation, advancing its time in equal steps. Its advances are tied to wall clock time. The rate of its advance of logical time relative to wall clock time is the property `Manager.rate`. Between each TIME ADVANCE GRANT † and its next TIME ADVANCE REQUEST, the federate sleeps for an interval, ensuring its next advance request occurs at the correct point in wall clock time. See Figure 5-12 in Chapter 5 and its discussion. The Manager federate is waiting, while in the time advancing state, for the rest of the federates to do their calculations so they can advance time; if the rest of the federation is too slow, the Manager federate will advance time as quickly as it can. The Manager federate can successfully pace the federation only if the federation is capable of running faster than the desired rate. You can tell if the federation is keeping pace by watching the display of time state in the Manager: if the Manager is always advancing, the federation is behind. If the Manager is in the granted state some of the time, the rest of the federation is waiting for it, and the federation is running at the desired rate.

When the Manager receives the interaction SimulationEnds, it leaves the time-advance loop. It achieves the synchronization point ReadyToResign and waits for the rest of the federation. It then waits for the other federates to resign. As each federate resigns, its corresponding Manager.Federate instance is removed. When the number of instances in the Manager's federate table has decreased to one (you should see rows disappear in the federate table), the Manager resigns, destroys the federation execution, and posts "All done" to the log area.

6.9   THE VIEWER FEDERATE

The Viewer federate acts as a passive recipient and display of simulation data from the rest of the federation. The rest of the federation runs correctly without the Viewer federate. If you wish to run the federation without the Viewer, you should adjust the property `Manager.numberOfFederatesToAwait` so the Manager will not wait for it to join.

The Viewer's user interface is depicted in Figure 6-13. The log area displays the usual messages from the federate. The ring in the middle of the viewing area represents the restaurant's canal. The icons inside the canal of hands cutting a roll of sushi represent chefs. Boat

icons travel around on the canal. The icons of a hand holding chopsticks outside the canal represent diners. The chef and diner icons have words superimposed on them that represent their current state. Servings are represented by small rectangular photographs of sushi servings.

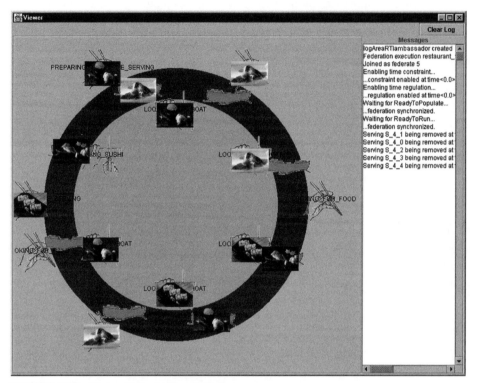

FIGURE 6-13   Viewer Federate User Interface.

The code to draw the display is in the method `paintComponent()` of class `Viewer-Panel`. It uses the Swing repaint facility. The code is designed to be simple rather than fast.

The Viewer subscribes to various object classes but publishes none. Its subscriptions are
passive. The Viewer is time-constrained so that it will receive data in time-stamp order and will
pace its clock to the rest of the federation. As delivered, the Viewer is also time-regulating,
which will prevent the rest of the federation from running ahead of it. If the rest of the federation
is running slowly enough that the Viewer federate will not otherwise lag behind, the Viewer can
run with time regulation disabled.

The Viewer advances time in equal steps. It updates its display at each time step using the
last received values of positions, and so on.

Extending the Federation for a New Purpose

7.1 USING THE FEDERATION FOR A NEW PURPOSE

One promise of the HLA is that simulations can be reused: new tricks for old code. Reuse comes about by recombining existing simulations in novel ways, creating new federations. The restaurant federation example has concentrated on this use of the HLA up to this point. Reuse also comes about from taking an existing federation and extending it for new purposes. In this chapter we show how to extend the restaurant federation, adding new capability but not changing any code in the sample implementation. You should have read Chapters 4 and 5 first.

Somehow a rumor has sprung up on the Internet that sushi is particularly susceptible to bacteria growth. The Internet community has reacted with its usual degree of responsibility and good judgement, and amplified the rumor beyond recognition. The Center for Concerned Sushi Patrons, the originators and keepers of the Consumption federate, are alarmed by the allegation that bacteria in sushi grow particularly well in a sushi boat restaurant. Their goal is to quash the rumor before it achieves the status of urban legend. They wish to add a model of bacteria growth to the restaurant federation to study the problem.

They could add a bacteria model to the Consumption federate, but the phenomenon doesn't really belong in the Consumption federate: it encompasses the lifecycle of sushi servings. Besides which, the original developers of the Consumption federate have moved on to web technology start-ups, and new developers will take too long to learn the code. The Center for Concerned Sushi Patrons has access to the entire existing restaurant federation but can't change the behavior of any of the federates.

The situation described in this section, that is, the need to extend an existing federation, is one for which the HLA is designed. In this chapter we'll discuss the mechanics of extending the restaurant federation to incorporate a new bacteria growth federate, without changing the previous federates. There are several aspects of the federation design, with corresponding HLA service groups, that must be considered.

7.1.1   STRATEGY: ADD NEW FEDERATES FOR NEW FUNCTIONS

There are really two new functions that must be added to the existing federation. They are:

- Model the growth of bacteria in the servings using the existing model of sushi production, transport, and consumption. The model will use the type, age, and position of each Serving.
- Report the combined output of the previous and new models.

To fulfill the first function, we'll add a new federate, the Biological federate, that will model growth of bacteria in sushi servings based on the data available in the existing federation. The Biological federate will model this aspect of all the Serving objects in the federation.

To fulfill the second function, we'll add a Reporting federate that will combine data from the previous federates and the new Biological federate. The reporting function certainly could be incorporated into the Biological federate. We'll keep it separate for two reasons. First, separating the Reporting federate will allow us to make some points in the example about federation design. Secondly, and more importantly, it separates modeling from presentation. Today's printed graphs and numbers, the output of analysis, may be replaced by demonstrations featuring dynamic visualization. It's good design to keep modeling and presentation separate.

The extended federation consists of the following:

- The previous Manager, Production, Transport, Consumption, and Viewer federates, unchanged
- The new Biological and Reporting federates
- A new FED, created by extending the previous FED
- The same RTI as before

7.1.2   THE FOM CAN BE EXTENDED WITHOUT DISRUPTING EXISTING FEDERATES

The design of the FOM, FED, declaration and object management services accommodate extension of a federation without changes to previous federates.

The previous federates can continue to function as before using the data (objects and attributes, interactions and parameters) that they were built for. The Biological federate will consume data about Servings and will produce new data describing Servings. The Reporting federate will require data about Servings from previous and new federates. Thus we need a way to continue to pass previous data (defined in the original FED) to previous and new federates that need it, and to pass previous and new data (newly defined in the extended FED) to new federates.

The HLA allows the FOM to be extended to handle this. We add a new class attribute to the Serving class that represents biological data: bacteriumCount. The previous class attributes, privilegeToDeleteObject, position, and type, remain unchanged. This addition to the FOM means a new FED file for our extended federation, presented below in abbreviated form. The additions and changes are in boldface.

```
;; restaurant_2.fed
;; The Sushi Boat Restaurant, extended version
(FED
  (Federation restaurant_2) ;; we choose this tag
  (FEDversion v1.3)         ;; required: specifies RTI spec version
  (spaces                   ;; we define no routing spaces
  )
  (objects
    (class ObjectRoot        ;; required
      (attribute privilegeToDelete reliable timestamp)
      ;; RTIprivate is required
      (class RTIprivate)
      ;;now we get to our stuff
      (class Restaurant
        (attribute position reliable timestamp)
        (class Serving
          (attribute type reliable timestamp)
          (attribute bacteriumCount reliable timestamp)
        )
        (class Boat
          (attribute spaceAvailable reliable timestamp)
          (attribute cargo reliable timestamp)
        )
      )
      ;; Manager class and subclasses are required
(class Manager. . . .)
    )     ;; end ObjectRoot
  )       ;; end objects

  (interactions
    ;;interactions unchanged from original federation
  )       ;; end interactions
)         ;; end FED
```

The publications of and subscriptions to class attributes of the previous federates remain unchanged, in keeping with the fact that we cannot change the previous federates' code. The publications and subscriptions for the new federates are presented in Table 7-1. Recall that the difference between active and passive subscription is that the former will cause class relevance advisories at the publisher, and the latter will not.

Table 7-1   Publications and Subscriptions for New Federates

	Biological	**Reporting**
Serving priviledgeToDeleteObject position type bacteriumCount	Published by default Active subscribe Active subscribe Publish	Published by default Passive subscribe Passive subscribe Passive subscribe

The most important point to make is this: *The previous federates operate just as they did with the previous FED; the existence of a new attribute for class Serving does not affect them.* The design of the HLA services always allows a federate to operate with a subset of the available attributes for a class. The Production federate can register Serving instances as it did before. Attributes are not specified in a registration. As the previous federates update attribute values, the fact that they do not provide a value for the new attribute bacteriumCount is irrelevant. The previous federates are now subscribing to a subset of the class attributes for Serving, but subscribing to a subset of the available attributes is legal. A subscribing federate will receive reflections only of attributes to which it has subscribed, so if a new federate is updating bacteriumCount, the RTI will ensure that a previous federate will not reflect a value of the new attribute. To sum up: the HLA services allow addition of new attributes to existing object classes without surprises for existing federates.

7.1.3   COOPERATIVE MODELING MEANS SHARING OWNERSHIP

In the original restaurant federation, responsibility for modeling a Serving is shared between the Production, Transport, and Consumption federates. The Production federate registers a new instance, thereby receiving ownership of those attributes it is publishing. When the Serving is to be loaded on a Boat, ownership of the position instance attribute is transferred to the Transport federate, which then becomes responsible for updating that attribute. When a Serving is taken off a Boat by a diner, ownership of the position instance attribute is transferred to the Consumption federate. So the responsibility for modeling the position of an instance of Serving, and hence ownership of that attribute, varies along the life of the instance. This evolution of ownership was diagrammed in Figure 4-8.

In the extended federation, the modeling of Servings is now shared between the Production, Transport, and Consumption federates on the one hand, and the Biological federate on the other. For a given instance of Serving, its position attribute is the responsibility of the Production (or Transport or Consumption) federate, and its bacteriumCount attribute is the responsibility of the Biological federate. As we've said before, the HLA is designed to support such shared responsibility.

Responsibility for modeling in the HLA means ownership of an instance attribute. In the steady state, then, an instance of Serving will have, at a given moment in the federation execution, its position attribute owned by the Production (or Transport or Consumption) federate, and its bacteriumCount attribute by the Biological federate. This is depicted in Figure 7-1.

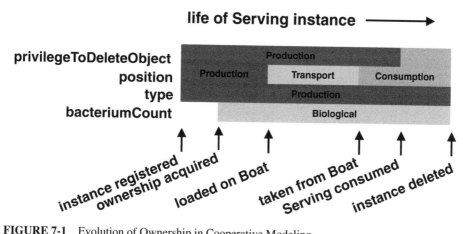

FIGURE 7-1   Evolution of Ownership in Cooperative Modeling.

Let's examine the lifecycle of a Serving instance in detail. A Serving instance comes into existence when the Production federate registers the instance. Because the Production federate is publishing the privilegeToDeleteObject, type, and position attributes, it gains immediate ownership of those instance attributes. Because it is not publishing bacteriumCount, that instance attribute becomes eligible for ownership but is unowned.

The Biological federate is subscribing to the type and position attributes, so it discovers the newly registered instance. (The fact that it is publishing privilegeToDeleteObject is irrelevant; the Biological federate will not seek to acquire ownership of that attribute, but will leave responsibility for deleting the instance with the older federates.) Upon discovering the instance, the Biological federate will attempt to acquire ownership of the bacteriumCount attribute for the discovered instance so that it can begin to update it. It can invoke ATTRIBUTE OWNERSHIP ACQUISITION IF AVAILABLE for this purpose. The RTI will call back immediately with ATTRIBUTE OWNERSHIP ACQUISITION NOTIFICATION † because the attribute is unowned. This point is marked "ownership acquired" in Figure 7-1. After this the Biological federate begins updating *that attribute* of the instance. (Recall that if the Biological federate attempts to update the other attributes, it will cause an exception, because it doesn't own those attributes.)

In the course of the federation execution, ownership of the position attribute of the instance is transferred from the Production federate to the Transport federate, and eventually to the Consumption federate. The Biological federate is unaware of these transfers.

The Reporting federate has subscribed to the class attributes type, position, and bacteriumCount. Therefore it will discover each new Serving instance as it is registered. It will reflect new values for all the instance attributes. The only indication that these attributes are being updated by different federates (and this is not an infallible indication) is that the Reporting federate will receive distinct reflect callbacks for position and bacteriumCount. (Recall that the original federates do not update the type attribute after sending an initial value.)

When the Consumption federate deletes the Serving instance, the Biological and Reporting federates get a corresponding REMOVE OBJECT INSTANCE † callback.

Let's summarize this section. The modeling of a Serving instance involves cooperation between the Production, Transport, and Consumption federates, on the one hand, and the Biological federate on the other. This is reflected in the ownership of the instance attributes of each Serving. The new instance attribute, bacteriumCount, is initially unowned when the instance is registered. The Biological federate detects the registration of the instance and immediately acquires ownership of the instance attribute bacteriumCount. It then updates its value, using the Serving's type, age, and position, through the life of the Serving instance.

7.1.4   TIME MANAGEMENT ACCOMMODATES NEW FEDERATES

We've alluded to the dependence of the Biological federate's modeling on data from the previous federates. In this section we explore the consequences of that dependence on time management.

We discuss the Reporting federate first, since it's the easy case. The Reporting federate is a passive viewer. It only receives data and produces none. Therefore it can be time-constrained but not time-regulating. As a time-constrained federate it can receive TSO events, and will get all attribute updates with time stamps. Because it is not time-regulating, it will not affect the progress of logical time of other federates. However, it must advance its clock to receive updates. The easiest thing for it to do is to invoke TIME ADVANCE REQUEST once, asking to go to the final time, or to the federation ending time if one is defined. (See Chapter 5 for discussion of the lifecycle protocol.) The Reporting federate will then enter the Time Advancing state, and will receive TSO events in order.

The case of the Biological federate is not as simple, but it is still straightforward. It must be both time-constrained and time-regulating, since it is both consuming and producing TSO events. The time stamps on its received data are important because the age of a Serving and its type and position play a part in the bacteria calculations.

Bacteria calculations for an instance cause an update to the bacteriumCount attribute. These calculations are updated each time the federate receives a new value for the instance's position attribute. Thus the Biological federate operates in a loop in which it reflects a position update, performs bacteria calculations, and updates the corresponding bacteriumCount attribute.

It would be desirable if the bacteriumCount updates bore the same time stamp as the position update. That is not possible using only the time management services that we've introduced thus far. It is possible using zero-lookahead time management services of the HLA, and we'll discuss these services in Chapter 8, "Advanced Topics." For now, we'll assume that the Biological federate sets a constant, small (but positive) lookahead.

The Biological federate must be able to produce bacteriumCount updates with times very close to the times of the corresponding position updates, and those times may be irregular. If the Biological federate advanced its time with TIME ADVANCE REQUEST, the times it would be granted to—which determine the times of its output events—would be limited by the times to which it is granted. Therefore the Biological federate should use NEXT EVENT REQUEST to advance its logical time. The Biological federate has no need to be granted to a particular time other than the time of the next event, so each time it invokes NEXT EVENT REQUEST, it can request an advance to the federation ending time, if one is defined, or to the final time. The Biological federate operates then in a loop with these steps:

```
loop
   NEXT EVENT REQUEST to the federation ending time or final time;
   await REFLECT ATTRIBUTE VALUES t̸ callback,
      containing update of the position attribute
      for Serving instance k at time t;
   await TIME ADVANCE GRANT t̸ to t;
   compute bacteriumCount for instance k at time t + lookahead;
   UPDATE ATTRIBUTE VALUES bacteriumCount
      for instance k at time t + lookahead;
end loop;
```

One more detail remains to be mentioned. The Transport federate is time-stepped, so it updates the position of all known Boats (and hence Servings) in equal steps. Its pattern then is to produce at regular intervals a group of updates with the same time stamp. How does this affect the Biological federate? Using NEXT EVENT REQUEST, the Biological federate will receive all events at t before it gets the TIME ADVANCE GRANT $t̸$. Thus the federate will get the reflect callbacks in batches corresponding to the Transport federate's update batches. The Biological federate can receive the batch (which is delimited by the grant) and produce its outputs as a batch. However, the function of the Biological federate does not depend on the time advance mechanism used by the Transport federate. As described, the Biological federate will function correctly regardless of the approach used by the Transport federate.

What are the other federates doing while the Biological federate is computing? If they were waiting on the Transport federate, they are probably still waiting for a grant. Since the Biological federate's lookahead is small, its output time while it's computing (logical time plus lookahead) probably doesn't allow the other federates to proceed. This has the effect of serializing the position computations in one federate with the bacteria computations in the Biological federate, but, since the latter depend on the former, that's unavoidable. The HLA is maintaining causal consistency across the federation.

7.1.5   The New Federates Easily Join the Lifecycle Protocol

We should consider briefly the consequences for the lifecycle protocol of adding the new federates. It turns out that careful design and application of the HLA services in the protocol makes the addition of new federates no additional work. We assume that the new federates fulfill their responsibilities in the protocol. The lifecycle protocol depends on three mechanisms:

- Federation synchronization points
- The Manager's use of the MOM to know when all expected federates have joined
- Time synchronization

All three mechanisms are designed to support the addition of new federates. Only the use of the MOM is sensitive to the number of federates, and only to the extent that the Manager must be told to wait for the proper number to join. Otherwise, everything works as before.

7.1.6   A FOM CAN ALSO BE EXTENDED THROUGH SUBCLASSES

There is another way to extend a FOM besides adding attributes and parameters: you can define subclasses of existing object and interaction classes.

Refer back to Figure 3-5, which illustrated the extension of an object class. Recall that the available attributes for an object class are the attributes defined for the class and all its super-classes. Thus the available attributes for the class CivilAircraft are privilegeToDeleteObject, position, and drinkCartsOnBoard. Suppose you had an existing federate that subscribes to the attribute position of class Aircraft. Suppose you add a federate that registers an instance of CivilAircraft. The existing federate will discover the instance as class Aircraft. When a federate discovers an instance as a superclass of the class at which it was registered, we say that the instance was *promoted*. When the new federate updates the position and drinkCartsOnBoard attributes for the instance, the existing federate will reflect the new value for position. The RTI will prune the attributes delivered on a REFLECT ATTRIBUTE VALUES † callback to the attributes the receiving federate subscribed, which must be attributes available to the class it subscribed. Similar observations apply to interaction classes. Refer to the interaction class tree in Figure 7-2. Suppose a federate subscribes to the interaction class A, and another federate sends an interaction of class B, supplying parameters p1 and p2. The first federate will receive the interaction as class A. Interactions undergo promotion just like object instances. The RTI will prune the parameters supplied when the interaction was sent to only those available to the class at which the first federate receives the interaction, in this case, only p1.

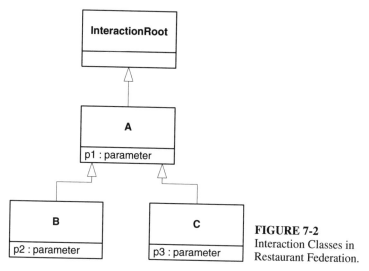

FIGURE 7-2
Interaction Classes in
Restaurant Federation.

Why, in our example of extending the restaurant federation, did we extend the FOM by adding an attribute to an existing class, rather than by defining a subclass with the additional attribute? Because we can't change the behavior of existing federates, the Production federate would continue to register instances of Serving, but those instances would not have the new instance attribute bacteriumCount defined in the new subclass, AugmentedServing, and, therefore couldn't accomplish what we wanted for the extended federation.

The class promotion mechanisms are useful for federates that operate on object instances as generalizations of instances, or interactions created by other federates.

7.2 SUMMARY

It is natural for an HLA federation to be extended for a new purpose. The HLA is designed with extension of federations in mind. The structure of the FOM and the design of the services support extension in natural ways.

This completes the discussion of the restaurant federation. Chapter 8, "Advanced Topics" describes data distribution management and further applications of time management (zero look-ahead, optimistic federates), federation management (save and restore), and the MOM.

Advanced Topics

8.1 Introduction

The topics covered in this chapter are "advanced" in the sense that they will be clearer after you have a good grasp of the fundamentals of the HLA. So we recommend reading this chapter after you've read Chapters 1–6, or are an experienced High Level Architecture (HLA) federate and federation developer.

8.2 Zero Lookahead

In the earlier discussion of time management services, we alluded to the existence of five different time advance requests. We discussed two of them, TIME ADVANCE REQUEST and NEXT EVENT REQUEST, in detail and deferred the rest. We also deferred discussion of the use of zero lookahead. Now we take up zero lookahead and in the process discuss two more time advance services, TIME ADVANCE REQUEST AVAILABLE and NEXT EVENT REQUEST AVAILABLE. The remaining time advance service, FLUSH QUEUE REQUEST, will be covered in the discussion of optimistic federates.

We discuss the zero-lookahead services under two scenarios for their use. We certainly don't claim that these are the only uses of zero lookahead, but they will serve to explain the mechanisms. As always, we invite your creative invention of other uses.

8.2.1 Zero Lookahead and Cooperative Modeling

Recall that, when we extended the restaurant federation to add calculations of bacteria counts, we engaged in cooperative modeling of the extended Serving entities. The Serving object class acquired a new attribute, bacteriumCount, in addition to its previous type and position attributes. Modeling the new Serving instances now involved cooperation between the Production, Transport, and Consumption federates, on the one hand, and the new Biological federate on the other. For each instance, the former federates retained responsibility for (and thus ownership of) the position and type attributes, and the Biological federate owned the bacteriumCount attribute. The Biological federate accomplished the cooperative modeling as follows:

- It discovered each Serving instance as it was registered.
- It took ownership of the corresponding bacteriumCount instance attribute.
- When it reflected an update of the position attribute, it computed a new bacteriumCount value and updated the attribute value.

In the earlier section, the Biological federate advanced its time using NEXT EVENT REQUEST. Its time loop was as follows:

```
while simulation running loop
    invoke NEXT EVENT REQUEST to federation ending time;
    await  REFLECT ATTRIBUTE VALUES † for
        position attributes; //perhaps mutiple REFLECT ATTRIBUTE VALUES †
    await  TIME ADVANCE GRANT †;
    compute new bacteriumCount for each instance;
    UPDATE ATTRIBUTE VALUES for the bacteriumCount;
end loop;
```

We remarked at the time that it was desirable that the updates of bacteriumCount should bear the same time stamp as the position updates that triggered them, but that this wasn't possible. Using NEXT EVENT REQUEST to advance time did not allow the Biological federate's lookahead to be zero. Thus the Biological federate's updates were required to bear time stamps of at least its granted time plus lookahead.

The zero-lookahead services allow us to overcome that limitation. The changes needed to the code are very small, but the consequences are significant. The only changes needed are:

- The Biological federate uses zero for its lookahead, rather than a positive quantity.
- The federate invokes NEXT EVENT REQUEST AVAILABLE, rather than NEXT EVENT REQUEST.

Why use NEXT EVENT REQUEST AVAILABLE rather than NEXT EVENT REQUEST? Both forms of advance allow zero lookahead.[1] The two forms are similar in that, if an event is available with a time less than the requested time, the RTI will grant an advance to the event time, rather than the requested time. (It's this behavior that the Biological federate uses to move its logical time from event to event.) The chief difference for the present application is the time stamps allowed on events the federate sends after it gets the TIME ADVANCE GRANT †. If the federate requested the advance with NEXT EVENT REQUEST AVAILABLE, it can produce events with

---

1. We didn't mention use of zero lookahead with NEXT EVENT REQUEST because it behaves differently and it isn't applicable to our present problem; we'll discuss it in the next section.

times stamps at the granted time (plus zero lookahead); if the federate requested the advance with NEXT EVENT REQUEST, it is only allowed to produce events with time stamps strictly greater than the granted time (plus lookahead).

There is another difference in the behavior of NEXT EVENT REQUEST and NEXT EVENT REQUEST AVAILABLE of which you should be aware. It turns out not to matter in this application, but is important in the next to be discussed.

When a federate advances with NEXT EVENT REQUEST, it is guaranteed that by the time it receives TIME ADVANCE GRANT †, it has received the event (if any) with the least time stamp that could possibly be sent in the federation, *and any other events with the same time*. In the original extension of the federation, the Biological federate was using NEXT EVENT REQUEST and the Transport federate was updating all its Serving instances for each time step at the same logical time. So its updates were being generated in batches. The Biological federate received the corresponding reflects in batches: each time it was granted an advance, it had gotten all the reflects that would arrive bearing that logical time.

When a federate advances using NEXT EVENT REQUEST AVAILABLE, it is guaranteed to get the event (if any) with the least time stamp that could possibly be sent in the federation, and whatever events with the same time stamp *that happen to be queued for delivery* before the RTI issues the grant. It is not guaranteed to get all events at the granted time.[2] When the RTI issues the TIME ADVANCE GRANT † as the result of a NEXT EVENT REQUEST AVAILABLE, it knows that it is still possible that other federates may generate more events at the granted time. The purpose of the NEXT EVENT REQUEST AVAILABLE service, and the analogous TIME ADVANCE REQUEST AVAILABLE, is to allow federates to engage in conversation at a constant logical time.

This does not turn out to make a difference in this application because of the way the time advance loop operates in the Biological federate. Each time the federate gets a grant, it processes the updates it has received, whether one or many, and then requests to advance time again. If there are straggling events, the federate will receive those and be granted (again) to the same time. So the federate may go through several cycles of request and grant at a constant point in logical time before it receives and processes all updates at that time. But it will receive all of them, and will never receive any events late.

There are two more points to discuss, and we're done with this application. First, it's important that the Biological federate continually try to advance its time. It is time-regulating, and must be if it is to create time-stamped events. Because it's time-regulating, the other time-constrained federates (Production, Transport, and Consumption) that are updating the original Serving attributes, cannot advance their clocks unless the Biological federate keeps trying to advance. As soon as all the events in a given update batch have been delivered to the Biological federate, its output time rises (to at least the time of the next event to be delivered to it), and the other federates can advance.

2. If it's helpful, think of the service as "Request the next event and others that are *available* for delivery at that time."

Secondly, you'll notice that, during each cycle, the Biological federate does not update bacteriumCount instance attributes until it has received a grant. What would happen if the federate tried to update the bacteriumCount attribute as it received each position update in the Time Advancing state (that is, before the grant)? The RTI would throw an exception; while in the Time Advancing state, the federate's minimum allowed time stamp is its requested time (plus zero lookahead). So the federate must wait each cycle until it has received the grant. In the Time Granted state, its minimum allowed time stamp is the granted time (plus zero lookahead).

To sum up: A federate acting as a "follower" in a cooperative modeling scheme that wishes to produce its updates at the same logical time as its triggering updates can do so. It sets a lookahead of zero and uses NEXT EVENT REQUEST AVAILABLE to request time advances. And everything works out.

8.2.2   Zero Lookahead and Episodic Simulation

In this section we consider the use of zero-lookahead time services for supporting "episodic" simulation, a term we use here to describe any federation where there are episodes in which significant numbers of events are exchanged among federates at a single logical time. This might come about to support the "activity scanning" style of discrete event simulations [Neelamkavil 1987]. Episodes might also occur because a single event in the actual system being modeled might be modeled as several distinct events at the same time. For example [Fujimoto 1999], a ship contacting a mine is a single event in an actual system, but it might be modeled as the ship contacting the mine (from the perspective of the ship) and the mine being struck by the ship (from the mine's perspective)—the first event causing the second to be scheduled at the same logical time.

To perform episodic simulation, a federate needs two mechanisms:

1. Having arrived at the logical time of the episode, the federate needs a way to exchange an indeterminate number of events with other federates, all at the episode's logical time.
2. The federate needs a way to signal other federates that it wishes to end the episode, and to ensure that it has received all events at the episode time before leaving the episode.

The HLA furnishes both mechanisms; they both involve zero lookahead.

The first mechanism we've seen in the preceding section. The federate advances to the time of the episode by invoking NEXT EVENT REQUEST AVAILABLE with zero lookahead. This causes the federate to receive all events before the episode time, plus events at the episode time that happen to be available for delivery upon the invocation. When the federate receives TIME ADVANCE GRANT †, it can process the events it has received and issue events at the episode time. The federate may repeatedly invoke NEXT EVENT REQUEST AVAILABLE at the episode time to receive more events.

At some point the federate will signal that it is ready to end the episode and advance its time beyond the episode time. Before it can actually advance, it will need assurance that it has received all events at the episode time; hence the need for the second mechanism. The RTI allows invocation of NEXT EVENT REQUEST with zero lookahead. To end the episode, the federate invokes NEXT EVENT REQUEST with zero lookahead to advance (again) to the episode time. With zero lookahead, this service guarantees that the federate will receive all possible events before or at the episode time before the grant. (Recall that the "available" flavor guarantees all events before, and only some of the events at, the granted time.) By invoking NEXT EVENT REQUEST, even with zero lookahead, the federate is stating that it will produce no more events at the episode time; indeed, after the invocation the RTI will only accept events from the federate strictly greater than the granted time. All time-regulating federates contributing events at the episode time must eventually use NEXT EVENT REQUEST to allow the other federates to proceed.

The processing of a federate during an episode can be summarized in the following code.

```
invoke ENABLE TIME REGULATION with zero lookahead;
while simulation is running loop:
   determine time stamp of next local event; call it tslocal;
   //advance to logical time of next event
   invoke NEXT EVENT REQUEST AVAILABLE with tslocal;
     await events via REFLECT ATTRIBUTE VALUES, RECEIVE INTERACTION or REMOVE
OBJECT INSTANCE;
   await TIME ADVANCE GRANT;
   let now be the granted time; //the episode time

   //perform zero-lookahead operations, e.g. queries
   invoke UPDATE ATTRIBUTE VALUES, SEND INTERACTION at now or DELETE OBJECT
INSTANCE;

   //federate may repeat calls to NEXT EVENT REQUEST AVAILABLE to now
     //and issue further UPDATE ATTRIBUTE VALUES, SEND INTERACTION or DELETE
OBJECT INSTANCE at now

   //retrieve remaining events at now; signal intent to advance logical
     //time without actually advancing it
   invoke NEXT EVENT REQUEST at now;
     await remaining events at now
       via UPDATE ATTRIBUTE VALUES, SEND INTERACTION or DELETE OBJECT INSTANCE;
   await TIME ADVANCE GRANT;
   process local and external events in federate-determined order,
     providing changed information via
     UPDATE ATTRIBUTE VALUES, SEND INTERACTION or DELETE OBJECT INSTANCE;
end loop;
```

As presented thus far, we've assumed that the federate moves to a new episode by seeking the next available event, hence using NEXT EVENT REQUEST AVAILABLE. The HLA also supports episodic time-stepped federates. The service TIME ADVANCE REQUEST AVAILABLE is analogous to TIME ADVANCE REQUEST, in that the invoking federate will receive a grant only when the RTI can safely allow an advance to the requested time (rather than to the time of the next external event); it is analogous to NEXT EVENT REQUEST AVAILABLE in that the federate is guaranteed to receive all events before, and only some events at, the granted time. For a federate to step from episode to episode in determinate amounts, the federate moves to each new episode using TIME ADVANCE REQUEST AVAILABLE (with zero lookahead). The federate still uses NEXT EVENT REQUEST AVAILABLE within the episode to receive events at the episode time. The federate invokes NEXT EVENT REQUEST to the episode time with zero lookahead to signal its intent to end the episode.[3]

To sum up: The HLA offers time management services that support episodic federates. A group of federates can advance to the same logical time, indulge in an episode of exchange of events at the logical time, and then agree to end the episode and move on. Not all federates in the federation need to behave episodically; the RTI will coordinate the entire federation appropriately. However, it should be clear by now that the behavior of each federate with respect to time management is a significant part of federation design.

8.2.3   A FINAL REMINDER ON LOOKAHEAD

We've said little throughout our discussion about how a federate establishes a lookahead value. A federate must always have a value of lookahead if it is to be time-regulating; a value must be supplied when the federate invokes ENABLE TIME REGULATION. (And zero is a legitimate value at that point.) Its lookahead can change, however: the federate can invoke MODIFY LOOKAHEAD to request a new value. But the modification is subject to this constraint: a federate cannot suddenly decrease its lookahead in such a way that it is now free to send events that might be in another federate's past. In such a case, the RTI maintains an *actual lookahead* for the federate whose value is between the previous value and the requested value, and which is safe for the federation. As the federate advances time, the RTI decreases the federate's actual lookahead until it reaches the requested value. The federate can discover its actual lookahead at any point by invoking QUERY LOOKAHEAD.

8.3   APPROACH TO TIME MANAGEMENT FOR OPTIMISTIC FEDERATES

Our discussion thus far of time management has concerned conservative synchronization, where events are delivered to a federate only when it is "safe"; that is, there is no possibility of an event arriving in the federate's past. Optimistic approaches allow computation into an assumed future (with the consequent possibility that events arrive out of order) and incorporate a means of detecting and erasing the consequent errors [Jefferson 1985]. The optimistic approach makes several assumptions. The first is that a simulation can be speeded up if it can be decomposed into a number of logical processes that can run in parallel on multiple processors. The second is that

---

3.   The service TIME ADVANCE REQUEST can be invoked with zero lookahead. It behaves as you would expect from our discussion: the RTI always grants to the requested time; after the grant, the federate is guaranteed to have received all events before, and only some events at, the granted time; after the grant, the federate may send events with times strictly greater than the granted time.

the processes can make better progress if they compute independently out into the future. They may have to roll back their state when events arrive out of order that contradict an earlier state of their computation. For some problems, the decomposition into logical processes is straightforward, and the state rollbacks are either fast enough or infrequent enough that the optimistic approach is advantageous.[4]

Let us sketch an example. Assume a model of air traffic control in oceanic regions. The trajectories of aircraft could be computed on multiple processors into the future, and the events that correspond to their periodic position updates could be generated into the future. Occasionally, however, a directive from air traffic control will cause a trajectory to change from what it would have been. When air traffic control sends a directive to an aircraft, its pre-computed trajectory becomes invalid from the point in time of the directive. The events corresponding to position updates beyond the time of the directive must be retracted, and the trajectory computed again. The efficiency of such an optimistic scheme depends on the balance between the benefit of computing optimistically and the work occasioned by rolling back state.

The point of this section is that the HLA supports federates that use optimistic as well as conservative synchronization, and supports federations that mix the approaches. The HLA's support of optimistic federates takes the form of two mechanisms:

- A way of getting events "early," that is, before the federate's logical time has advanced to the time of the events
- A way of retracting events and being informed of retractions by other federates

These mechanisms are intended to be generic to all forms of optimistic synchronization and are not tied to a particular implementation framework. Any optimistic federate will require significant internal machinery, for example, for rolling back state, that is not the HLA's concern. The HLA furnishes an optimistic federate with the mechanisms needed to coordinate with other optimistic or conservative federates.

An optimistic federate will operate time-constrained and time-regulating. Thus it has a logical time like other federates. And its logical time has the same meaning as for other time-constrained federates: it defines the boundary of the immutable past for the federate. For the optimistic federate, federate state beyond its logical time is mutable, and events sent or received beyond its logical time may be retracted. But events (and state) before the federate's logical time are immutable. The optimistic federate also has a lookahead value, which may be zero. Lookahead functions for the optimistic federate as it does for other time-regulating federates.

8.3.1   ADVANCING TIME AND GETTING EVENTS EARLY

We arrive finally at the fifth and last of the time advance services, FLUSH QUEUE REQUEST. This service is intended specifically to support optimistic federates. As with the other time advance services, the federate invokes FLUSH QUEUE REQUEST, asking to advance to a stated time. The

---

4. The optimistic approach assumes that it's faster, if more complex, to ask forgiveness rather than permission.

federate enters the Time Advancing state, and remains there until the RTI calls back with TIME ADVANCE GRANT †. The federate then returns to the Time Granted state with a new logical time. While in the Time Advancing state, the federate may not produce events with timestamps less than the requested time plus lookahead. While in the Time Granted state, the federate may not produce events with time less than the federate's last granted time plus lookahead. The federate will receive receive order (RO) events only while in the Time Advancing state, unless it has enabled asynchronous delivery.

Here's what's distinctive about FLUSH QUEUE REQUEST. When the federate invokes the service (thereby moving into the Time Advancing state), the RTI delivers all time stamp order (TSO) events in its queue for the federate immediately, regardless of the logical time of the events. The RTI flushes its TSO queue (hence the name of the service), irrespective of the possibility that other events may arrive later whose logical times are between or later than events already delivered.

If the RTI can guarantee that no more events will arrive before the requested time (because the federate's LBTS is sufficiently high), it will grant the requested time to the federate. Otherwise, it will grant the latest time (before the requested time) that it can. The granted time may equal the federate's current logical time, that is, the federate's logical time may not move.

The choice of the federate's requested time, each time it invokes FLUSH QUEUE REQUEST, resembles the choice it must make when invoking NEXT EVENT REQUEST AVAILABLE. It cannot request to move any farther ahead than it can guarantee its state will be immutable, *regardless of late events or retractions it may receive*. Other time-constrained federates, whether optimistic or conservative, cannot advance their logical time beyond what the federate requests, so its choice is important. FLUSH QUEUE REQUEST resembles NEXT EVENT REQUEST AVAILABLE in the following ways:

- Lookahead is allowed to be zero.
- The time granted by the RTI may be less than the time the federate requested.
- After the federate is granted to a new time, it is still possible that the federate will receive events at the granted time.
- The federate will receive no more events whose time is before the granted time.

The obvious difference between the two services is in the events delivered while the federate is in the Time Advancing state: for NEXT EVENT REQUEST AVAILABLE, no events are delivered beyond the granted time; for FLUSH QUEUE REQUEST, all queued events are delivered, regardless of time.

8.3.2   RETRACTING EVENTS

Optimistic federates must be able to receive and act upon retractions of events from other federates and must be able to retract events themselves. They do this through "retraction designators," as they are called in the interface specification.[5]

---

5.   The corresponding data type in the APIs is called an EventRetractionHandle.

Every time a federate invokes a service to send an event (UPDATE ATTRIBUTE VALUES, SEND INTERACTION, or DELETE OBJECT INSTANCE) and supplies a time stamp, the RTI returns a retraction designator. Every time a time-constrained federate receives a TSO event (REFLECT ATTRIBUTE VALUES †, RECEIVE INTERACTION †, REMOVE OBJECT INSTANCE †), the RTI supplies a time stamp with the event and a retraction designator. The retraction designator uniquely identifies each event within a federation execution to the federate. An optimistic federate must store retraction designators that it generates or receives, together with the information needed for it to adjust its state.[6]

A federate retracts an event by invoking the concisely named RETRACT service, supplying a retraction designator. If the federate attempts to retract an event in its past, the RTI will throw an exception.

A great deal may happen when an event is retracted. Consider briefly our earlier example of air traffic control. A federate modeling the trajectory of an aircraft must roll back its state if it receives an air traffic control directive that invalidates some of its optimistic computations. That may in turn invalidate other trajectories that were influenced by the first. One retraction may lead to many retractions exchanged among the modeling processes. This is reflected in the HLA.

- If the event was the deletion of an object, the existence of the object and the ownership of its attributes must be adjusted. The instance is reconstituted. Each federate that owned attributes of that instance when it was deleted reacquires ownership of the instance attributes.

- When an event is sent, there may be several resulting events received by various federates. (For example, one UPDATE ATTRIBUTE VALUES event may cause REFLECT ATTRIBUTE VALUES † at several federates.) When a sent event is retracted, the received events that had resulted from the retracted events must be adjusted. Those resulting events that remain in the RTI's TSO queue for delivery to some federate are annihilated. Those resulting events that have been delivered to some federate cause the RTI to invoke REQUEST RETRACTION † on the federate.

A federation may thus experience a chain of retractions if it contains more than one optimistic federate, in the following fashion. An optimistic federate receives a late event, causing it to roll back its state. The rollback causes the federate to retract certain events it sent. The retractions cause the RTI to request retraction of resulting events that were delivered to other federates. These requests may cause the other federates to roll back and retract other events.

8.3.3 SUMMARY

The HLA supports federates that engage in optimistic or aggressive computation, thereby producing tentative events. An optimistic federate is both time-constrained and time-regulating. An

---

6. Conservative federates also receive retraction designators when they send or receive events. But because they will never have occasion to retract an event, or to receive a request to retract, they need not store the retraction designators.

optimistic federate must be able to retract events and receive and act upon retractions. The HLA supports optimistic federates in a federation with other optimistic and conservative federates.

8.4   SAVE AND RESTORE

The services for federation save and restore are part of the federation management group. Our discussion of them in this section begins with an overview, and then covers details of save and restore.

8.4.1   OVERVIEW

Among the kinds of applications intended for HLA federations are those that involve many computers running around the clock for a long time, where "long" is long enough for computers to break, power to fail, or people to trip over cables. Also among the applications intended for the HLA are those involving analysis of alternatives that diverge from a common state. Save and restore mechanisms are intended to support both kinds of applications.

The save and restore mechanisms help with long-lived federations by affording a means of saving the state of the entire federation at significant points in the federation execution. If a failure occurs later for any reason, the federation can be restored to the point of the last save, and the federation execution can proceed from that point.

The save and restore mechanisms facilitate analysis of alternatives in the following way. Often the alternatives to be analyzed branch from a common state. All the alternatives to be considered begin with the same conditions. Those conditions may require substantial simulation to achieve, and it would be burdensome to have to repeat the computations required to reach the initial conditions for each alternative to be considered. The federation save mechanism can be used to save the state of the federation when the initial conditions have been achieved. As each alternative is simulated in turn, the federation restore mechanism can be used to put the federation in the initial condition. This has the effect of setting not only logical time but all the federation state to the point of restoration.

The HLA partitions the architecture of a distributed simulation into two parts: that which is generic to distributed simulation is assigned to the RTI; that which is specific to a particular simulation is assigned to a federate. This partition is preserved in the HLA's approach to save and restore. The HLA partitions responsibilities for save and restore accordingly:

- The RTI is responsible for coordinating all the activities of a save or restore for an entire federation. This is a generic function.
- The RTI is responsible for saving or restoring its own state. This is another generic function.
- Each federate is responsible to save or restore its own state under direction from the RTI. These are functions specific to each federate and cannot be performed by the RTI.

Thus a proper implementation of save and restore in a federation is synergistic and cooperative. All the federates and the RTI must do their part, and they must work together.

This is how the save and restore mechanisms work in broad terms. A federation execution is executing, with a set of federates. One federate, perhaps a manager, requests a federation save. The requesting federate supplies a label that identifies the save and is attached to all data generated by the save. The RTI informs each federate that it should initiate saving its internal state, and desists from any further RTI-initiated services. Each federate is responsible for saving its state in some persistent form. Exactly how the federate does this is its concern, rather than the RTI's. Each federate indicates to the RTI that its save is complete. Meanwhile the RTI saves its state. When the RTI has heard that all federates have finished, it announces to each federate that the federation has been saved, and the RTI and federates resume the normal activity of the execution.

A restoration occurs after a save. It might occur before the saved federation execution finishes, or later. Suppose the saved federation execution has not finished and all the federates are still joined that were joined at the time of the save. Some federate requests the restoration of the saved federation execution, supplying the label of the desired save. The RTI instructs each federate to assume the identity of one of the federates in the saved execution. The RTI provides enough information that the federate can find the persistent state data corresponding to a federate in the saved execution. When each federate has restored the internal state corresponding to the named federate, it notifies the RTI. When the RTI has heard from all federates, and has finished restoring its state, it declares the federation restored, and normal activity resumes from the point of restoration.

If the saved federation execution had finished before the restoration, a new federation execution must be created with the same name as the saved execution, and an appropriate number of federates must have joined the new federation execution. Some federate requests the restoration, and the restoration proceeds as before.

If the federate requesting a save supplies a logical time, the save is said to be *timed*. Otherwise, the save is said to be *untimed*. In a timed save, the RTI uses the logical time of the save with all time-constrained federates to define when the save is taken. All federates and the RTI define the state they save by the logical time, ensuring consistency across the federation. We will make this more precise shortly.

An untimed save occurs as quickly as possible in wall clock time after it is requested. Its operation is subject to network and processing latencies in the federation. The behavior of a federation save is also defined for a federation that mixes time-constrained and unconstrained federates.

8.4.2   DETAILS OF SAVE

A federation save is initiated when some federate, perhaps a manager of some sort, invokes REQUEST FEDERATION SAVE. The requester must supply a "save label" (a character string in the APIs) that will serve to distinguish this save from others in this federation execution. The save label is typically a date and time or something descriptive like `just_before_lunch_break`. The requester may also specify a logical time. If a save was requested previously with a logical time that has not yet arrived, it is legal for a new save to be requested, in which case the new request supplants the previous. Thus if you'd scheduled the usual five o'clock save, and lightning is threatening at three, you can enter a new request for a nearer time. A federate's view of the save protocol is presented in Figure 8-1.

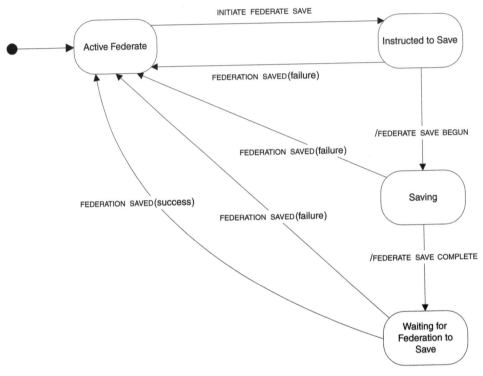

FIGURE 8-1   Federate's View of Federation Save Protocol.

A federate is notified that it should save its state when the RTI invokes INITIATE FEDERATE SAVE † on the federate. In the diagram, the federate moves from the state "Active Federate" to "Instruced to Save." When does the RTI notify federates? That depends on whether the save is timed or untimed, and whether the federate is time-constrained, as summarized in Table 8-1.

Table 8-1   Notification of Federates to Save

	Federate time-constrained	Federate not time-constrainted
Save is timed	When federate can advance to save time	As soon as possible after last time-con-strained federate is notified
Save is untimed	As soon as possible	As soon as possible

If the save is timed, each time-constrained federate is notified when it is safe for the federate to advance to the logical time of the save. The invocation of INITIATE FEDERATE SAVE † on the federate has the force of a time advance grant, in the following ways. The invocation can occur only when the federate is in the Time Advancing state—that is, has some time advance service like TIME ADVANCE REQUEST or NEXT EVENT REQUEST pending—and the request to advance is to a time at or beyond the save time. The service INITIATE FEDERATE SAVE † does not convey the save time, so the federate does not actually know the save time. The federate's state is characterized by its last granted logical time, by having a certain time advance service pending, and having received certain events. The restored state of the federate will be the same: granted most recently to the same logical time, with the same advance request outstanding, and the same events having been received.

If the save is timed and the federate is not time-constrained, it will be notified as soon as possible (in wall clock time) after the last time-constrained federate is notified. If the save is untimed, all federates are notified as soon as possible.

What are a federate's responsibilities when it is notified of a save? First, it desists from normal service invocations on the RTI. In Figure 8-1, the federate moves to the state "Instructed to Save." Then it invokes FEDERATE SAVE BEGUN. The federate moves to the state "Saving."

The federate saves its state in some persistent form, such as disk files, database entries, or persistent objects. If the federation save is to be used after the federation execution has finished and the federation execution has been destroyed, the state must persist beyond the execution. The federate must identify its saved state using the following information:

- The name of the federation execution
- The save label supplied when the RTI invoked INITIATE FEDERATE SAVE †
- The federate designator it received when it joined the federation

This information should be used to form a file path name, a database key, or a persistent object identifier.

After all federates have been notified of the save, the RTI saves its state. Where and how the RTI saves its state depends on the implementation.

When the federate has finished saving its state, it calls the RTI with FEDERATE SAVE COMPLETE, indicating whether it succeeded, and moves to the state "Waiting for Federation to Save." After all federates have invoked FEDERATE SAVE COMPLETE, the RTI calls each federate back with FEDERATION SAVED †. That call includes an indication whether the entire federation save was successful: if it was successful, that means that all federates indicated a successful save.[7] In Figure 8-1 the federate moves back to the "Active Federate" state.

---

7. In the APIs, the FEDERATE SAVE COMPLETE call on the RTI maps typically to two methods on the interface RTIambassador: federateSaveComplete and federateSaveNotComplete. Similarly the RTI-initiated service FEDERATION SAVED † maps to two methods on the interface FederateAmbassador: federationSaved and federationNotSaved.

In any of the states "Instructed to Save," "Saving," or "Waiting for Federation to Save," the federate may receive FEDERATION SAVED † with an indication of failure. This means that the save is being aborted. In any such case, the federate moves to "Active Federate" and resumes normal activity.

The RTI guarantees that it will not invoke any service on a federate between its invocations of INITIATE FEDERATE SAVE † and FEDERATION SAVED †. This is to ensure consistency of the federate's state. Likewise, the federate is prohibited from invoking most services on the RTI during that period, with the obvious exceptions of FEDERATE SAVE BEGUN and FEDERATE SAVE COMPLETE. A federate can resign during the period, but this will cause failure of the overall save.

8.4.3   DETAILS OF RESTORATION

Like a federation save, a federation restore begins when one federate, probably acting as a manager, requests the restore by invoking REQUEST FEDERATION RESTORE, supplying a save label. Only one restore is allowed to be active at a time: if several federates request restores simultaneously, the RTI will grant success to one and failure to the others.

Before it goes any farther, the RTI will check that the restore is feasible. It checks for the following conditions:

- The restore is for a federation execution of the same name as the present federation execution.
- The federation execution has joined to it the same census of federates as before: the same types and numbers of each type (we'll discuss types below).
- The RTI can locate its saved information corresponding to the save label.

The RTI calls back the requesting federate with CONFIRM FEDERATION RESTORATION REQUEST †.[8] If all is well, the callback will indicate success; otherwise, failure. A failed restoration request has no effect on the federation execution.

If the request for restoration succeeds, the RTI immediately invokes FEDERATION RESTORE BEGUN † on each federate. Restoration is depicted from the federate's perspective in the state chart in Figure 8-2. In the figure, the federate moves from the "Active Federate" to the "Prepared to Restore" state. The federate ceases immediately making any calls on the RTI. The federate awaits the indication it should begin restoration.

---

8.   As with other such RTI-initiated services, this is represented in the APIs by two methods on FederateAmbassador: requestFederationRestoreSucceeded and requestFederationRestoreFailed.

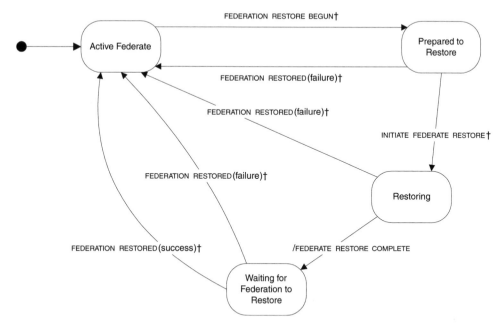

FIGURE 8-2   Federate's View of Federation Restore Protocol.

That indication takes the form of INITIATE FEDERATE RESTORE † invoked on the federate. With it, the RTI supplies the save label and the federate designator that determines the identity the federate is to assume. As we've said, this federate designator is likely to differ from the federate designator the federate has had heretofore. The federate now moves to the "Restoring" state. The federate's job now is to:

• Locate the save information it needs, using the federation execution name, save label, and new federate designator
• Restore its state accordingly

When the federate is finished, it invokes FEDERATE RESTORE COMPLETE, and indicates whether it succeeded. The federate moves into the state "Waiting for Federation to Restore." The federate waits to receive FEDERATION RESTORED † from the RTI.

If the FEDERATION RESTORED † callback indicates that the restoration succeeded, the federate should resume normal activity with its new identity. If the restoration failed, the federate returns to the "Active Federate" state but it probably cannot do anything. The federation execution is in an awkward state and probably requires manual intervention through a manager federate. The restoration might be attempted again after the cause of the failure is resolved; or a different restoration might be attempted; or the federation execution might be brought to an end. The federate can receive FEDERATION RESTORED † (with an indication of failure) in the states

"Prepared to Restore" and "Restoring." In these cases as well the federate returns to the "Active Federate" state, but cannot proceed.

The RTI guarantees that it will invoke no services on a federate (besides INITIATE FEDERATE RESTORE †) between invoking FEDERATION RESTORE BEGUN † and FEDERATION RESTORED †. The federate must not invoke any services on the RTI after it receives FEDERATION RESTORE BEGUN † (except FEDERATE RESTORE COMPLETE), until it receives FEDERATION RESTORED †. The federate may resign during that period; its resignation will cause the restoration to fail.

8.4.4   FEDERATE TYPE

Let's return to the notion of *federate type*. Recall that restoration is possible only if the federation execution has joined to it federates of the same number and type as the prospective restored federation. A federate's type is supplied by the federate when it joins a federation execution. It typically takes the form of a string of characters. The purpose of federate type is to allow federation designers to specify what federates might play the role of each federate in a restored federation execution.

A federate of a given type is considered by the RTI to be equivalent to any other federate of the same type for the purpose of restoring a federation execution. Thus if a federation consisted of, say, some federates of type a and others of type b when the federation execution was saved, the RTI will restore the federation execution so that each presently joined federate of type a will assume the identity of a type a federate in the restored federation, and each type b will assume the role of a restored type b. The meaning of federate type is left to the developers; the RTI interprets the type to mean "this federate can successfully assume the role of any federate of this type." Types generally are distinguished by differing requirements for hardware or software.

8.5   DATA DISTRIBUTION MANAGEMENT (DDM)

Data distribution management, or DDM, is the sixth and final group of HLA services, the other groups being federation management, declaration management, object management, ownership management, and time management. Like the other groups, DDM includes both RTI- and federate-initiated services. The goal of DDM is to afford the federation designer more precise and flexible tools for determining the flow of information between federates than are otherwise available with declaration management. A federation need not use DDM; the examples presented thus far (which haven't mentioned DDM) are complete and correct. DDM is in that sense entirely optional. However, DDM is a powerful mechanism that any federation developer should consider.

DDM is more closely related to some of the service groups than others. It's closely related to declaration and object management services. Discussion of DDM has had to wait for the current chapter because you need to understand declaration and object management services first. However, DDM is independent of logical time. DDM is similar to ownership in its independence from time management.

Our approach to explaining DDM will be to motivate the use of the DDM services in the next section. Then we'll give an overview of the DDM mechanisms. Finally we'll discuss the details of using DDM.

8.5.1   WHY THESE SERVICES?

DDM does much the same thing as declaration management, but with a greater degree of specificity. To appreciate the role of DDM, let's review the purpose of declaration management.

Declaration management accomplishes three things:

- It allows producers of data to declare their intent to produce data, and to know, via advisories, whether the data they propose to produce is of interest to the federation.
- It allows consumers of data to declare their interest in certain kinds of data, limiting the data that the RTI must send them and they must process.
- It allows producers and consumers a certain anonymity: producers need not be aware of the number or identity of the consumers; the consumers need not be aware of the number or identity of the producers. This makes federations easier to extend.

Declarations of interest in declaration management are expressed in terms of *kinds* of data: object class attributes and interaction classes. There is no way to make declarations in finer terms, for example, in terms of specific instances or sent interactions.

DDM accomplishes the same three purposes as declaration management. It allows producers to declare their intent and to know whether their proposed data will be used. It allows consumers to declare their desire for data, thereby limiting the data they receive. And DDM decouples producers and consumers, making them effectively anonymous. However, the declarations supported by DDM are more specific; declarations apply to specific instance attributes and to each sending of an interaction.

DDM operates in addition to declaration management. A federation that uses DDM must also use declaration management. However, DDM is optional: a federation need not use DDM at all.

The HLA is designed generally to apply to a range of simulation problems. We've seen that nothing in the object model template or the specification of the RTI is peculiar to a domain of application. The HLA is as applicable to sushi restaurants as it is to manufacturing simulation or ground warfare. The design of DDM upholds that generality. The services are defined in terms of abstractions that can be applied to many domains of application.

We should note that both declaration management and DDM are designed to allow patterns of production and consumption to vary as a federation evolves. The examples we'll present of the use of DDM highlight the fact that DDM "declarations" can change in the course of a federation execution. Although our use of declaration management in Chapter 4 is static (all publications and subscriptions made at the outset and never changed), that is merely our design choice for that federation. The declaration management services fully support their dynamic use. A federate may change publications or subscriptions at any time in a federation execution.

8.5.2   THE GENERAL IDEA

Recall how publication and subscription operate in the declaration management services. For interaction classes, subscribers indicate their interests by subscribing to interaction classes. When a federate sends an interaction, the interaction has a class associated with it. The RTI decides what federates receive the interaction by matching interaction classes; a federate that has subscribed to interactions of the sent class (or a superclass) will receive the interaction. Thus declaration management functions by:

- Associating a piece of information with subscribers (the class they subscribe)
- Associating a piece of information with published data (the class of a sent interaction)
- Matching the subscribers' and the data's information

DDM refines this model by adding new information to subscriptions and published data, and by extending the way that data and subscribers are matched. The new information is called a region. Regions are associated with interaction classes and instance attributes.

An example will help to explain this. Suppose you're building a simulation of civil air traffic control in the continental United States. Your simulation will contain at any given time hundreds of civil and military aircraft. These aircraft communicate via radio with air traffic controllers on the ground. Suppose your simulation models the behavior of these radios, both transmitters and receivers. A transmission by an aircraft might be modeled as an HLA interaction sent by a federate modeling aircraft transmitters and received (potentially) by all the federates modeling receivers. This approach to modeling requires each receiver model to determine whether it actually receives the transmission, and the degree of degradation of the transmission.

Clearly not all receivers need to hear all transmissions; with the transmitters and receivers in current use, transmissions are not received more than a few hundred miles away. And receivers operate on a given radio frequency, receiving transmissions only on their set frequency. It would be helpful, the federation designer thinks, if the RTI could distinguish transmission interactions so that they are received only by federates whose receivers are within a reasonable distance and are tuned to the frequency of the transmission.

Let's define regions and their related notions of dimensions and routing spaces. In HLA terms, a *dimension* is a portion of a coordinate axis defined and named (in the FOM) by the federation developer. The FOM may define many dimensions; each dimension is independent of the others. A *routing space* is a sequence (an ordered list) of dimensions defined and named in the FOM. A *region* is a portion of a routing space defined by taking parts of each dimension in the routing space. Because the names for dimensions and routing spaces are defined in the FOM, they appear in the FED, in a fashion we'll discuss shortly.

For the air traffic control example, we'll begin by discriminating data by geography, and we'll consider discrimination by frequency later. We define dimensions called Latitude and Longitude. We define a single routing space called TransmissionSpace that contains dimensions Latitude and Longitude. We'll say that the FOM for the air traffic control example contains an interaction class called Transmission. The FED defines an ordering and transportation type for class Transmission, as it does for all interaction classes. To use DDM with this class, we must also declare in the FED that the class is *bound* to the routing space TransmissionSpace. This means that regions of TransmissionSpace can be associated with the interaction class Transmission to control its distribution.

The DDM services use region information in a way that is analogous to the use of class information in declaration management. At a high level, DDM works as follows with our example. A federate modeling one or more receivers subscribes to the interaction class Transmission, specifying a region of the routing space TransmissionSpace. That region corresponds to an area in Latitude and Longitude that includes the area of coverage of all the receivers the federate is modeling, as in Figure 8-3.

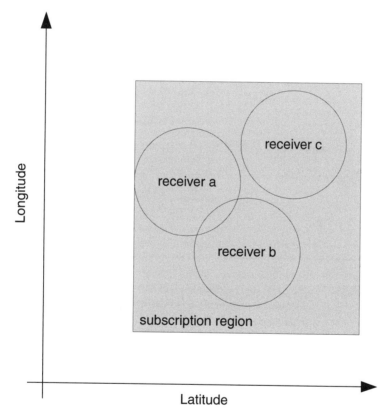

FIGURE 8-3   Simple Subscription Region.

Now consider some federate that models a transmitter. When the federate sends an interaction of class Transmission, it associates with it another region of TransmissionSpace. That region corresponds to an area in Latitude and Longitude that includes the area of coverage of the transmitter. When the interaction is sent, the RTI checks the region associated with the sent interaction against the region associated with the Transmission class for each subscribing federate. If, for a given federate, the sending and subscription regions overlap, that federate receives the interaction. If the regions do not overlap, the federate does not receive the interaction. This is illustrated in Figure 8-4. Because the region associated with the sent interaction overlaps with the subscription region for federate 1, federate 1 will receive the interaction. Because there is no overlap with the subscription region for federate 2, federate 2 will not receive the interaction.

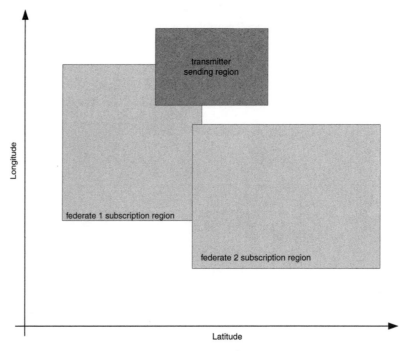

FIGURE 8-4   Subscription and Sending Regions.

The region associated with sending a Transmission interaction can change as the aircraft carrying the modeled transmitter moves. The region can vary from one send to the next. The federate designer has control over how often the region changes.

Note that the discrimination provided DDM is inexact: receivers must still check precisely whether they receive a transmission. The inexactness is due to the approximate nature of the subscription region, and the fact that subscriptions are defined for an entire federate, rather than for individual modeled receivers. The subscription region can be made more precise (at the cost of greater computation) by means we'll discuss later.

Note also that declaration management is still operating: the receiving federates must subscribe to the Transmission interaction class (or a superclass), and each sending federate must publish the interaction class before sending it. DDM functions as a refinement of declaration management rather than as a replacement.

Note finally that DDM decouples the senders and receivers appropriately. A design goal of the HLA is that each federate need not be aware of other federates except as the requirements of modeling dictate. This is critical if federates are to be usable in a variety of federations. The DDM matching criterion of overlapping regions achieves this separation. Transmitters define the size of the region associated with sending an interaction according to the strength of the transmitter they model, without regard to potential receivers. Likewise, receivers define the size of their subscription regions according to their sensitivity, without regard to transmitters.

DDM applies as well to updating object instance attributes. Each class attribute listed in the FOM may be bound to a routing space. (Note that class attributes are bound, not object classes.) A federate subscribing to one or more class attributes may associate a region with each subscribed attribute. The owner of an instance attribute (attribute of a specific instance of an object class) may associate a region with updates of that instance attribute; such updates are reflected only by federates that have previously subscribed to the corresponding class attribute with a region that overlaps the updating region. The region associated with updating an instance attribute can vary from instance to instance of the same class, and can vary from one update to the next.

The example thus far uses a routing space that corresponds to a physical area. While such an example is intuitive, it may be misleading if left by itself. Dimensions of routing spaces in DDM need not correspond to physical spaces: in many useful applications of DDM, dimensions may be quite abstract. To reinforce this point, let's extend the example. Radio receivers typically only hear transmissions on the frequency they are tuned to, and we can exploit that fact to lessen the number of transmissions that must be sent around the federation and received. To enlist the help of DDM, we'll add another dimension, Frequency, to the routing space TransmissionSpace. We divide this dimension into discrete (non-overlapping) segments that correspond to the frequencies in use. When a Transmission interaction is sent, we associate with the sending of the interaction a region of TransmissionSpace. The region covers the transmitter's broadcast area in the dimensions of Latitude and Longitude as before. The region corresponds to the transmitter's frequency in the Frequency dimension. The goal now is that a federate modeling a receiver will receive only interactions on the frequency of the receiver. The federate's subscription region will extend in Latitude and Longitude as before, and will extend in the Frequency dimension corresponding to the receiver's frequency. Now the subscribing federate will receive Transmission interactions only if the sending region overlaps the subscription region in Latitude and Longitude, and coincides in Frequency. The point here is to demonstrate discrimination in a combination of geographic (spatial) and abstract concerns.

8.5.3 DETAILS OF THE SERVICES

Before plunging into service calls, we must review the FED entries needed to support DDM. The FED for a federation must name the dimensions and routing spaces to be used. And it must specify the binding of class attributes and interaction classes to routing spaces. The definitions of dimensions and routing spaces appear in the FED before the object classes. We show below a partial FED file that contains the entries needed for our transmitter-receiver example.

```
;; ddm_example.fed
;; Example of DDM entries
(FED
  (Federation DDM_Example)
  (FEDversion v1.3)
  (spaces
    (space TransmissionSpace    ;; names are case-insensitive
      (dimension Latitude)      ;; order of appearance is significant
      (dimension Longitude)
      (dimension Frequency)
    )
    ;; another space could go here
  )
  (objects
    . . . .
  )
  (interactions
    (class interactionRoot reliable receive
      (class RTIprivate reliable receive)
      (class Manager

        . . .

      )
      (class Transmission best_effort timestamp TransmissionSpace
        (parameter contents)
      )
    )
  )
)
```

This FED file defines one routing space called TransmissionSpace.[9] The space defines three dimensions. The order of their appearance is significant, as the APIs refer to a specific dimension by its index. Notice that the interaction class Transmission is bound to a space by virtue of the routing space name appearing in its declaration after the ordering and transportation types.

You'll recall that the declaration management and object management services refer interaction classes, object classes, attributes, and parameters by handles. A federate discovers the handles by invoking support services like GET OBJECT CLASS HANDLE, supplying the class name that appears in the FED. These things are true of dimensions and routing spaces. In the following discussion, we'll assume the federate will retrieve the handles it needs through the appropriate support services.

9. Names of routing spaces and dimensions, like other FED-defined names, are case-insensitive. Federation designers are prohibited from declaring dimension or routing space names that begin with "HLA."

The first step in using any DDM service is to create a region, which a federate does by invoking CREATE REGION. In the C++ and Java APIs, what is returned from this service is a reference to an instance of the programming-language class Region. Before the federate can use its newly acquired Region, it must fill in its definition.

And this brings us face-to-face with a topic we've avoided to this point, namely: How are dimensions actually represented? We've seen examples of dimensions defined conceptually on a continuous parameter (latitude and longitude), and on a discrete set (frequency, considered as a channel). The HLA must be as applicable to these dimensions as to Dalton distances in genomics or enumerated types of sushi. There cannot be anything in an RTI implementation that rests on assumptions about the nature of routing space dimensions.

This is really the same problem as that of representations for attribute and parameter values. The HLA approach to the dimension problem is the same as for the others: dimensions are represented abstractly in the RTI, and the mapping of federate-specific values to and from their abstract representation is left to the HLA component that knows how to perform the mapping, that is, the federates. In the case of attribute values, the abstract representation is an uninterpreted sequence of octets; in the case of dimensions, the representation is a range of integers $\{i = MIN, MIN + 1,..., MAX\}$, where MIN and MAX are properties of a particular RTI implementation. Thus, for a given RTI implementation, each declared dimension has the same representation. The federation designers must decide what dimensions will be declared, and how the definition of a region in simulation-specific terms will map to the RTI representation in each dimension.

The definition of a region is built up as follows. Given a dimension, a *range* of a dimension is a subset of the dimension characterized by a lower and upper bound. For a range with upper bound u and lower bound l, $l < u$, $MIN \leq l$, $u \leq MAX$, the range is the integers $\{i = l,..., u - 1\}$. Note that the lower bound is a member of the range but the upper bound is not. An *extent* for a routing space is a sequence of ranges, one for each dimension in the space, in the order of declaration of the dimensions in the space. An extent defines a rectangular volume inside the routing space. A region consists of a set of one or more extents.

Federation designers must decide how their conceptual dimensions map to the RTI's representations. To return to our example, suppose we are using an RTI whose dimensions are defined on the integers in $[0, 2^{31}]$. The continental United States spans about latitude 25N to 48N, and longitude 67W to 125W. We will map decimal degrees of latitude to the range [25000000, 48000000] in the Latitude dimension, and decimal degrees of longitude to [67000000, 125000000] in the Longitude dimension. Thus a region intended to cover the city of Denver, Colorado (roughly latitude 39.6N to 39.8N, longitude 104.8W to 105.3W) is represented by the range [39600000, 39800000) in the Latitude dimension and [104800000, 105300000) in the Longitude dimension. The frequencies used in air-to-ground radios for air traffic control in the United States range roughly from 118 MHz to 137 MHz, in increments of 0.05 MHz. In our design, frequencies are intended to be discrete. Each frequency is represented by a point in the Frequency dimension, computed by multiplying the frequency in megahertz by a million. Thus the frequency of the north approach controller for Denver International Airport, 119.3 MHz, will be represented as the range [119300000, 119300001). (Recall that the upper bound of the range is not included.)

Before a region can be used to affect transmission of data, it must be created and filled out. A federate creates a region by invoking CREATE REGION, specifying the routing space it inhabits. As we said before, in the C++ and Java APIs, the service returns a reference to an instance of the programming-language class Region. The federate invokes methods on the Region instance to set its extents. In our example, we supply an extent consisting of three ranges, one for each of the dimensions. After a region is set up initially (or modified later), the RTI must be informed of the changes. The service MODIFY REGION in the interface specification is represented in the C++ and Java APIs by the interface method notifyOfRegionModification(), which carries the Region reference as a parameter.

In the Java API, this sequence of steps might look as follows:

```
int spaceHandle = rti.getRoutingSpaceHandle("TransmissionSpace");
int latitudeDimHandle =
  rti.getDimensionHandle("Latitude", spaceHandle);
int longitudeDimHandle =
  rti.getDimensionHandle("Longitude", spaceHandle);
int frequencyDimHandle =
  rti.getDimensionHandle("Frequency", spaceHandle);
hla.rti.Region currentRegion =
  rti.createRegion(spaceHandle, 1); //1 extent
//extent has index 0
currentRegion.setRangeLowerBound(0, latitudeDimHandle, 39600000L);
currentRegion.setRangeUpperBound(0, latitudeDimHandle, 39800000L);
currentRegion.setRangeLowerBound(0, longitudeDimHandle, 104800000L);
currentRegion.setRangeUpperBound(0, longitudeDimHandle, 105300000L);
currentRegion.setRangeLowerBound(0, frequencyDimHandle, 119300000L);
currentRegion.setRangeUpperBound(0, frequencyDimHandle, 119300001L);
rti.notifyOfRegionModification(currentRegion);
```

Thus far we've spoken of regions that consisted of a single rectangular subspace of a routing space, a single extent. In fact, a region can contain multiple extents, and thus can have the shape of the union of rectangular volumes. This is illustrated in Figure 8-5. In this figure, a subscription region (the gray area) is composed of three extents, each corresponding to one receiver modeled by the federate.

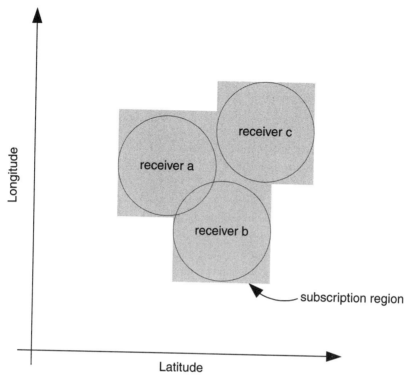

FIGURE 8-5   Subscription Region of Several Extents.

Once a region has been created and filled out, and the RTI has been notified that it has been modified, the federate can use it. A federate modeling radio receivers in our example will invoke SUBSCRIBE INTERACTION CLASS WITH REGION, supplying the handle of the class Transmission and a reference to the region. This call establishes a subscription in the same way SUBSCRIBE INTERACTION CLASS does, except that the subscribing federate receives only those interactions sent with regions that overlap its subscription region. A federate that invokes SUBSCRIBE INTERACTION CLASS WITH REGION for an interaction class does not invoke SUBSCRIBE INTERACTION CLASS first; the former service substitutes for the latter.

A federate modeling radio transmitters publishes the Transmission class as before. The Federate then creates and fills out a region corresponding to the area of coverage of its transmitters. When the federate wishes to send an interaction with that region, it invokes SEND INTERACTION WITH REGION, supplying the region and the data associated with the declaration management SEND INTERACTION service (interaction class, parameters, user-supplied tag, and perhaps a logical time). The effect is as if the federate had invoked SEND INTERACTION, except that the only federates that will receive the interaction are those that subscribed with an overlapping region. The federate is free to modify the associated region before each invocation of SEND

INTERACTION WITH REGION. It does this by modifying its local programming-language represen-tation of the region and calling the appropriate notifyOfRegionModification(). However, changes in sending or subscription regions may require significant computation from the RTI (there may be a great deal of matching to do). Deciding the best strategy for updating regions will require knowledge of the problem being simulated and the performance characteristics of the RTI implementation.

Notice that, as defined in our example, there is no necessary connection between the meaning of a Transmission and the regions supplied for sending. The semantic connection—for instance, the fact that the modeled transmitter is being carried by an aircraft with a current loca-tion—is entirely the federate's responsibility. On the other hand, the abstractness of the DDM mechanism invites clever application. If you wish, you may think of the RTI as maintaining a matrix for each declared routing space. The matrix shows, for each pair of regions defined in that space in the federation execution, whether the pair overlaps.

Suppose a transmitter federate sends a Transmission interaction into a region, and there is a federate that has subscribed the Transmission interaction class without any region, that is, using the SUBSCRIBE INTERACTION CLASS service from declaration management. That federate will receive the interaction and any other Transmission interactions sent into any region. From the standpoint of DDM, a subscription using SUBSCRIBE INTERACTION CLASS is considered to be a subscription to a *default region* of the routing space to which the interaction is bound. That default region by definition encompasses the entire routing space.

The analogous thing is true when the interaction is sent. If the interaction is sent with SEND INTERACTION, using no region, it is considered to have been sent into the default region. All sub-scribers to the interaction class will receive the interaction regardless of their subscription region.

As you read through the list of services in DDM you'll find that they contain counterparts for many of the services in Declaration and Object Management. Where there is a DDM coun-terpart, the Declaration or Object Management version may be considered to act like the DDM version with the default region.

Thus far we've discussed only DDM services for interactions. The services for attribute updates are similar but not identical. DDM applies to updates of individual attributes, rather than object classes. In this respect it is analogous to the Declaration and Object Management services for attributes.

To use DDM with an instance attribute, its class attribute must be bound to a routing space in the FED, just as an interaction class is. The class attribute's FED declaration will include a routing space after its transportation and ordering types. Attributes of an object class may be bound to the same, or different, routing spaces. They may use the same spaces as interaction classes. Not all attributes of a class need be bound to a routing space.

A federate wishing to reflect attribute value updates can subscribe with a region using SUBSCRIBE OBJECT CLASS ATTRIBUTES WITH REGION. This service is analogous to SUBSCRIBE OBJECT CLASS ATTRIBUTES and substitutes for it. But the effect of the subscription for the named attributes is limited to updates made into an overlapping region. The declaration management rules still hold regarding passive and active subscriptions. The declaration management rules also hold regarding the effect of a subscription to one class on an update to an instance of a sub-class.

A federate wishing to update instance attribute values can do so into a region. However, there is no counterpart of UPDATE ATTRIBUTE VALUES specific to DDM. A federate wishing to use DDM precedes the call to UPDATE ATTRIBUTE VALUES with an invocation of ASSOCIATE REGION FOR UPDATES, specifying an object instance, a region, and a set of attributes. That association is then in force for all updates of those instance attributes until the association is changed, by another invocation of ASSOCIATE REGION FOR UPDATES, or an invocation of UNAS-SOCIATE REGION FOR UPDATES.

The services SUBSCRIBE OBJECT CLASS ATTRIBUTES WITH REGION, SUBSCRIBE INTERAC-TION CLASS WITH REGION and ASSOCIATE REGION FOR UPDATES have an additional feature not found in their declaration management counterparts. They each allow the accumulation of a group of regions in the subscription. See the interface specification for details.

Remember that when a federate registers a new instance of an object class, all federates subscribed to attributes of the class discover the object. There is a way to allow DDM to affect the discovery of new instances. Suppose it is intended that updates of the new instance attributes are to be controlled by DDM; there are federates that wish to reflect new values only where their subscription region overlaps the (eventual) update region. In that case, the reflecting federates probably only wish to discover those instances for which they will receive updates. This can be accomplished if the registering federate uses REGISTER OBJECT INSTANCE WITH REGION, the counterpart of REGISTER OBJECT INSTANCE. Use of REGISTER OBJECT INSTANCE WITH REGION is equivalent to REGISTER OBJECT INSTANCE followed by ASSOCIATE REGION FOR UPDATES, except that this service is atomic and therefore affects discovery of the new instance. The service takes as parameters a set of pairs of attributes and regions they are to be associated with. Not all attributes being published by the registering federate must be specified; omitted attributes are associated with the default region of the routing space to which they are bound.

There is a final DDM service to mention. It is the equivalent of REQUEST ATTRIBUTE VALUE UPDATE when invoked with an object class rather than an instance. That declaration man-agement service is provided for a federate to solicit updates of a set of attributes for all instances of the specified class. In response to REQUEST ATTRIBUTE VALUE UPDATE, the RTI will stimulate the owner of each of the instance attributes of each registered instance of the class. This opera-tion can be affected by DDM by invoking REQUEST ATTRIBUTE VALUE UPDATE WITH REGION. Rather than stimulating updates for all instance of the class, this service causes the RTI to stimu-late updates only for some instances. With this service the federate supplies a region as well as an object class and set of attributes. The RTI will solicit an update from only those federates that own one of the specified attributes of an instance of the class, and that have a region associated for update with that instance attribute that overlaps the specified region.

8.5.4   INTERPRETING SILENCE

DDM can create a circumstance for a federate, possibly awkward, that would not exist without it. A federate has discovered an instance and has been reflecting updates of some of its attributes. After a time it ceases to receive any more reflections. Is the silence because the owners of the attributes are not updating them, or is it because the updating and subscription regions no longer overlap? If the receiving federate has just modified its subscription region, it might suspect that the change has ended the reflections. But the owner may have changed its updating region. The subscribing federate cannot tell from the mere absence of reflections which is the case.

There are several services designed to help with this. They constitute two mechanisms:

- A way to elicit advice from the RTI about the state of production of data
- A way the RTI can help a federate manage its local store of objects

Let's consider advice from the RTI first. The HLA has a phrase for the conditions under which a subscriber will see updates of an instance attribute; the attribute is said to be in scope. Specifically, an instance attribute is *in scope* for a subscribing federate if all the following are true:

- Some federate owns the instance attribute (and thus must have published the corresponding class attribute).
- The instance is known to the subscribing federate (and thus the subscriber must have subscribed to the corresponding class attribute).
- If either the owner or the subscriber is using regions, the regions overlap.

If an instance attribute is not in scope, it is *out of scope*. If an instance attribute is in scope, updates may flow to a subscriber. If an attribute is out of scope, updates will certainly not arrive.

The HLA defines services ATTRIBUTES IN SCOPE † and ATTRIBUTES OUT OF SCOPE †. If requested, the RTI will invoke these on a federate that is subscribing to some class attributes. ATTRIBUTES OUT OF SCOPE † carries an object identifier and a set of attributes. It tells the federate that those instance attributes have become out of scope. The subscribing federate then knows that the ensuing paucity of reflected values for those instance attributes is due to one of two causes:

- Either the subscribing federate or owning federate(s) has modified or substituted regions so that they no longer overlap. The owner(s) may continue to produce updates, but the subscriber will not get the reflections.
- The owning federate(s) has lost ownership of the attributes, by unpublishing the corresponding class attributes, or by unconditionally divesting themselves of the instance attributes. In either case, the former owner(s) can no longer update the attributes.

When the conditions are established again for the subscriber to reflect updates, because the regions once again overlap or another federate owns the attribute, the RTI will invoke ATTRIBUTES IN SCOPE † on the subscriber.

Federates do not receive ATTRIBUTES IN SCOPE † and ATTRIBUTES OUT OF SCOPE † by default. Federates must invoke the Support service ENABLE ATTRIBUTE SCOPE ADVISORY SWITCH to receive them. This contrasts with class relevance advisories (START REGISTRATION FOR OBJECT CLASS † and STOP REGISTRATION FOR OBJECT CLASS †), which are enabled by default.

You may notice that ATTRIBUTES IN SCOPE † and ATTRIBUTES OUT OF SCOPE † are not listed among the DDM services, but among the object management services. This is a hint that these services are effective without DDM. You can see from the definition of "in scope" that both declaration management conditions (publications, subscriptions) and DDM conditions are involved. A subscribing federate can use the scope advisories either with declaration management alone or with declaration management and DDM. The subscribing federate then becomes aware of instance attributes passing from being owned to being unowned and back.

8.5.5   MANAGING INSTANCES IN THE PRESENCE OF DDM

Let's discuss a federate's management of instances in the presence of DDM. Every federate that subscribes to object attributes maintains in some form its private representation of objects it discovers from the RTI. A subscribing federate typically keeps a collection of known instances, some of whose attributes are owned by other federates. The federate will add an instance to its collection upon receipt of DISCOVER OBJECT INSTANCE † for the instance and will remove it when it receives REMOVE OBJECT INSTANCE †. Meanwhile the federate will maintain a current set of values for the subscribed attributes as it receives REFLECT ATTRIBUTE VALUES † callbacks. When DDM is in use, the federate can use the scope advisories to tell when it is possible that it will reflect new values for attributes.

If a subscribing federate has been advised that all the subscribed attributes of a given reflected instance are out of scope, the instance might as well not exist as far as that federate is concerned. It is, perhaps literally, "off the radar scope." It occurred to the designers of the HLA that it would be convenient if such a case could be treated as if the instance actually went out of existence; specifically, that the RTI would invoke DISCOVER OBJECT INSTANCE † for the instance when at least one of the subscribed attributes came back in scope. That way the federate could treat in the same way initial discovery of an instance and the return of attributes to being in scope. There is a federate-initiated service, LOCAL OBJECT DELETE INSTANCE, to cause this behavior.

A subscribing federate typically invokes LOCAL OBJECT DELETE INSTANCE, supplying an instance handle, when all attributes for an instance have gone out of scope. When the federate invokes LOCAL OBJECT DELETE INSTANCE, the RTI will behave as if it had never informed the federate of the existence of the instance. Later, when at least one of the subscribed attributes comes back in scope, the RTI will call back with DISCOVER OBJECT INSTANCE †, and the federate can use that as its trigger to reinstate the instance in its collection. The subscribing federate need not own the attribute privilegeToDeleteObject of the instance to invoke LOCAL OBJECT DELETE INSTANCE; in fact the RTI will raise an exception if the federate owns any attributes of the instance. And we should mention that one federate invoking LOCAL OBJECT DELETE INSTANCE doesn't affect any other federate.

What happens if a federate invokes LOCAL OBJECT DELETE INSTANCE for an instance some of whose attributes are in scope? The RTI will call back immediately with DISCOVER OBJECT INSTANCE †.

As with the scope advisories, LOCAL OBJECT DELETE INSTANCE is a declaration management service, not a DDM service. Its behavior is defined even if DDM is not in use, just as for the scope advisories. Thus if DDM is not in use in a federation, and a subscribing federate enables scope advisories, the federate will be told attributes have gone out of scope if their owner ceases publishing them or otherwise gives up ownership. The subscriber can invoke LOCAL OBJECT DELETE INSTANCE; it will discover the object when some other federate acquires ownership of one of the attributes.

8.6   MORE ON HOW TO USE THE MOM

In this section we take a tour of the facilities offered by the management object model (MOM). You'll recall that we introduced the MOM as part of the lifecycle protocol for federations. We used it as a way for a manager federate to perceive other federates joining and resigning. The goal of this section is to introduce the kinds of things one can do with the MOM, rather than to explore all its details.

The MOM is a general facility for managing HLA federations, furnishing information about the federation and the means to affect its state. The MOM is present in every federation execution. Its information and abilities are generic to HLA federations and their management; the MOM contains nothing specific to a given simulation.

By "the MOM" we really mean two things:

- The "MOM proper," an object model in the HLA sense
- The software that animates it

Unfortunately, both things are called "the MOM" in discussions of the HLA and we will abide by that usage. However, we will make it clear, if it isn't from context, which is meant.

The MOM proper is an object model in the HLA sense: it contains object and interaction classes, attributes, and parameters. The MOM proper itself consists of two parts:

- A standard part, which is defined by the HLA Interface Specification
- User extensions

The standard part of the MOM is defined by the HLA Interface Specification, and must be part of every FOM. A FED that does not contain at least the standard MOM is invalid, and should elicit an exception from an RTI. The standard part of the MOM defines object and interaction classes. The standard MOM object classes are depicted in Figure 8-6. The standard MOM interaction classes are depicted in Figure 8-7.

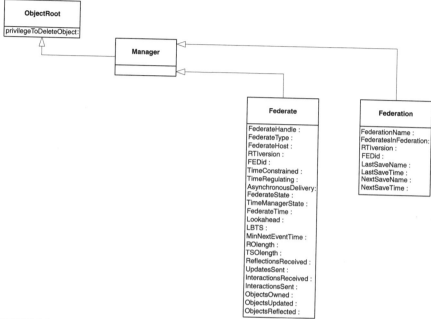

FIGURE 8-6 MOM Object Classes.

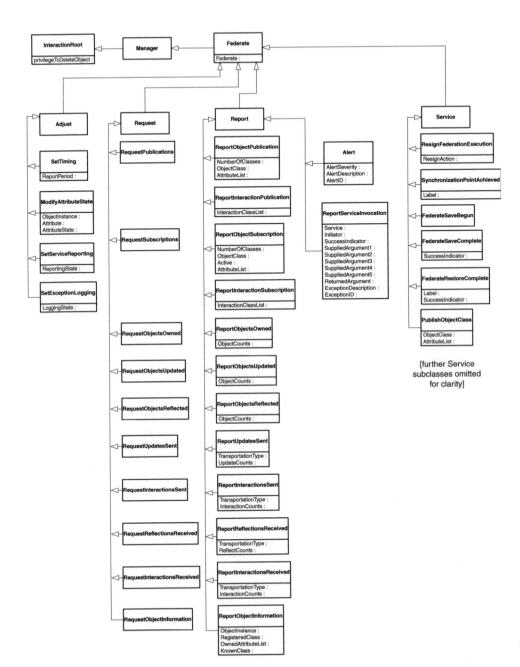

FIGURE 8-7   MOM Interaction Classes.

The standard object classes must appear in a FED as subclasses of ObjectRoot. The topmost object class of the standard MOM is ObjectRoot.Manager. The interaction classes of the standard MOM must appear as subclasses of InteractionRoot. The topmost interaction class of the standard MOM is InteractionRoot.Manager. The order of the Manager classes relative to other subclasses of ObjectRoot and InteractionRoot, respectively, is immaterial.

In addition to the standard MOM, the MOM of a given federation may contain user extensions designed by the federation developer. These extensions consist either of:

- Object or interaction classes added as subclasses to ObjectRoot.Manager or Interaction-Root.Manager; or
- Attributes or parameters added to standard MOM classes.

You have seen a user extension to the standard MOM: the interaction SimulationEnds in the Extended Example.

For the MOM to be useful, there must be software that animates it, registers instances of MOM object classes, updates the values of attributes, responds to sent MOM interactions, and sends its own interactions. Responsibility for animating the MOM differs for the two parts of the MOM proper:

- The RTI is responsible for animating the standard MOM. Every implementation of the RTI must, according to the interface specification, animate all the standard MOM.
- Some federate or federates of a federation must animate any user extensions to the MOM.

Owing to the design of the HLA, federates that merely use the MOM (standard or extensions) needn't worry about where the software resides that animates the MOM; they merely interact with it through its object model as they would with any other part of the FOM. In the sample implementation, the Manager federate subscribes to ObjectRoot.Manager.Federate without concern for the source of instances of the class. Likewise, the Manager federate subscribes to the interaction class SimulationEnds (a user extension) without concern for the source of those interactions. However, the federation designers must ensure that some federate is responsible for publishing and then sending the interaction, since it is a user extension.

8.6.1   STAY CURRENT ON THE STATE OF FEDERATES AND THE FEDERATION

The most obvious thing you can do with the MOM is to acquire and keep current information on the state of the federation and individual federates. To facilitate this, the MOM represents the federation and federates as instances of HLA object classes with attributes that a federate can subscribe to in the same way as with any other object classes in the FOM. The RTI registers a single instance of Manager.Federation when the federation execution is created. If a federate subscribes to one or more of the attributes of the class, it will discover the instance. The interested federate will need to solicit updates of attributes by invoking REQUEST ATTRIBUTE VALUE UPDATE.

The RTI also registers an instance of Manager.Federate when each federate joins, and deletes the instance when the federate resigns. Thus an interested federate can subscribe to one or more of the Manager.Federate attributes, and will discover a fresh instance for each federate that joins (including itself), and will be told to remove an instance when the corresponding federate resigns. As we said in the lifecycle discussion, this is the canonical means of knowing what federates are in a federation. Because the RTI updates the attributes of a new instance of Manager.Federate only once (by default), and the update probably occurs before the interested user federate has joined, the interested federate must solicit a fresh update by invoking REQUEST ATTRIBUTE VALUE UPDATE. Alternatively, the RTI can be requested to produce periodic updates by a mechanism we'll discuss in the next section.

It's important to remember that, as far as the interested federate is concerned, these MOM objects are like any other HLA object instances. All the services that apply to other instances behave identically for these. However there are rules for the RTI's animation of the standard MOM. The rules for the standard MOM state that the RTI will not relinquish ownership of any standard MOM attributes, so a federate will be frustrated in any attempt to acquire ownership. When a federate publishes a MOM interaction class, it will immediately receive a callback of TURN INTERACTIONS ON † for the class (assuming the federate has enabled the advisory), since the RTI effectively subscribes to all the MOM interaction classes it must receive.

8.6.2   CONTROL MOM'S REPORTING

The other uses of the MOM, covered in this and the succeeding sections, all operate by sending and receiving interactions.

We mentioned before that MOM instance attributes are not updated by default. However, the RTI updates the attributes of Manager.Federate periodically if instructed to do so. The instruction comes in the form of an interaction of class InteractionRoot.Manager.Federate.Adjust.SetTiming, hereinafter "SetTiming." If some federate sends an interaction of the class SetTiming, the RTI will begin to produce periodic updates of the attributes of Manager.Federate. The SetTiming interaction must be sent with its parameter ReportPeriod and with the parameter Federate that SetTiming inherits. The value of the Federate parameter determines which Manager.Federate instance the instruction applies to. If you want periodic updates of more than one instance of Manager.Federate, you must send multiple interactions. It doesn't matter what federate sends the interaction. And, of course, the updates produced by the RTI will be reflected by all federates that are subscribed to any of the attributes. Periodic updates can be turned off for a given federate by setting a ReportPeriod of zero.

8.6.3   OTHER REQUESTS FOR INFORMATION

A variety of other information may be obtained about other federates through the MOM, beyond what is available from the Manager.Federate instances. The other information is obtained by sending one of the several subclasses of interaction class Manager.Federate.Request. Each subclass elicits a certain kind of information, which is returned in an interaction of a subclass of

Manager.Federate.Report. Each Request class has a corresponding Report class. An inquiring federate uses these classes according to this pattern:

1. The inquiring federate publishes the desired Request class.
2. The inquiring federate subscribes to the corresponding Report class.
3. The inquiring federate sends the interaction of the desired class, specifying in the Federate parameter which federate the inquiry applies to, and other information as necessary.
4. The RTI intercepts the sent interaction, and sends the corresponding Report interaction with the desired information. (The federate that is the subject of the inquiry never receives the Request interaction.)
5. The inquiring federate receives the Report interaction.

The Report interaction contains a Federate parameter that states what federate the information applies to. This is important, because any federate that is subscribed to a particular Report class will receive all interactions of the class (as it should), regardless of what federate sent the request.

8.6.4   ASK MOM TO CLEAN UP MESSES

Sometimes federates and their operators don't do what's expected and they cause problems for the rest of the federation. For instance, a federate might cease advancing time because of a software failure. If the federate is time-constrained, the rest of the federation cannot advance. It might be the case that the federation could proceed usefully without the erring federate, if the RTI could be persuaded either to treat the erring federate as resigned or as non-time-constrained. The MOM offers a comprehensive set of facilities for intervention in a federation for situations of the sort we've described. In keeping with the HLA approach of "mechanism not policy," the MOM offers facilities for intervention but does not dictate their use.

There are 32 subclasses of the interaction class Manager.Federate.Service. The subclasses include, for instance, the interactions ResignFederationExecution, EnableTimeConstrained, and TimeAdvanceRequest. These interactions correspond to 32 selected RTI- and federate-initiated services. These interactions invoke the corresponding service on behalf of another service, in the following sense. They are acted upon by the RTI. For those interactions corresponding to a federate-initiated service, the RTI responds as if the named federate had invoked the service. For those interactions corresponding to RTI-initiated services, the RTI will invoke the corresponding service on the named federate. As with all other service invocations, an exception generated causes a corresponding Alert interaction to be sent.

The HLA Interface Specification lists all the Service interaction classes, together with their parameters. You can see that the Service interactions constitute a powerful toolkit for repairing a damaged federation.

Another such facility is represented by interaction subclass ModifyAttributeState of Manager.Federate.Adjust. A manager federate can send this interaction to change the ownership of an instance attribute from owned to unowned or the reverse. In any distributed system that keeps multiple copies of the same information (ownership of instance attributes in this case), it is possible for the copies to diverge. This facility is designed to repair such divergences.

We should emphasize that the facilities described in this section are not for the casual user! Their effective use requires thorough knowledge both of the RTI and of the federates involved. They are provided for experts to salvage a federation from difficulties caused by hardware or software failure. Good federation design does not depend upon routine use of these facilities.

8.6.5   GET THE BLOW-BY-BLOW FOR DEBUGGING

The MOM offers tools for monitoring a federation's activity. Among them are:

- A log file of exceptions thrown by the RTI
- A means of tracing all the service calls made on or by the RTI
- An Alert interaction sent each time an exception is raised

The interaction class Manager.Federate.Adjust.SetExceptionLogging can be sent to turn on or off the logging of exceptions. The file to contain the log is determined by the RTI implementation. Usually its location and name are influenced by RID parameters. The federate parameter indicates which federate's exceptions should be logged.

The RTI can be made to report, via an interaction, each service that is invoked on the RTI by a given federate, or invoked by the RTI on the federate. The interaction class Manager.Federate.Adjust.SetServiceReporting enables or disables the sending of these reporting interactions. The Federate parameter determines the federate for which services are reported. An interaction of the class Manager.Federate.Report.ReportServiceInvocation is sent for each service invocation. These interactions carry the parameters supplied for the service; the value returned, if any; and the exception raised, if any.

We mention finally the interaction class Manager.Federate.Report.Alert. The RTI sends this interaction every time it throws an exception. A federate wishing to receive these interactions need only subscribe to the interaction class. The RTI may also send this interaction for alerts of lesser severity; the nature of these depends on the RTI implementation.

8.6.6   EXTEND THE MOM FOR YOUR OWN PURPOSES

When we extended the restaurant federation, we showed that an existing FOM could be extended for new purposes. The same is true of the MOM. Federation designers are free to extend the MOM in much the same way they can extend any existing FOM.

But recall that we said the MOM is really two things: the "MOM proper" and the animating software. You can extend the "MOM proper" in both ways we mentioned earlier for extending a FOM: by adding subclasses of object or interaction classes, and by adding new attributes or parameters to existing classes. However, you must implement the animation behind your extensions. If you add a new attribute to a MOM object class, the RTI cannot furnish values for it. You are now modeling the MOM instance cooperatively. (You're cooperating with the RTI.)

One of your federates must notice the registration of an instance of the class, acquire ownership of your new attribute, and update its value. You're generally in the same position as you'd be if you were extending a federation and leaving the existing federates untouched; the RTI's behavior will not change, and your code must cooperate with the RTI.

References and Accompanying CD-ROM

1. THE ACCOMPANYING CD-ROM

The software and documentation on the accompanying CD-ROM is described in the file `index.html` in the top directory of the CD-ROM.

2. REFERENCES

[Belanger *et al.* 1997] Belanger, Jean-Pierre, Carl Byers, and Lily Lam, "OSIM: Experience of an In-Flight Refueling Federation Development Using Commercial Tools," *Simulation Interoperability Workshop Proceedings*, Paper Number 97F-SIW-108, September 1997, pp. 667-676.

[Braudaway and Harkrider 1997] Braudaway, Wesley K., and Susan M. Harkrider, "Implementation of the High Level Architecture Into DIS-Based Legacy Simulations," *Simulation Interoperability Workshop Proceedings*, Paper Number 97S-SIW-089, March 1997, pp. 577-584.

[Campione and Walrath 1996] Campione, Mary, and Kathy Walrath, *The Java Tutorial: Object-Oriented Programming for the Internet*, Addison-Wesley, 1996. See also `http://java.sun.com/docs/books/tutorial.html` (April 1999).

[Carothers *et al.* 1997] Carothers, Christopher, Richard Fujimoto, Richard Weatherly, and Annette Wilson, "Design and Implementation of HLA Time Management in the RTI version F.0," *Proc. 1997 Winter Simulation Conference*, pp. 373-380.

[Dahmann *et al.* 1997] Dahmann, Judith S., Jeffrey Olszewski, Richard Briggs, Russell Richardson, and Richard M. Weatherly, "High Level Architecture (HLA) Performance Framework," *Simulation Interoperability Workshop Proceedings*, Paper Number 97F-SIW-137, September 1997, pp. 849-862.

[DMSO 1995] Defense Modeling And Simulation Office, U.S. Department of Defense. "Department of Defense Modeling and Simulation Master Plan." U.S. Government Printing Office, Washington, DC, 1995. See also `http://www.dmso.mil/dmso/docslib/mspolicy/msmp/` (October 1995).

[DoD 1996] U. S. Department of Defense, Under Secretary of Defense for Acquisition and Technology, USD (A&T), memorandum. *DoD High Level Architecture (HLA) for Simulations*, 10 September 1996. See also `http://hla.dmso.mil/hla/policy/` (April 1998).

[DMSO 1998a] Defense Modeling and Simulation Office, U.S. Department of Defense. "HLA Compliance Checklist, Federate, Version 1.3." See `http://hla.dmso.mil/hla/policy/` `cmp_cl11.html/` (June 1998).

[DMSO 1998b] Defense Modeling and Simulation Office, U.S. Department of Defense. "Test Procedures For High Level Architecture Interface Specification, Version 1.3." See `http://` `hla.dmso.mil/hla/policy/pro_v11.doc` (June 1998).

[DMSO 1998c] Defense Modeling And Simulation Office, U.S. Department of Defense. "Test Procedures For High Level Architecture Object Model Template, Version 1.3." See `http://` `hla.dmso.mil/hla/policy/pro_v3-0.doc` (June 1998).

[Fujimoto 1993] Fujimoto, Richard M, "Parallel Discrete Event Simulation: Will the Field Survive?" *ORSA J. Computing*, vol. 5, no. 3, Summer 1993.

[Fujimoto 1999] Fujimoto, Richard M., *Parallel and Distributed Simulation Systems*, Wiley, 1999.

[IEEE 1995] IEEE Standard for Distributed Interactive Simulation—Application Protocols (Revision and redesignation of IEEE Std 1278-1993). Designation: 1278.1-1995.

[IEEE 1999] IEEE draft standards P1516 (HLA Rules), P1516.1 (Interface Specification) and P1516.2 (OMT). See `http://standards.ieee.org` (March 1999).

[Jefferson 1985] Jefferson, D. R. "Virtual Time," *ACM Transactions on Programming Languages and Systems*, 7(3): pp.404-425, July 1985.

[Kiviat 1969] Kiviat, Philip J., Digital Computer Simulation Computer Programming Languages, The Rand Corporation RM-5883-PR, January 1969.

[Lea 1996] Lea, Douglas. *Concurrent Programming In Java: Design Principles and Patterns*, Addison-Wesley 1996.

[Levine and Fowler 1993] Levine, Linda, and Priscilla Fowler, *Technology Transition Push: A Case Study of Rate Monotonic Analysis (Part 1)*, Technical Report CMU/SEI-93-TR-29, The Software Engineering Institute, December 1993.

[Levine and Fowler 1995] Levine, Linda, and Priscilla Fowler, *Technology Transition Pull: A Case Study of Rate Monotonic Analysis (Part 2)*, Technical Report CMU/SEI-93-TR-30, The Software Engineering Institute April 1995.

[McLeod Institute 1999] McLeod Institute of Simulation Science, *HLA Lecture Notes*, `www.ecst.csuchico.edu/~hla/` (April 1999).

[MITRE 1999] The MITRE Corporation, *Support for sample implementation*, see `http://www.mitre.org/technology/hla-book` (April 1999).

[Neelamkavil 1987] Neelamkavil, Francis. *Computer Simulation and Modeling*, Wiley, 1987.

[Nicol and Fujimoto 1993] Nicol, David, and Richard Fujimoto, "Parallel Simulation Today," *Annals of Operations Research*, vol. 53, April 1993, pp. 249-285.

[Objectspace 1999] *Java Generic Library (JGL)*, See also `http://www.objectspace.com/products/jgl/` (April 1999).

[OMG 1996] Object Management Group, *The Common Object Request Broker: Architecture and Specification*, revision 2.2, February 1998. See `http://www.omg.org/library/c2indx.html.` (April 1999)

[OMG 1998] Object Management Group, *Facility for Distributed Simulation Systems*, OMG document number formal/99-05-01. See also `http://www.omg.org/cgi-bin/doc?formal/99-05-01` (December 1998).

[Paterson *et al.* 1998] Paterson, Daniel J., Eric Anschuetz, Mark Biddle, and Dave Kotick, "An Approach to HLA Gateway/Middleware Development," *Simulation Interoperability Workshop Proceedings*, Paper Number 98S-SIW-005, March 1998, pp. 21-30.

[Pitch 1999a] Pitch AB, *pRTI Exploration Edition*, `http://www.pitch.se/pRTI/explore/` (April 1999).

[Pitch 1999b] Pitch AB, *pRTI*, `http://www.pitch.se/pRTI/` (April 1999).

[Scrudder *et al.*1998] Scrudder, Roy, William Waite, Marcus Richardson, and Robert Lutz, "Graphical Representation of the Federation Development and Execution Process," *Simulation Interoperability Workshop Proceedings*, Paper Number 98F-SIW-103, September 1998, pp. 584-606.

[Scrudder *et al.*1998b] Scrudder, Roy, Robert Lutz, and Judith Dahmann, "Automation of the HLA Federation Development Process," *Simulation Interoperability Workshop Proceedings*, Paper Number 98F-SIW-101, September 1998, pp. 581-587.

[Shaw and Garlan 1996] Shaw, Mary, and David Garlan, *Software Architecture: Perspectives on an Emerging Discipline*, Prentice-Hall, 1996.

[UML 1997] Object Management Group, "UML Summary," OMG document number ad/97-08-03. See `http://www.omg.org/cgi-bin/doc?ad/97-08-03` (March 1997).

[Wieland 1998] Wieland, Frederick, "Parallel Simulation for Aviation Applications," *Proceedings of the 1998 Winter Computer Simulation Conference*, Washington, D.C., December, 1998.

INDEX

LICENSE AGREEMENT AND LIMITED WARRANTY

READ THE FOLLOWING TERMS AND CONDITIONS CAREFULLY BEFORE OPENING THIS DISK PACKAGE. THIS LEGAL DOCUMENT IS AN AGREEMENT BETWEEN YOU AND PRENTICE-HALL, INC. (THE "COMPANY"). BY OPENING THIS SEALED DISK PACKAGE, YOU ARE AGREEING TO BE BOUND BY THESE TERMS AND CONDITIONS. IF YOU DO NOT AGREE WITH THESE TERMS AND CONDITIONS, DO NOT OPEN THE DISK PACKAGE. PROMPTLY RETURN THE UNOPENED DISK PACKAGE AND ALL ACCOMPANYING ITEMS TO THE PLACE YOU OBTAINED THEM FOR A FULL REFUND OF ANY SUMS YOU HAVE PAID.

1. **GRANT OF LICENSE:** In consideration of your payment of the license fee, which is part of the price you paid for this product, and your agreement to abide by the terms and conditions of this Agreement, the Company grants to you a nonexclusive right to use and display the copy of the enclosed software program (hereinafter the "SOFTWARE") on a single computer (i.e., with a single CPU) at a single location so long as you comply with the terms of this Agreement. The Company reserves all rights not expressly granted to you under this Agreement.

2. **OWNERSHIP OF SOFTWARE:** You own only the magnetic or physical media (the enclosed disks) on which the SOFTWARE is recorded or fixed, but the Company retains all the rights, title, and ownership to the SOFTWARE recorded on the original disk copy(ies) and all subsequent copies of the SOFTWARE, regardless of the form or media on which the original or other copies may exist. This license is not a sale of the original SOFTWARE or any copy to you.

3. **COPY RESTRICTIONS:** This SOFTWARE and the accompanying printed materials and user manual (the "Documentation") are the subject of copyright. You may <u>not</u> copy the Documentation or the SOFTWARE, except that you may make a single copy of the SOFTWARE for backup or archival purposes only. You may be held legally responsible for any copying or copyright infringement which is caused or encouraged by your failure to abide by the terms of this restriction.

4. **USE RESTRICTIONS:** You may <u>not</u> network the SOFTWARE or otherwise use it on more than one computer or computer terminal at the same time. You may physically transfer the SOFTWARE from one computer to another provided that the SOFTWARE is used on only one computer at a time. You may <u>not</u> distribute copies of the SOFTWARE or Documentation to others. You may <u>not</u> reverse engineer, disassemble, decompile, modify, adapt, translate, or create derivative works based on the SOFTWARE or the Documentation without the prior written consent of the Company.

5. **TRANSFER RESTRICTIONS:** The enclosed SOFTWARE is licensed only to you and may <u>not</u> be transferred to any one else without the prior written consent of the Company. Any unauthorized transfer of the SOFTWARE shall result in the immediate termination of this Agreement.

6. **TERMINATION:** This license is effective until terminated. This license will terminate automatically without notice from the Company and become null and void if you fail to comply with any provisions or limitations of this license. Upon termination, you shall destroy the Documentation and all copies of the SOFTWARE. All provisions of this Agreement as to warranties, limitation of liability, remedies or damages, and our ownership rights shall survive termination.

7. **MISCELLANEOUS:** This Agreement shall be construed in accordance with the laws of the United States of America and the State of New York and shall benefit the Company, its affiliates, and assignees.

8. **LIMITED WARRANTY AND DISCLAIMER OF WARRANTY:** The Company warrants that the SOFTWARE, when properly used in accordance with the Documentation, will operate in substantial conformity with the description of the SOFTWARE set forth in the Documentation. The Company does not warrant that the SOFTWARE will meet your requirements or that the operation of the SOFTWARE will be uninterrupted or error-free. The Company warrants that the media on which the SOFTWARE is delivered shall be free from defects in materials and workmanship under normal use for a period of thirty (30) days from the date of your purchase. Your only remedy and the Company's only obligation under these limited warranties is, at the Company's option, return of the warranted item for a refund of any amounts paid by you or replacement of the item. Any replacement of SOFTWARE or media under the warranties shall not extend the original warranty period. The limited warranty set forth above shall not apply to any SOFTWARE which the Company determines in good faith has been subject to misuse, neglect, improper installation, repair, alteration, or damage by you. EXCEPT FOR THE EXPRESSED WARRANTIES SET FORTH ABOVE, THE COMPANY DISCLAIMS ALL WARRANTIES, EXPRESS OR IMPLIED, INCLUDING WITHOUT LIMITATION, THE IMPLIED WARRANTIES OF MERCHANTABILITY AND FITNESS FOR A PARTICULAR PURPOSE. EXCEPT FOR THE EXPRESS WARRANTY SET FORTH ABOVE, THE COMPANY DOES NOT WARRANT, GUARANTEE, OR MAKE ANY REPRESENTATION REGARDING THE USE OR THE RESULTS OF THE USE OF THE SOFTWARE IN TERMS OF ITS CORRECTNESS, ACCURACY, RELIABILITY, CURRENTNESS, OR OTHERWISE.

IN NO EVENT, SHALL THE COMPANY OR ITS EMPLOYEES, AGENTS, SUPPLIERS, OR CONTRACTORS BE LIABLE FOR ANY INCIDENTAL, INDIRECT, SPECIAL, OR CONSEQUENTIAL DAMAGES ARISING OUT OF OR IN CONNECTION WITH THE LICENSE GRANTED UNDER THIS AGREEMENT, OR FOR LOSS OF USE, LOSS OF DATA, LOSS OF INCOME OR PROFIT, OR OTHER LOSSES, SUSTAINED AS A RESULT OF INJURY TO ANY PERSON, OR LOSS OF OR DAMAGE TO PROPERTY, OR CLAIMS OF THIRD PARTIES, EVEN IF THE COMPANY OR AN AUTHORIZED REPRESENTATIVE OF THE COMPANY HAS BEEN ADVISED OF THE POSSIBILITY OF SUCH DAMAGES. IN NO EVENT SHALL LIABILITY OF THE COMPANY FOR DAMAGES WITH RESPECT TO THE SOFTWARE EXCEED THE AMOUNTS ACTUALLY PAID BY YOU, IF ANY, FOR THE SOFTWARE.

SOME JURISDICTIONS DO NOT ALLOW THE LIMITATION OF IMPLIED WARRANTIES OR LIABILITY FOR INCIDENTAL, INDIRECT, SPECIAL, OR CONSEQUENTIAL DAMAGES, SO THE ABOVE LIMITATIONS MAY NOT ALWAYS APPLY. THE WARRANTIES IN THIS AGREEMENT GIVE YOU SPECIFIC LEGAL RIGHTS AND YOU MAY ALSO HAVE OTHER RIGHTS WHICH VARY IN ACCORDANCE WITH LOCAL LAW.

ACKNOWLEDGMENT

YOU ACKNOWLEDGE THAT YOU HAVE READ THIS AGREEMENT, UNDERSTAND IT, AND AGREE TO BE BOUND BY ITS TERMS AND CONDITIONS. YOU ALSO AGREE THAT THIS AGREEMENT IS THE COMPLETE AND EXCLUSIVE STATEMENT OF THE AGREEMENT BETWEEN YOU AND THE COMPANY AND SUPERSEDES ALL PROPOSALS OR PRIOR AGREEMENTS, ORAL, OR WRITTEN, AND ANY OTHER COMMUNICATIONS BETWEEN YOU AND THE COMPANY OR ANY REPRESENTATIVE OF THE COMPANY RELATING TO THE SUBJECT MATTER OF THIS AGREEMENT.

Should you have any questions concerning this Agreement or if you wish to contact the Company for any reason, please contact in writing at the address below.

Robin Short
Prentice Hall PTR
One Lake Street, Upper Saddle River, New Jersey 07458

pRTI™ Exploration Edition
License Agreement

pRTI™ Exploration Edition
Copyright (c) 1998-1999 Pitch AB.

Notice

Pitch licenses Pitch Portable RTI (pRTI™) Exploration Edition (hereafter referred to as the "Software") to you only upon the condition that you accept all of the terms contained in this license agreement. If you do not agree to these terms and conditions, then Pitch is unwilling to license the Software. Please read the License carefully before using the Software. By using the Software you agree to the terms and conditions of this License.

License and Warranty

The Software is the property of Pitch and is protected by copyright law. While Pitch continues to own the Software, you will have certain rights to use the Software after your acceptance of this license. Your rights and obligations with respect to the use of this Software are as follows:

YOU MAY:
(i) for educational purposes, use one copy of the Software;
(ii) for personal use, make one paper copy of the documentation which accompanies the Software

YOU MAY NOT:
(i)   distribute the documentation which accompanies the Software;

(ii) use the Software for any commercial purpose;
(iii) sublicense, rent, lease or distribute any portion of the Software;
(iv) reverse engineer, decompile, disassemble, modify, translate, make any attempt to discover the source code of the Software, or create derivative works from the Software.

DISCLAIMER OF WARRANTY:

Software is provided "AS IS," without a warranty of any kind. All expressed or implied representations and warranties, including any implied warranty of merchantability, fitness for a particular purpose or non-infringement, are hereby excluded.

LIMITATION OF LIABILITY:

In no event will Pitch be liable for any lost revenue, profit or data, or for direct, indirect, special, consequential, incidental or punitive damages, however caused and regardless of the theory of liability, relating to the use, download, distribution of or inability to use software, even if Pitch has been advised of the possibility of such damages.

Feedback Comments

Pitch shall be free to utilize your input or not with respect to any future versions of the Software. All such comments shall constitute confidential information of Pitch.

General

This Agreement will be governed by Swedish Law. This Agreement may only be modified by a license addendum which accompanies this license or by a written document which has been signed by both you and Pitch. Should you have any questions concerning this Agreement, or if you desire to contact Pitch for any reason, please write: Pitch AB, Nygatan 35, S-582 19 Linköping, Sweden.

About the CD-ROM

The CD-ROM has everything you need to learn the HLA, with or without programming:

- A complete implementation of the simulation described in the tutorial, both Java source code and executable files, so you can run it or use it as a starting point for your own simulation system
- A Test Federate, software that invokes HLA services manually. You can use the Test Federate to explore the HLA without writing any software.
- An implementation of the HLA Runtime Infrastructure (RTI) for use with the sample code or your own experiments
- The HLA specification (all three parts) to complement the tutorials in the book

System Requirements

The CD software is written entirely in Java and is designed to run on any Java platform. The CD-ROM contains the Java Runtime Environment (JRE) 1.1.7 for Windows 9x/NT and instructions for installation on Windows 9x/NT and Sun Solaris.

How to Use the CD

The file `index.html` in the CD top directory has links to all the content and explains how to install and use the software.

Technical Support

Prentice Hall does not offer technical support for the software on the CD-ROM. However, if there is a problem with the CD, you may obtain a replacement copy by sending an email describing your problem to:

`disc_exchange@phptr.com`